*The Canon and the
Common Reader*

The Canon and the Common Reader

Carey Kaplan and
Ellen Cronan Rose

*The University
of Tennessee Press*
Knoxville

Library of Congress Cataloging in Publication Data

Kaplan, Carey.
  The canon and the common reader / Carey Kaplan and
Ellen Cronan Rose.
     p.   cm.
  Includes bibliographical references and index.
  ISBN 0-87049-674-3 (cloth : alk. paper)
  ISBN 0-87049-675-1 (pbk. : alk. paper)
  1. English literature—History and criticism—Theory, etc.
2. American literature—History and criticism—Theory, etc.
3. Feminism and literature. 4. Canon (Literature) 5. Books and
reading. I. Rose, Ellen Cronan, 1938– . II. Title.
PR21.K37   1990   7/11 1
820.9—dc20   90-38034   CIP

For our fathers,
James Pigott Cronan and
Bertram David Halperson

Contents

Tables

Acknowledgments

We wish to express our gratitude to the following people and institutions. We cannot begin to rank the worth of their contributions to this project.

Lisa Alther read, advised, and kept us honest. Ralph Cohen, editor of *New Literary History*, graciously gave us permission to quote extensively from the journal's special *Feminist Directions* issue. Members of the Drexel University Seminar for Feminist Inquiry provided a tactful and rigorous critique of an early draft of chapter seven, "Who Speaks for the Academy?" Heather Dubrow read, critiqued, and helped us improve an early draft of chapter six, "Playing the Numbers." Joan Hartman and Lillian Robinson read the entire manuscript and used the "mother tongue" of feminist collegial discourse to help us re-vision and revise. Cheryl Iverson was an ideal common reader and suggested useful directions for the afterword. Jay Kaplan gave continuous encouragement. Jane Marcus shared unpublished material with us and led us to relevant scholarship. Carol Martin gave invaluable secretarial assistance. Beth Mintz helped us conceptualize chapter six, "Playing the Numbers," and generously advised us about statistical methodology, as did Bill Rosenberg. Carol Orr, Kim Scarbrough, and Stan Ivester of The University of Tennessee Press made producing this book an unadulterated pleasure. Eve Raimon helped with concepts, language, and research; read all the chapters in draft; and encouraged us throughout. Robert Raimon delighted in being a gadfly and amateur clipping service. St. Michael's College gave financial support and unstinting encouragement. Jack

Weston inspired the first half of chapter two, "Dr. Johnson's Canon and His Common Reader."

We also want to thank our families for their love, faith, and laughter: Michael and Peter Halperson; Emily, Amanda, and Barnabas Rose.

Some of the material in chapter five, "The Power of the Common Reader," was used in a different form and context in Ellen Cronan Rose, "From Supermarket to Schoolroom: Doris Lessing in the United States," in Claire Sprague, ed., *In Pursuit of Doris Lessing: Nine Nations Reading* (London: Macmillan, 1990).

Preface

We began writing this book when we met, in 1979. We didn't know at the time, of course, that we were writing a book. We thought we were simply talking about a contemporary British novelist, Margaret Drabble, whom we found personally important but who was not part of canonical literature. Subsequently, over years of drinks, dinners, and a continuing correspondence, we discovered that we read books and wrote articles about Drabble and that renegade, Doris Lessing, because we wanted to explain what these books had to say about our lives.

All this was in the heady days of the Women's Movement when anything seemed possible—even a wide-open curriculum that might include the writers we loved and who helped define our lives, as well as the writers we knew we must study and teach in order to appear literate to our male colleagues. We met at a conference, "Women and Society," improbably but generously sponsored by St. Michael's College, whose participants included psychologist Carol Gilligan, historian Sara Evans, critic Mary Anne Ferguson, Nobel Prize winner Rosalyn Yalow, writers Tillie Olsen and Grace Paley. Elaine Showalter had just published *A Literature of Their Own*. Feminist scholarship in general was flourishing. We felt powerful, empowered.

A few years later, chastened by subsequent professional experiences, we began to question why some books were regularly taught and others not; why some books were considered "literature," others merely "good reads." We were bewildered that contemporary novel courses routinely included Barth, Borges,

Coover, Hawkes, Kundera, Nabokov, Pynchon, and almost never Atwood, Drabble, Lessing, Morrison, Paley.

We both published on Lessing and Drabble; we both taught the conventional curriculum, with feminist modifications. One of us stayed put in a small Roman Catholic–affiliated liberal arts college while the other engaged in a sad odyssey from one prestigious institution to another—Dartmouth, MIT, Haverford—all of them willing to employ her for a year or even six years, none willing to grant her tenure. To stave off embitterment, we tried not to think about the professional liabilities associated with our chosen area of study. Nevertheless, one late December evening, after presiding over a meeting at the Modern Language Association convention of the Doris Lessing Society, of which she was then president, Ellen found herself weeping on Carey's shoulder in a Washington restaurant as she contemplated the consequences of having abandoned her gypsy-scholar peregrinations for the dubious security offered by a business school's program designed to retrain academics for the world of commerce. "I don't want to be recycled," Ellen wailed. "I've published a dozen articles and three books and I'm a damn good teacher."

While this soap opera may appear self-indulgent and irrelevant, it explains the genesis of *The Canon and the Common Reader*.

A year later, when Ellen had been miraculously returned to the academy, at yet another meeting of the Modern Language Association the two of us discussed, less emotionally, the implications of our professional lives. Because our academic interests lay outside the traditional canon, we had been excluded from the institutional power structure. Questions we asked each other that night included: What's wrong with Drabble and Lessing? Why don't people teach Ursula Le Guin and Alice Walker? Why do students think of assigned texts as boring? How did we get the reading lists we have? Why did we, along with everyone else we knew, believe unquestioningly in an immutable canon of "great works" by "great authors"? What did "great" mean? What was a "classic"? And who decided?

We also began to speculate about our role, as members of the academic establishment, in creating—or alienating—future readers. Who were we trying to teach, what were we trying to teach them, and why?

Our students come from a variety of backgrounds, although they are in no way an exhaustive cross-section of the American college population (we have few adult students and even fewer poor ones). The English majors Ellen taught at Dartmouth included men who have gone on to write speeches for President Bush, cover national politics for the *Wall Street Journal*, broadcast from Beirut and Warsaw for ABC News. Not only did these men enjoy studying the traditional literary canon while they were students, they continue to return to it for inspiration and solace in times of trouble. Ellen will never forget the phone call she received one December afternoon in 1984, when the Middle East was quite literally threatening to blow itself out of existence, from a former student whose Dartmouth honors thesis on Conrad she had directed. "Where are you?" she asked the faint voice on the other end of a long-distance connection. "I'm in Jerusalem," he said, "reporting on the fighting. It's three o'clock in the morning and I'm reading *Lord Jim*. I thought you'd understand."

Carey has taught at the same school for 17 years. The most noticeable change in the student body at Saint Michael's College over the years is that it is wealthier than it was 10 years ago. Carey's students are still 85% Roman Catholic, 95% white, 80% from Massachusetts, New York, New Jersey, Connecticut, Vermont, and Rhode Island. Most have had very little exposure to cultures outside their suburban, Roman Catholic, well-to-do Irish-American or Italian-American world. Saint Michael's students are less ready than their counterparts at Dartmouth to challenge authority, more ready to believe they do not know much. Still, they are eager to learn, excited about new ideas (especially ideas they regard as outré, like feminism or deconstruction) and, given a benign environment, interested in lively discussion.

By contrast, students who pass through literature courses at Drexel University where Ellen now teaches do so, for the most part, reluctantly. What they anticipate (as a result of high-school English classes?) as the study of boring, long-winded, irrelevant "classics" looms as an impediment to what they have come to Drexel for as future accountants, engineers, and computer scientists (acquisition of professional skills) and as a waste of (scarce) reading time they would rather spend on Stephen King or *Infoworld*.

Demographic projections suggest that the future Establishment "old boys" who still major in English at schools like Dartmouth will be overwhelmingly outnumbered in the near future by a new student constituency, prefigured by the students we now teach at Drexel and St. Michael's. Most of our students will not become prominent in the worlds of politics and letters. Many will not even read the *New York Times Book Review*. And yet, we are sure that what they learn in our classes will influence how they read and what they read, or even how they see films and television, for many years. What they learn in our introductory and survey classes, often the only literature courses they will have after high school unless they are English majors (and there are no English majors at Drexel), will influence even their sense of what books and cultural productions are available out there. We are, we feel, probably producing common readers who will fit into various overlapping communities of readers. What ought we try to teach them? What shall we do (what *can* we do), we wonder, to entitle these students to the legacy of meaning and value that young graduate of Dartmouth derived from Conrad in strife-torn Jerusalem and that, as women, we find in novels by Doris Lessing and Margaret Drabble?

These are questions we asked over and over again during the years in which we learned the pleasures of collaboration by putting together two collections of essays on Doris Lessing. After they were published and we were once again sitting at dinner—this time over a bottle of champagne—we knew it was time to write about the issues of canonicity we had never stopped considering.

The book we have written grapples with these issues in language that reflects our conviction that academic writing should be accessible to common readers as well as academics. Today's common reader, though, as this book demonstrates, is not easily definable, certainly not unitary. In our eclectic, pluralistic, post-modern era, we can no longer assume a reader as stable as Dr. Johnson's imagined common reader, whom we discuss in chap-ter two. Today we find communities of readers, communities that sometimes, but not always, overlap and intersect. There is no single reader to represent our culture, no ideal common reader.

While we believe that some common readers will be inter-ested in the issues we address in the chapters that follow, we expect that certain readers will find what we have to say par-ticularly congenial. Our implied (and idealized) reader is middle-class, probably white, probably female, probably feminist in sym-pathies, has some higher education, knows something about the world of academic literary studies, is at least noddingly familiar with the current debate about education in America, and leans to the left politically.

This book enters the current controversy about the literary canon—generally understood as the list of authors and works in-cluded in basic literature courses because they are deemed to comprise our cultural heritage—from a unique angle. We begin, in chapter one, by examining a 1987 report by the National En-dowment for the Humanities, *American Memory: A Report on the Humanities in the Nation's Public Schools,* to initiate discus-sion of the way in which an ossified canon has become impli-cated in the education controversy.

Since this report assumes an unvarying and ideal notion of culture and, by extension, what ought to be taught—a concept with which we disagree strongly—we return, in chapter two, to Samuel Johnson, who first established a "canon" of English lit-erature, for clarification about what makes a work canonical. We discover that, in judging which works were of great and endur-ing value, Dr. Johnson rejoiced "to concur with the common reader; for by the common sense of readers uncorrupted with literary prejudices, after all the refinements of subtlety and the dogmatism of learning, must be finally decided all claim to poet-ical honours."

In chapter three, we attempt to characterize today's common readers, who are not only less protected from the corruptions of literary prejudice promulgated by formal education than were Dr. Johnson's but also more heterogeneous. Nonetheless, they share with their eighteenth-century forebears a fervent belief that books matter. Now as then, common readers are intelligent, sincere, and discerning; they deserve respect.

Unfortunately, as we demonstrate in chapter four, that is not what they have historically received from the academic literary establishment. In fact, the history of canon formation and reformation can be conceptualized as a 200-year-long oscillation between common readers and the cultural/academic elite over who owns culture.

We believe, however, that an increasingly powerful coalition of dissenting voices within the academy is challenging the academic establishment to examine its ideological premises and alter existing power relationships. Radical teachers, revisionist scholars, new historicists, and feminists are, in their diverse ways, encouraging formation of new alliances between the academy and the common reader.

In chapter five, we use our decades-long interest, as feminist scholars, in Doris Lessing to describe the process by which a writer enters the canon today. The case of Doris Lessing, like that of Alice Walker, evinces the power exerted by the common reader—augmented by feminist and African-American scholars—in determining what is, at a given historical moment, "canonical."

But how powerful an advocate of the common reader *is* feminist scholarship? In chapter six, we employ statistics to determine the extent to which feminist scholarship has had a measurable impact on the academy, paying particular attention to the professional organization of literary scholars, the Modern Language Association, and selected prestigious scholarly journals. This chapter is disquieting because it concretely shows the degree to which the academy is no more responsive than the National Endowment for the Humanities to the pluralistic society evolving in the United States.

Further evidence of the academy's indifference to the common reader can be adduced from the current infatuation of many academics with literary theory that does not seek to elucidate literature, but rather to obfuscate and make it inaccessible to nonspecialists. In our seventh chapter, we trace the genealogy of mainstream literary theory from Sir Philip Sidney to Geoffrey Hartmann. We contrast this theoretical discourse to the newly emerging discourse of feminist literary theory which, we argue, empowers and dignifies the common reader. As yet, however, although feminist scholarship has challenged, it has not succeeded in transforming the academy.

If we were writing fiction, we could write a happy ending to the story we tell in this book. Or, eschewing romance in favor of sterner genres, we could at least write a resounding conclusion. But if—as we believe and argue throughout *The Canon and the Common Reader* and especially in the afterword—the process of canon formation and reformation is an organic and ongoing process, we are compelled to forego peroration and closure. We cannot predict who will be tomorrow's canon-makers and common readers, only that they will surely contest each other's right to own, and define, culture.

*The Canon and the
Common Reader*

The American Dream
A Nightmare from Which We Must Awaken

In 1987 the National Endowment for the Humanities issued a position paper on education in the United Stated entitled *American Memory: A Report on the Humanities in the Nation's Public Schools*. The situation in the nation's public schools was, from the point of view of the NEH, grim. "Culture" was losing a battle to "skills": "The culprit is 'process'—the belief that we can teach our children *how* without troubling them to learn anything worth thinking about." What is being objected to is "a practical, often vocational approach" to education (*American Memory* 12, emphasis in the original). For example, the authors of this document deplore using "modern foreign languages as a key to employment opportunities." They are dismayed that "schools and colleges that once concentrated on literature now offer such courses as 'Spanish for Hotel Management'" (12). They, however—rising above such mundane concerns—know what is worth thinking about: "questions of good and evil, freedom and responsibility, that have determined the character of people and nations. These needs cannot be met . . . in a curriculum that takes a hit and miss—and mostly miss—approach to literature" (10-11). To the crass materialism of the back-to-basics people, these writers oppose a high idealism that, in fact, is more crudely utilitarian than those vocational courses they scorn. "World competition," they aver, "is not just about dollars but about ideas" (10). It seems that they are motivated in their pedagogical endeavors by a deepseated but unacknowledged desire to keep the world safe for (their version of) democracy.

The title of this document, *American Memory*, perpetuates

the popular fantasy that we have a common, unitary national memory. Actually memory is both partial and selective. For example, Babbitt's America is unavailable to Portnoy; John Wayne westerns conveniently forget the Trail of Tears. Our national myth of "the Civil War" forgets that for the South it is still "the War of Northern Aggression." Indeed, ironically, *American Memory* begins complacently with a quotation from Abraham Lincoln, forgetting that for much of the nation even today, Lincoln is no hero.

This quotation from Lincoln's First Inaugural Address, embalming as it does notions of death, war, and patriarchal hegemony, deserves close analysis:

> The mystic chords of memory, stretching from every battlefield and patriot grave to every living heart and hearthstone all over this broad land, will yet swell the chorus of the Union when again touched, as surely they will be, by the better angels of our nature. (i)

The bizarre syntax (is it "the mystic chords of memory" that are to be "touched" by "the better angels of our nature"? or "every living heart"?) disguises the sinister vision of "living" hearts and homes bound by the chords/cords of war and death and the disturbing ambiguity hinting that "the better angels of our nature" may herald another war. In other words, the (mythical) Union exalts war over peace, death over life, headstones over hearthstones, men over women, and the mystical over the corporeal.

Why do the authors of *American Memory* choose such avatars as Lincoln, Milosz, Cicero, Santayana, Dante, Chaucer, Dostoevsky, Austen, Whitman, Hawthorne, Melville, Cather, Kundera, Arnold, Priestley, Jefferson, Longfellow, Alcott, Dickens, Shakespeare, Aesop, Daedalus, King Arthur, George Washington, Madison, Joan of Arc, Douglass, Welty, Homer, and Twain to embody (or is it disembody?) the American cultural heritage they think it so crucial to preserve?

Might it have something to do with power? Despite the mandated quota of women and an African American, their list does not include Native Americans, Hispanics, or Asian-Americans, although it does include Europeans of all eras. Nevertheless, the authors blandly if disarmingly, by way of the subjunctive, suggest that "if history gives us perspective on our lives, then shouldn't every young person be encouraged to study it? If literature connects us to permanent concerns, then shouldn't every young person read it?" Rhetorical questions such as these lead to sweeping generalizations:

> By their nature, the humanities disciplines ought to be the easiest to bring to everyone. While some students will need more help than others with the language of Shakespeare's plays, for example, the themes that animate the plays—love, honor, betrayal, revenge—are familiar to all and interesting to all. (10)

The authors of this passage acknowledge that because Shakespeare's language is difficult some students will need help learning it; they will get that help because Shakespeare is considered "necessary." What of the necessity to understand the equally specialized language of, say, Langston Hughes or Zora Neale Hurston?

The authors of *American Memory* are committed to timeless, eternal "classics" that institutionalize and ossify the world they already control. To alter the canon might alter power relations; to acknowledge pluralism might disperse authority; to accept the consequences of true democracy might topple oligarchy. This document, as part of the current discourse on education in the United States, is curiously parochial. By contrast, the Institute for Reconstructing American Literature, which convened at Yale University in the summer of 1982, was dedicated to cultural pluralism, to expanding the canon of American literature taught in universities and colleges to include the diverse experiences of women, African Americans, Hispanics, immigrants, gays, lesbians, and other groups not traditionally studied. And the topic for the National Council of Teachers of English 1988 Summer Institute for Teachers of Literature to Undergraduates was "Gender Studies and the Canon." Far from abjuring "tradition," the organizers of the summer institute contrasted the canon "at its worst" ("a Great List cast forever in concrete") to their vi-

sion of the canon "at its best"—"the aesthetic and cultural embodi-
ment of a given time continuously scrutinized" (NCTE brochure).[1]

What might be the consequences to the NEH of broadening
their definition of culture? What are they afraid of? Their overtly
benign intention is, like Arnold's, "to make the best that has been
thought and known in the world current everywhere" (10). The
cultural imperialism implicit in quoting this passage in 1987
escapes them, but not readers, when they provide the following
justification by Santayana for preserving the cultural heritage:
"When experience is not retained, *as among savages,* infancy is
perpetual" (6, emphasis ours). These quotations, far from issuing
a clarion call that will rally us to excellence in national education, sound the sour note of cultural jingoism.

The rhetorical force of such locutions as "our age," "our nation," "the past," and "our culture" indicates what Raymond Williams characterizes by the Gramscian notion of "hegemony . . . a
lived system of meanings and values [that] constitutes a sense
of reality for most people in the society" (Williams 110). Most but
not all. What this rhetoric obscures is the authors' resistance to
their own discovery of a shift in the national self-perception.
They are appalled to learn that 45% of people polled in a Hearst
survey "thought that Karl Marx's phrase 'from each according to
his abilities, to each according to his need' is in the U.S. Constitution" (5). Having registered horror, they retreat into the solace of clichéd patriotic rhetoric, ignoring what Williams more
clearsightly realizes:

> The reality of any hegemony, in the extended political and cultural
> sense, is that, while by definition it is always dominant, it is never
> either total or exclusive . . . . Any hegemonic process must be espe-
> cially alert and responsive to the alternatives and oppositions which
> question or threaten its dominance. The reality of cultural process
> must then always include the efforts and contributions of those who
> are in one way or another outside or at the edge of the terms of the
> specific hegemony. (113)

At least since the Industrial Revolution, the humanistic hegemony
has felt itself threatened by a scientific/technological counter-

hegemony, as reflected in the anxious manifestos of such writers as Wordsworth and Arnold. Additionally, with the growth of global consciousness, the western claim to both the new scientific and the old humanistic hegemony has become embattled. Just as the American political response to this threat has been increased isolationism (coupled with Caribbean colonialism, with its implicit invocation of the Monroe Doctrine), so the cultural response is regressive nostalgia. The authors' goal is an imaginary Tocquevillian America:

> Knowledge of the ideas that have molded us and the ideals that have mattered to us functions as a kind of civic glue. Our history and literature give us symbols to share; they help us all, no matter how diverse our backgrounds, feel part of a common undertaking. (7)

But what distinguishes our common undertaking is the very cultural diversity *American Memory* forgets.[2] Surely the National Endowment for the Humanities should lead the nation to a public education that celebrates difference even as it rightly honors our cultural heritage.

Unfortunately, the NEH, the most powerful body speaking for the study of the humanities in the United States, seems marooned in a time warp. As its position papers *American Memory* and *Humanities in America* amply demonstrate, the NEH, at least in its official and written manifestations, yearns for a stable, unchanging, primarily univocal and Anglo country in which the sonorous and ostensibly safe voices of the past never clash with the multivocal cacophony of the present.[3]

We have analyzed this recent NEH policy statement in such detail in order to introduce a general discussion of academic processes whereby canons are formed.[4] Though usually defined as a list of "authors and works generally included in basic . . . literature college courses and textbooks, and those ordinarily discussed in standard volumes of literary history, bibliography or criticism" (Lauter, "Race and Gender" 19), the canon is not, as Gerald Bruns reminds us, "a literary category but a category of power" (81). The general education canon of texts that constitute the western heritage (and its American apotheosis) is, as we have seen, a gage thrown onto the ground by the National Endowment for the Humanities in its determination to defend "culture" against the encroaching barbarians and retain control of the national (self-)consciousness.

While in the nation's public schools, this battle over who defines and owns culture—the mandarins or the barbarians—is waged over "vocational" versus "humanistic" curricula, in colleges and universities it also erupts in debate at the departmental level about which texts to include on required reading lists for English majors or in "standard" offerings like the history of the novel. Given realistic time constraints (how many texts can you ask a student to read in a 15-week semester?), the choice to include a novel by Elizabeth Gaskell or Toni Morrison may entail dropping one by Thomas Hardy or Thomas Pynchon.

This battle over the syllabus pits not only authors and texts against each other, but also scholars and definitions of scholarship. Frequently, though by no means always, it manifests itself as generational conflict—between older, established scholars (of such "classic" authors as Shakespeare, Milton, or Joyce) and young radicals determined either to deconstruct, contextualize, and historicize the classics (and the idea of a great tradition) or, more modestly, to argue that the list be expanded to include works by women and other previously marginalized writers.

For a heady moment in 1987, we ourselves felt a surge of power when *Doris Lessing: The Alchemy of Survival*, a collection of essays we edited, won the NEMLA/Ohio University Press prize for "the best book-length manuscript on literary criticism or literary history written in 1986 by a member of the Northeast Modern Language Association (NEMLA)." A year earlier, the Modern Language Association's Committee on Teaching and Related Activities had approved our prospectus for a volume on *The Golden Notebook* for the MLA series, Approaches to Teaching World Literature. For the two of us, who remembered vividly the days when it took considerable chutzpah to add *The Golden Notebook* to a syllabus for a course in contemporary fiction or to consider submitting an article on Lessing to a scholarly journal, such signs of canonical respectability were a moving tribute to a generation of scholars who had risked ridicule (and jobs) to validate scholarship on the "popular" novelist Doris Lessing.

Moreover, we believed our experience with Lessing reflected what we were hearing everywhere, that the canon was opening to include women and minorities.[5] Elated, we decided to write an article, maybe even a book, about women's inclusion. As our research progressed, however, we discovered that the dynamic of canon formation and reformation was more complicated than we and others had assumed. Our assumptions had been naively linear, perhaps because of our personal history in the academy during the 1950s and 1960s.

A generation of academics who flourished in the middle decades of this century promulgated a notion of "the canon" as monolithic. As English majors in the 1950s we assumed that the members of the group who defined the canon were "of sound mind and body, duly trained and informed, and generally competent." As women aspiring to join the professoriat, we accepted their valuation of "all other subjects" as "defective, deficient, or deprived, suffering from crudeness of sensibility, diseases and distortions of perception, weakness of character, impoverishment of background-and-education, cultural or historical biases, ideological or personal prejudices, and/or undeveloped, corrupted or jaded taste" (Smith, "Contingencies of Value" 22). Without the Civil Rights Movement, the Vietnam War, and the Women's Movement, we would never have dared voice our repressed interest in, for example, such then marginal texts as *Jane Eyre*, never have sought to find such lost texts as *The Awakening*, never have proposed writing a doctoral dissertation on a popular contemporary woman writer like Doris Lessing, because had we done so, we would have become the despised Others. But in the ferment of the 1960s, everything was "thrown into question: our established canons, our aesthetic criteria, our interpretive strategies, our reading habits, and most of all, our selves as critics and as [would-be] teachers." In particular, "for those of us [women] who studied literature, a previously unspoken sense of exclusion from authorship, and a painfully personal distress at discovering whores, bitches, muses, and heroines dead in childbirth where we had once hoped to find ourselves, could—for the first time—begin to be understood as more than 'a set of disconnected, unrealized private emotions'" (Kolodny, "Dancing" 140–41).[6]

In other words, as women scholars, we experienced an academic version of consciousness raising, which Catherine Mac-Kinnon accurately names the epistemology of feminism.[7]

In the 1970s the accepted "canon" was challenged by women who were both academics and feminists. Unable to reconcile our experience as women with the literature we had been taught as undergraduate and graduate students, we unearthed "lost" women writers and began to rewrite course syllabi, first-year anthologies, and even PhD reading lists to represent the experience of that half of the human race that had previously been excluded. The exhilaration the two of us felt when we succeeded in validating Doris Lessing as an acceptably "canonical" writer was shared by others, while others still, most notably Christine Froula, suggested that feminist scholars had not so much opened the canon as called the authority of canonizers into question. "How," Froula asked, "are the dynamics of canonists selecting, readers interpreting, teachers teaching, and students learning affected by what is beginning to be a critical mass of women in the academy?" Her answer was that the "impact of formerly silenced voices on the . . . 'system of power' that controls which texts are taught and how they are taught" had mounted a "radical challenge" to the "concept of a canon as such" (150–51).

The research into canon formation and reformation that spun off from our euphoria about the Lessing project forced us to question both Froula's (and our) blithe assumption that the "critical mass" of women in the academy *had* significantly challenged the "system of power" that determines canonicity and the correlative, if implicit, assumption that the feminist challenge of the 1970s to canonical authority was unprecedented.[8]

Froula's argument that feminist scholarship mounts a "radical challenge" to the "concept of a canon as such" depends on an analogy between the literary canon and the gospel created by the early church fathers in founding the Roman Catholic Church. But when we looked at literary history, beginning with Samuel Johnson in the eighteenth century, we discovered that the canon approximates more closely the yeasty ferment of post-Reformation protestantism, in which sects proliferated and the final arbiter of truth was the individual conscience.

One of the problems in contemporary discussion of what is or should be taught in college literature courses and thereby both validated for critical attention and sanctioned for cultural reverence by such agencies as the NEH is academics' curious and obsessive adherence to the term "canon," implying as it does "an authoritative list of books accepted as Holy Scripture" (*Webster's Ninth New Collegiate Dictionary*).

Before the middle of the eighteenth century, English literature did not have sufficient self-consciousness to see itself as a subject for serious scholarly research and discourse; that activity was appropriate only for "the classics," i.e., Homer, Aristotle, Virgil, Ovid, Seneca, and Horace. Indeed it was not until 1737 that *Beowulf* achieved recognition and textual stability. Dr. Johnson, whose definition of lasting literature in the "Preface to Shakespeare" constitutes the popular notion of canon ("what has been longest known has been most considered, and what is most considered is best understood"), was neither doctrinaire nor prescriptive in his literary judgments. Rather, in the course of compiling *The Lives of the Poets*, his edition of Shakespeare, and especially the *Dictionary*, he inscribed his personal taste, on the assumption that he was a more than usually knowledgeable and astute "common reader." As such, he could confidently recommend such noncanonical figures as at that time both Shakespeare and Richardson were because both spoke to the human heart; for the same reason, he could also express reservations about the then-revered Milton because the "perusal [of *Paradise Lost*] is a duty rather than a pleasure" ("Life of Milton").

The "canon" of English literature as we know it from school

syllabi, standard anthologies, and literary histories was not firmly established until 1904, when Walter Raleigh designed a reading list for the first course in English literature (as distinguished from English language) taught in British universities.[9] And subsequently, even this canon opened to admit new genres like the novel and whole new national literatures like American.

Given this history, the incorporation of formerly unstudied women writers into the canon and the revaluation of others are neither revolutionary nor unprecedented; they are part of an organic and ongoing process. When the tutelary muse of women's studies, Virginia Woolf, wrote a series of essays for the *Times Literary Supplement* celebrating a list of those writers she personally revered, many of them women, she was quite self-consciously invoking the model of her journalistic forebear, Dr. Johnson, with whom she rejoices

> to concur with the common reader; for by the common sense of readers, uncorrupted by literary prejudices, after all the refinements of subtilty and the dogmatism of learning, must be generally decided all claim to poetical honours. (Dr. Johnson, "Life of Gray," quoted as epigraph to Virginia Woolf, *The Common Reader* and *The Second Common Reader*)

Like him, she relied on both literary longevity and personal taste. In other words, she opened the canon to new voices like Dorothy Wordsworth's at the same time that she revalued and reaffirmed such undisputed scriptures as Montaigne's *Essays*. Like Johnson, too, she championed the common reader, who "differs from the critic and the scholar" because "he reads for his own pleasure rather than to impart knowledge or correct the opinions of others" ("The Common Reader" 1). And again like Johnson, she neither condescended nor dictated to common readers. "After all," she asks, "what laws can be laid down about books?"

> The battle of Waterloo was certainly fought on a certain day; but is *Hamlet* a better play than *Lear*? Nobody can say. Each must decide that question for himself. To admit authorities, however heavily furred and gowned, into our libraries and let them tell us how to read, what to read, what value to place upon what we read, is to destroy the

spirit of freedom which is the breath of those sanctuaries. ("How Should One Read" 234)

The "considered criticism" of Dr. Johnson, she allowed (and of Virginia Woolf, she implied), might "light up and solidify" the common reader's "vague ideas":

But [great critics] are only able to help us if we come to them laden with questions and suggestions won honestly in the course of our own reading. They can do nothing for us if we herd ourselves under their authority and lie down like sheep in the shade of a hedge. ("How Should One Read" 244)

When we look again at literary history, we discover a 200 years' tug of war between the common reader at one end of the rope and a representative of the cultural elite (Woolf's "furred and gowned" authorities) at the other. The latter's name changes from one generation to the next: Coleridge called him "the clerisy," Matthew Arnold "the remnant," F. R. Leavis "the minority." But he always represents the culturally privileged Subject fighting against the Other, who also changes from Johnson's common reader to Arnold's Philistine to a black American ghetto kid, all of them always accompanied by a legion of disenfranchised women.

Although the players have, today, changed names, the tug of war goes on. Or perhaps it is more accurate to think of an oscillation, since "tug of war" suggests good guys vs. bad and the possibility of victory and an end to the game. This oscillation between the powerless and the powerful is fecund, productive, and ongoing. From it have erupted new discourses, new disciplines, new ways of viewing the world, as well as the continuing empowerment of previously excluded communities.

We should say here that our notion of "oscillation" differs from the Marxian concept of dialectic although we are indebted to the cultural analysis articulated most cogently by Raymond Williams. The notion of dialectic suggests at least temporary closure; oscillation, on the other hand, implies a process as ceaseless as respiration. Furthermore, dialectic is teleological while oscillation, goalless, does not endorse the myth of progress. Rather it connotes unending process. Dialectic is linear, oscillation is cyclic: for example, Dr. Johnson's common reader is not synthesized into some new being at the end of the eighteenth century but, like Orlando, having changed clothes and some allegiances, returns in 1925 to be addressed by a new and strangely metamorphosed Great Cham, Virginia Woolf. The difference between the two common readers is equally evident. Johnson's, not haunted by an academic bogeyman, is more powerful: "uncorrupted by literary prejudices after all the refinements of subtilty and the dogmatism of learning [he] must . . . finally decide all claim to poetical honors." Woolf's common reader, representing larger numbers but less powerful, "reads for his own pleasure rather than to impart knowledge or correct the opinions of others" and is "guided by an instinct to create for himself out of whatever odds and ends he can come by, some kind of whole—a portrait of a man, a sketch of an age, a theory of the art of writing" (The Common Reader" 1).

Yet perhaps there *is* something unprecedented about the contemporary version of this historical drama. Within the last 20 years, a number of the previously disenfranchised—African-American men and other minorities as well as women—have joined the Establishment. Yet the battle rages on, now between the augmented and paradoxically weakened Establishment on the one hand and a new aristocracy on the other—literary theorists, most of them men.

Why should enlarging an elite weaken it? One might suppose that including the previously excluded would enrich and strengthen the ruling hegemony. However, Barbara Johnson of Harvard suggests an answer: "The minute women start to rise in a field is concommitant with the demise of the overall prestige of the field" (quoted in Kolbert 117). Unconsciously threatened by such feminization and loss of caste, the male academic elite has found a new source of power in theory. Theorists from Michel Foucault to Harold Bloom use quasi-scientific discourse designed to exclude any but the specialist in order to discuss the deployment and transmission of power.

But much feminist theorizing about literature differs substantially from "masculinist" theorizing, most dramatically by empowering the (common) reader and affirming connections between writers and readers, texts and contexts.

For, insofar as it originated in and retains its links to the Women's Movement of the late 1960s and early 1970s, feminist scholarship—even at its most theoretical—vehemently and on principle opposes the arbitrary separation between classroom and community. As Marilyn Boxer noted in an important review essay on the theory and practice of women's studies in the United States, significantly titled "For and About Women":

> Feminist thought characteristically replaces dichotomous with dialectical modes of analyzing self and other, person and society, consciousness and activity, past and future, knowledge and practice. . . . It also fortifies abstract understanding with active commitment to improve the condition of women. (687)

The first women's studies courses were developed by feminist faculty women, "supported and sometimes led by feminist students, staff or community women" (663). Even now, two decades later, "the conviction remains strong that women's studies must be explicitly political, consciously an academic arm of women's liberation, and actively part of a larger social movement that envisions the transformation of society" (676).[10] This conviction, of course, constitutes a radical critique of the separation between theory and practice, the university and its surrounding community, the scholar and the common reader, that characterizes established institutional rhetoric and serves, not incidentally, to empower and mystify an academic elite.

In its determination to challenge the academic establishment to examine its ideological premises and alter existing power relations, feminist scholarship is not unique. It is only one of a congeries of dissenting forces within the academic hegemony, allied in solidarity with African-American, Chicano, Asian-American, gay and lesbian, working-class, and other historically marginalized groups. But because we are personally more familiar with feminist scholarship than with other radical academic practices, we tend in this book to use it as synecdoche and exemplum. When, for example, in chapter seven, we contrast "masculinist" and "feminist" theoretical discourse, we are placing a dominant discursive practice in antagonistic relation to a subversive (and, we argue, emancipatory) one. Readers with histories that differ from ours should feel free to supply their own dramatis personae for the prototypical drama we script.

Who will be the common reader of the 1990s, who the canon-maker? While the professors bloody each other in department meetings, at professional conventions, and on the pages of scholarly journals, the authors of *American Memory* yearn for a lost common culture and assert that its recovery, preservation, and transmission depend on formal study of a fixed canon of "classic" texts. The National Endowment for the Humanities appears to endorse this notion by publishing *American Memory*, yet it also affirms the innate intelligence and taste of ordinary people by sponsoring such projects as the Vermont Library Reading Project, which we describe in chapter three. Oscillating between mandarin elitism on the one hand and cultural populism on the other the NEH, avatar of the Establishment's literary values, exemplifies the mysterious process by which humans make culture.

We believe it is vital to situate the current controversy about canon reformation within a broader historical context. We therefore begin our extended discussion of the oscillation between the needs and desires of the common reader and the ideological interests of a cultural/academic elite by returning to Samuel Johnson and the eighteenth-century origins of the canon.

2

Dr. Johnson's Canon
and His Common Reader

On 29 March 1777 Samuel Johnson's daily devotions were inter-
rupted by the arrival of 3 friends and publishers, representing
a much larger syndicate of 36 London booksellers and publishers, who asked him to "write little Lives, and little Prefaces, to
a little edition of the English Poets" (Boswell, *Life of Johnson* 3:
109). Johnson agreed to the task, set to work, and ultimately produced the multivolume *Lives of the Poets*, an achievement that
not only stands by itself separate from the poets it memorializes
and criticizes but marks the real beginning of the canon of English literature—the canon that continues substantially unchanged
today, replicated in anthologies and taught in secondary schools
and universities.

Johnson was, of course, not creating his list of poets out of
whole cloth. He chose those writers he personally admired and
who educated society agreed were central to the tradition of
English letters. His contribution to the canon was characteristic
of his entire contribution to literature: he codified, standardized,
rationalized, and defined at length and for a popular audience
a tradition already implicit but unstated. Further, the length of
the *Lives* is just the opposite of what was initially requested. The
three volumes, which now always stand alone, separate from the
poetry itself, are magisterial in their amplitude and certainty.

Significantly, this moment of canon establishment was initiated by the owners of print technology in cooperation with the
writer. The king, the court, and the aristocracy are conspicuously
absent. Johnson was the writer approached by the publishers
because some 22 years earlier he had very nearly single-handedly

codified the English language itself, taking 8 years to complete a task worked on for decades by the Italian and French academies— both not incidentally empowered by their monarchs.

Representative of Johnson's continued centrality to issues of canonicity, in *Cultural Literacy* E. D. Hirsch rejoices that Johnson's "famous authoritative dictionary" was the "most important" single work in achieving the "standardization of English" (78). What Hirsch, from his aerie on the political right of this debate, wholeheartedly applauds, Robert DeMaria, Jr., writing from a Marxist perspective, describes as "a monument in the architecture of cultural dominance" (71) even as he applauds "the tendency toward democracy" (72) of Johnson's lexicography.

The point here is that, however Johnson's contributions to the standardization of language and canon formation are viewed, Johnson remains forceful and influential. The historical moment, then, that initiates his canon of English literature seems an appropriate starting place for this discussion of the relationships among canon-makers, the owners and manipulators of print technology, and common readers as defined first by Johnson and redefined over the centuries. Our choice of historical moment is somewhat arbitrary, as any such choice must be, but nonetheless useful as we define the terms that inform this book. Johnson, by virtue of his intelligence, knowledge, eminence, and willingness to pontificate, provides a logical stepping-off place for many current discussions of the canon on both the political left and right.

Because Johnson was *the* powerful canon-maker at a moment pivotal to the appropriation of literary production and print technology by publishers taking over from the aristocracy, both Johnson-bashing and Johnson-puffing have become staples of the burgeoning literature on canonicity. For instance, while E. D. Hirsch admires Johnson's standardization of the language, Jane Tompkins sets the Great Cham up at the very beginning of *Sensational Designs* as the straw man to topple in order to get on with her examination of the American literary canon. But Johnson is not a single-minded monolith, the foe of change, the champion of transcendent values. In reality, he was a mass of contradictions, strikingly complex both psychologically and intellectually: "The opposition of . . . two forces, the conservatism of intellectual attitude and the ebullient temperament[,] is at the root of most of his inconsistencies, and is perpetually fascinating" (Bronson 8).[1] Both Hirsch and Tompkins, speaking from antagonistic perspectives, accept conventional perceptions of Johnson, thus trapping themselves within an ahistorical misreading of the germinal moment of canon-making that Samuel Johnson represents.[2]

Johnson's deification as an intransigent Tory conservative and his concommitant co-optation by contemporary traditionalists have obscured his real achievements in defining the relationship between reader and writer in the era of print technology and in still relevant educational goals. This ossification of Johnson and the canon he initiated creates an unnecessary obstruction to the ongoing process of canon revision. If contemporary critics could perceive their kinship with Johnson and the ways in which he may be both the last of the neoclassicists and the first of the moderns, the current canon debate would appear more organic, more of a process, and less the cataclysmic revolutionary battle between the good guys and the bad guys imagined by Fredric Jameson, Jim Merod, and others.

As Alvin Kernan demonstrates in *Printing Technology, Letters, and Samuel Johnson*, Johnson's canon-making occurred at a critical historical moment, analogous to the historical moments of biblical canon formation. It was "a time of crisis when the old courtly literary order was falling apart in a flood of printed books and an increasing rational skepticism about the value of letters":

> The history of biblical canons reveals that the essence of canon-making is an effort to legitimate some central value or quality . . . in the face of a real threat to the existence of the institution. (161)[3]

Ironically, the crisis that Johnson confronted and that prompted his efforts at canon formation and language standardization was identical with the forces that allowed him to attain literary eminence. Literature by 1750 was a commercial enterprise; Johnson, grudgingly and ambivalently, wrote for money first, glory second. His ambivalence is nowhere more apparent than in his famous pronouncement, "No man but a blockhead ever wrote, except for money" (Boswell, *Life* 3: 19). It is true that, after he received his pension in 1762, he wrote far less than when his daily bread depended on his daily literary output. But it is during the post-pension years that he produced such major canon-making works as *The Lives of the Poets* and his edition of Shakespeare.

Johnson was indubitably proud of his position as premier man of letters of his time, deeply pleased by the honorary doctorate from Oxford, and constantly concerned to ennoble the writer. Thus, at the same time that Johnson was a self-described literary hack, much of his writing was devoted to legitimizing literature as a noble calling:

> No longer legitimated by its association with the old aristocratic social order, no longer justified by correspondence with prior and well-established moral, political, religious and philosophical systems, letters in a commercial age had to find and validate new ways of associating itself with truth in some form. (Kernan 161)

Johnson's self-imposed task was just this legitimation of literature, even while his essential integrity required him to acknowledge that his writings were not purely irresistable effusions of Truth and Beauty but also a means to make a living. Hence, Johnson's ambivalence, awareness of inevitable change and instability, and reluctance to pronounce for or expect absolutes are everywhere apparent in his criticism and his conversation. Johnson—the son of a barely lower-middle-class bookseller; a man who attended university briefly, on patronage, and who would not attend lectures because he had shabby clothes and no shoes; who made his way to eminence after many hard and hungry years on Grub Street—almost invariably qualifies and undercuts his most fiercely conservative statements. By dint of ferocious labor and by the force of his extraordinary mind, Samuel Johnson—the Other, the marginal, the outsider—scrabbled his way into the center of English letters. His pontifications, qualified and hedged as they so frequently are, reflect his awareness of the instability

of things, the relative nature of security and status, and the ten-
uousness of any imposed order:

> Johnson never can put aside his doubts nor quell his fear that beyond
> things there is nothing, and, always with a perturbed and partial
> awareness of how provisional were the meanings he constructed or
> defended, he constantly tried to fend off chaos by erecting firm so-
> cial and literary orders. (Kernan 239)

In addition to providing a new definition of the writer, Johnson also first invented and then frequently allied himself with
the common reader. In defining this new reader, Johnson opposed
the elitism of the pre-print era that saw literature as belonging
essentially to a courtly minority enjoying pleasures too recherché
for ordinary mortals. Were he living today, he would probably
oppose the removal of literature from ordinary people's enjoyment to a special (academic rather than courtly) realm in which
only the initiated can *understand*, never mind appreciate, sacred
texts that make up an unchanging canon.

For example, immediately after the strongly conservative statements Jane Tompkins adduces, particularly emphasizing Johnson's neoclassical approval of the "timeless" and "universal," two
notions that are anathema to reader-response and new-histori-
cist critics, Johnson characteristically qualifies his generalization:

> But because human judgement, though it be gradually gaining upon
> certainty, never becomes infallible; and approbation, though long
> continued, may yet be only the approbation of prejudice and fash-
> ion; it is proper to inquire, by what peculiarities of excellence Shake-
> speare has gained and kept the favour of his countrymen. (*Works* 7: 61)

Here Johnson does what he usually does in his critical writings:
after making some staggering and apparently irrefragable generalization, he backtracks and acknowledges change, human limi-
tation, and the forces of history. After stating that Shakespeare
has outlived his time and become immune to temporal forces,
Johnson undercuts himself and reminds both himself and his
readers that "human judgement" is never "infallible," and that
even long-continued public favor may be only the product of the

all-too-human vices of "prejudice and fashion." This qualifying ambivalence, highly typical of Johnson's writings, is frequently ignored because the Great Lexicographer has passed into legend, becoming a folk figure.

As Bertrand Bronson points out in "The Double Tradition of Dr. Johnson," "it is ironically unjust that Johnson should have come to typify in so many minds, a stubborn resistance to change" (167). Johnson was "in his maturity as in his early years, . . . a positive, not a negative nor a neutral, spirit" (164). Indeed, Johnson was a wild man into early middle age,

> a violent and outspoken opponent of the government and the reigning house:—a homeless, penniless, dangerous man, keeping questionable company, tramping the streets all night for lack of a lodging or money to pay for one; sustained by political passion, "brimful of patriotism," "resolved to stand by his country" by writing incendiary anti-ministerial pamphlets; the misreporter of Parliamentary debates and, in fact, wanted for questioning by the authorities. (164)

Although Johnson all his life adhered to firm moral, religious, and political opinions, on the deepest level he espoused freedom, liberty, and the enhancement of life for ordinary people, for his common reader.

The famous encounter with Sir Adam Fergusson, which Bronson adumbrates, offers one of the finest examples of Johnson's complexity and deep humanity. The encounter occurred at the Pantheon, one of the great eighteenth-century amusement parks in which all levels of society mixed. Sir Adam was concerned "lest such public amusements might encourage luxury in the populace" (165). Johnson, always a friend to any sweeteners of existence, responded, "Luxury, so far as it reaches the poor, will do good to the race of people; it will strengthen and multiply them. . . . Sir, I am a great friend to publick amusements; for they keep people from vice." The most interesting moment in this exchange came when Sir Adam talked of the necessity to preserve the power of the crown in the British Constitution. Johnson replied like the Tory he was, but with a characteristically complex layered reasoning:

> Sir, I perceive you are a vile Whig. Why all this childish jealousy of
> the power of the crown? The crown has not power enough. When
> I say that all governments are alike, I consider that no government
> power can be abused long. Mankind will not bear it. If a sovereign
> oppresses his people to a great degree, they will rise and cut off his
> head. There is a remedy in human nature against tyranny, that will
> keep us safe under every form of government. (166)

That Johnson here was not merely arguing for argument's sake,
as he was quite capable of doing on any subject save religion,
is evident from similar and reiterated statements in his writing
and conversation. *Rambler* 148, for example, utterly denies tyran-
nical parents any conventional rights over their children; the
same theme recurs in *The Vanity of Human Wishes* (lines 260–82).
His feelings in favor of self-determination and his aversion to
slavery made his attitude toward the American colonies ambivalent and sometimes surprising.

As canon-maker, as creator and exemplar of the writer-hero,
as advocate of the common reader, and as self-aware cultural
relativist Samuel Johnson is peculiarly contemporary. A cover article on canonicity by James Atlas in the *New York Times Magazine* of 5 June 1988, "The Battle of the Books," describes the would-be
new literary establishment at Duke University led by Stanley Fish:

> Fish and his radical colleagues . . . aspire to "space, importance and
> wealth," but on their own terms. Frank Lentricchia has a swimming
> pool in his backyard. In his work, though, he writes openly and with
> unashamed ardor, in the autobiographical fashion of the day, about
> his Italian-American origins, his grandfather in Utica, his working-
> class Dad.
>   "To become an intellectual from this kind of background means
> typically to try to forget where you've come from," he writes in *Criti-
> cism and Social Change*. "It means becoming a cosmopolitan gentle-
> man of letters, philosophy and art."
>   That's not Lentricchia's style. For the scholars of his generation,
> it's no longer a matter of proving their claim on literature; that struggle
> has been won. What they're demanding now is a literature that re-
> flects their experience, a literature of their own. (75)

Lentricchia and Johnson are not entirely incompatible, although
perhaps neither would wish to own the other as a literary sib-

ling. Both men stand at the end of long-established orders, trying to create new worlds in which former verities have weight
but in which they, the *nouveaux arrivés déclassés*, can find respect
both for themselves and the new classes they represent.[4] Lentricchia, like Johnson, is after all firmly allied with the old world of
letters even while he strives to expand and revise it. Atlas describes him "standing before his modern poetry class in a faded
blue workshirt open at the neck," making "his way through 'The
Waste Land' just the way the professors used to, line by line, point-
ing out the buried allusions to Ovid and Dante, Marvell and
Verlaine" (73). In his classroom, then, Lentricchia teaches the
great conservative modern classics and the more remote Latin
and Renaissance classics encoded within them at the same time
that he (far more self-consciously than Johnson) represents change,
opening of the canon, questioning of the values that keep Dante,
Ovid, and T. S. Eliot in the curriculum. Lentricchia here is not
so very different from Johnson in his goals if not in his achievements. Johnson, after all, knew Latin and Greek as well as any
man of his time but did not expect the common reader to share
his knowledge; Johnson opened the English canon to include his
contemporaries; Johnson was fascinated by such new genres as
the novel.

Moreover, just as Lentricchia and Johnson may share some attitudes toward literature and culture, so too, the cultural crisis
in America today may have relevant analogies to Samuel Johnson's mid-eighteenth-century England. Johnson's England was
faced with the crises brought about by print technology, increased
wealth and leisure time, and a new and relatively heterogeneous
reading public.[5] The United States today is increasingly pluralistic, increasingly aware of international and marginal literatures; colleges and universities find themselves addressing a
new student, a new common reader, whose interests may include not merely Plato and Rousseau but literature by women,
Hispanics, Native Americans, African Americans, Asian Americans, and other groups heretofore ostracized from curricula. In
fact, the new common reader may very well not care about lit-

erature and the humanities at all, valorizing instead science, the social sciences, and business as sources of useful knowledge and looking to music, video, film, and television for the entertainment and instruction formerly supplied by literature.

Johnson and today's new canon-makers have in common the need to define their own roles at historical moments when the definition, the significance, and the centrality of literature to society are in question. Kernan describes Johnson's *Lives* as "a powerful and influential statement about all the major literary questions that troubled letters in an age of radical change" (272).

Rapid growth of an enlarged and varied British reading public occurred during the years when Johnson was scraping a living as a Parliamentary reporter and hack writer for Edward Cave's *Gentleman's Magazine*. The homogeneity of the courtly audience of the Elizabethan era was gone. So was the wide-open theater that drew an audience from all walks of life (Stallybrass and White 87). Even the Tory literary hegemony of the first half of the eighteenth century had decayed. New groups were reading: dissenters, Whigs, women, domestics—groups literate for the first time in history and with leisure time to devote to reading. Thanks to advances in print technology, most people who were literate could gain access to at least a newspaper or periodical and a fairly private place in which to read it. These readers did not automatically participate in some generally accepted notion of what constituted literature and polite culture. They read what interested them or what the people around them read or what was available. Many of them moved from tracts on religion to tracts on politics (the best sellers of the eighteenth century) to books on etiquette to novels and romances to history, and so on, as interest and the availability of books, periodicals, and pamphlets dictated.

Today's canon-makers and critics are confronting a similar and even more pervasive shift. The crisis facing letters at the beginning of the 1990s is a geometrically multiplied vector of the eighteenth-century crisis. The reading public is not only huge today, as it was not in Dr. Johnson's time; it is multicultural, multilingual, not at all sure that value inheres in the humanities curriculum in place in universities for the past century and promulgated to the general public as a list of Great Books.

While on the political right Allan Bloom and E. D. Hirsch scramble to prove that the old world of letters was and is the best of all possible worlds and that only adherence to that world can give the teacher/scholar his central place in the scheme of things,[6] new historicists, reader-response theorists, and other radicals claim for the teacher/critic a different but no less central and possibly even more crucial role. The function of the critic, according to these groups, is to reform and re-create society, partly by writing and reading in a new way, usually within an explicit or implicit Marxist framework.[7] In spite of their ideological differences, both of these contemporary groups are grappling with the same crisis: how to retain power and significance in a world that increasingly gives power and significance not to the humanists but to the scientists, the industrialists, the politicians—none of whom can be assumed to share or even care about "common culture," opening the canon, or whether we are all confronting the impending disintegration of western civilization, a highly dubious concern of critics on both the left and the right because it masks the profound desire of both groups to retain and exercise power.

In this fragile balance of interests, feminist canon revision and its concomitant feminist literary theory, criticism, and pedagogy are dangerous to the unstable power structure. Since its inception, feminist critical theory has esteemed personal experience and popular taste. For the most part, feminist scholars— even the most theoretical of them—are committed to real social change. Feminist pedagogy, as we show in chapter four, constructs bridges between the community and the academy that deny the latter's exclusivity and superiority. Responding to this threat, some Establishment (mostly male) scholars have attempted to subsume feminism's agenda under a new obscurantism, often couched in the (again mostly male) language of war.

Thus, Fredric Jameson, arguing that new historicism or metacommentary will transform society, argues in typically epic rhetoric for the importance of the critic: "Interpretation is not an isolated act, but takes place within a Homeric battlefield, on which a host of interpretive options are either openly or implicitly in conflict" (13). Clearly, for Jameson, the outcome of this battle has significance for the well-being of humankind. Jim Merod, in *The Political Responsibility of the Critic*, is even more explicit about conferring power upon the teacher/scholar. Claiming that the critic must activate in students "the possibility of critical intervention in our culture at large" (13), and arguing persuasively against the perils of reading texts as universal statements about universal truths, Merod demands that teacher/critics "show that texts are strategies, that they carry values that exert a force in the social world" (11). Teachers, whose necessary task is to inculcate "the possibility of critical intervention in our culture at large" (13), must "deal with texts in a way that fosters intellectual ferment rather than making students' efforts conform to preexisting methods and critical dogmas" (11). Merod admonishes the teacher/critic to keep in mind "Marx's useful admonitions against methodological analyses of any sort that fail to promote active, socially productive political awareness" (15).[8] Whatever the perspective, the critic today perceives (typically) *himself* as fighting the good fight[9] against the forces of darkness, whether those forces are ones that deny Platonic universal values or ones that ignore the pluralism that make literature so centrally a part of ongoing social and political change. The hidden agenda, though, is power: who owns culture?

As we have just shown, within the academy this dispute over ownership of culture rages between groups roughly definable as politically left and right. In the larger dispute, however, as we suggest here and elaborate in chapter seven and the afterword, the two superpowers of science and the humanities slug it out for the money, prestige, perquisites, and visibility offered by the modern university, with science slowly asserting its dominance.

The humanities are so embattled that attacks from within by previously negligible groups may be particularly unwelcome.

Such attacks threaten a weakening factionalism for the already relatively weak humanities. Additionally, the humanities power structure finds itself faced with the dismaying necessity to somehow destroy, absorb, and/or co-opt these *déclassé* groups while at the same time continuing, as monolithically as possible, to battle the sciences. As we suggested in chapter one, moreover, the very disempowerment and disenfranchisement of these encroaching groups potentially diminish the status of the humanities establishment. Thus, both feminist canon reformation and feminist critical theory and practice pose substantial problems for the already tottering humanities hegemony.

Today's canon-makers and reformers, then, are asking questions similar to those confronted by Samuel Johnson in the eighteenth century: "crudely, who owns poetry, or more circumspectly, where does poetry originate and what determines its nature" (Kernan 272)? But Samuel Johnson's answer for his century—the writer in alliance with the common reader—is no longer adequate.

The "battlefield" of culture is wide open today, a darkling plain on which ignorant armies deploy a fascinating array of weaponry. Nonetheless, one may ask if the world at the end of the twentieth century is susceptible to some new version of the Johnsonian solution. A closer look at the historical process that created a literary canon perceived (wrongly) by most academics, whether railing or applauding, as fixed and constant, may help suggest some future direction.

To return, then, to Samuel Johnson and the origins of the contemporary literary canon and possibly to some insight into our current cultural crisis. Despite his Tory politics and his penchant for defining and cataloging, Johnson today might be more comfortable with Lentricchia and Jameson than with Bloom, Hirsch, and former Secretary of Education William Bennett. He certainly did not see himself freezing literature into monumental permanence. For example, Johnson is famous for debunking the neoclassical unities in the "Preface to Shakespeare." The opposite of rigid in his views about what constitutes literature, he was not doctrinaire about genre, rejoicing in Fielding's novels, weeping over *Clarissa* and ebulliently celebrating Fanny Burney's success with *Evelina*[10] at a time when many neoclassical critics were perceiving in the novel the certain downfall of civilization. When social critics were predicting revolution and chaos as a result of increased literacy among the lower classes, Johnson insisted on the positive value of more widespread learning. Additionally, he commended the dissenting, underclass tinker John Bunyan's *Pilgrim's Progress* as a book that every right-minded person ought to read and reread, ranking it with *Don Quixote* and *Robinson Crusoe* as one of the only three books "written by mere man that was wished longer by its readers" (Boswell, *Life* 2: 238 and 238 n.5).

Nonetheless, for many contemporary scholars, Samuel Johnson has become synonymous with a monolithic, immutable canon and with hidebound conservativism in matters academic as well as political. As the major literary figure of the second half of the eighteenth century and an avatar of neoclassical ideology, he represents for many a comforting security at a time when academic values he first enunciated and that, with modifications, have served nineteenth- and twentieth-century education well, seem especially at risk.

Lawrence Lipking, in his overview of canon-making in the eighteenth century, *The Ordering of the Arts in Eighteenth-Century England*, states that "Johnson set the standards for which earlier critics had asked, and against which future critics would be measured" (462). (In considering this pronouncement, it is important to keep in mind that only with Johnson did criticism become a middle-class pursuit, and only during and after his lifetime did the modern university begin to form.) An authoritative source to validate the new learning was essential. Since literary canons lack the ecclesiastical authority of the Scripture they seek to imitate, Johnson has been used by generations of critics as the source and model for literary order.[11] Even Lipking, while appearing to debunk Johnson's prophetic status, ultimately accepts it, using the same connotative language and religious implications as earlier critics:

> While Johnson could define poetry only in the same way as Dante
> defined the Holy Spirit, through the metaphor of light, his search for
> the spirit of poetry as realized in aspiring imperfect man constitutes
> the special quality of wisdom in his final literary biographies. (*Order-
> ing* 458)

"Too authoritative to invite argument," Lipking concludes, "the
Lives goes beyond conversation about poets, and authenticates
a regular right line of poetry" (459). Obviously, Johnson has post-
humously become the Moses of English literature, setting a standard upon which new critical claims and opinions are still based
and against which they are still measured.

For those critics and academics who defend the traditional
curriculum, the perceived central premise of Johnson's *Lives*,
that there exists a "unified culture in which all works of art" can
"be securely ranked and placed within one great idea of art" (Lipking 472), remains enormously seductive. The longing for order
and legitimacy, for, as it were, a literary Great Chain of Being
for which T. S. Eliot, among others, yearns (*Selected Essays* 4),
has converted Johnson's *Lives* into a Pentateuch of literature, individual portions of which one may question, as one questions
the literal interpretation of Genesis, but the essence of which is
ineluctable.

Although Johnson was rarely unwilling to pontificate, and
while he took great and personal interest in asserting the profound cultural and historical significance of language, literature,
and the writer, he was nonetheless aware of the ephemeral nature of his evaluation of writers who were, to him, very nearly
contemporaries (the *Lives* covers roughly the period 1660 to 1760).
As he explains in the "Preface to Shakespeare," in literature the
tests of time and continued popularity are everything:

> The reverence due to writings that have long subsisted arises . . . not
> from any credulous confidence in the superior wisdom of past ages,
> or gloomy persuasion of the degeneracy of mankind, but is the con-
> sequence of acknowledged and indubitable positions, that what has
> been longest known has been most considered, and what is most con-
> sidered is best understood. (*Works* 7: 60–61)

Here we can clearly see Johnson's characteristic combination of iconoclasm and traditionalism. His reverence for great literary works of the past, while consistent with eighteenth-century critical opinion, is based on a pragmatism consciously out of step with the entrenched dogma of neoclassical criticism that produced just the arguments Johnson dismisses as supports for continuing study of the classics.

Note, too, that Johnson refers implicitly to a large common readership that ultimately determines literary worth. Like the critics of today who are concerned with opening the canon, Johnson allows for change within the canon he is unwittingly establishing and repeatedly implies that it is not he alone who sets standards: "Surely to think differently at different times of poetic merit may be allowed. . . . Who is there that has not found reason for changing his mind about questions of greater importance" (*Lives* 3: 167)? As Clarence Tracy's essay, "Johnson and the Common Reader," insists:

> Criticism, as Johnson pointed out again and again, is not an exact science; the worth of a work of literature can never be demonstrated in the same way as a proposition in geometry can be proved. The principles upon which he said "the merit of composition must be determined" (*Lives* 1: 410) . . . must be inferred from a multitude of examples and tested during a lifetime of experience with readers. Even then they will remain tentative for a long time, if not for good, and will be modified, or absorbed, or rejected by other readers and critics in his own generation and later. For Johnson the judgment of literature was a communal undertaking, an effort of the whole civilized community. (422)

Thus, Johnson may comfortably and properly be accepted as the father of the literary canon academics, critics, and educators are agonizing about today. Moreover, such is his complexity that he can also be invoked as the originator of a flexible, mutable canon that always takes into account its readership. Johnson was far too eclectic and pragmatic, too much of a realist, to think that the canon he described would never change.

Furthermore, even the most radical of today's canon chal-

lengers agree with Johnson in perceiving themselves as part of
an enduring and valid culture; and, like Johnson, they also wish
to take account of the new, of their audience, of the constant
vicissitudes of our world. After all, as the *New York Times* avers,
Frank Lentricchia is still teaching that arch-elitist T. S. Eliot, and
even the radical canon reformers at Stanford University are not
throwing out the baby with the bath water. As James Atlas com-
ments in his *Times* article, despite William Bennett's opinion
that curriculum change has degraded a "great university" by means
of "the very forces which modern universities came into being
to oppose: ignorance, irrationality and intimidation," in reality
the new course that is causing all the fuss and furor includes

> the Old and New Testaments as well as the works of five authors:
> Plato, St. Augustine, Machiavelli, Rousseau and Marx. The other
> works assigned would concentrate on "at least one non-European
> culture," with "substantial attention to issues of race, gender and
> class." No one was proposing to "junk Western culture," insisted Stan-
> ford's president, Donald Kennedy. The point was simply to reflect
> "the diversity of contemporary American culture and values." (26)

Samuel Johnson's canon-making was not unlike the present
process. It was directed to ordinary, mostly middle-class readers
who looked to literature for information about how to perceive
their increasingly complex world. Indeed, one clear indication
of Johnson's interest in various individuals in various situations
is his invention of the modern biography, an analogue to the new
genre of the novel evolving at the same time. Johnson's definition
of biography was inclusive, arguing for preserving records of the
lives of both the famous and the obscure and insisting that no
detail of daily life was insignificant (Boswell, *London Journal*
293, 305).[12] Part of this interest in ordinary individual life and
happiness is reflected in the fact that, although Johnson supported both the state and the established church, he did not
write in the service of either, but for the common reader, whom
he saw as the ultimate judge of literary worth:

> I rejoice to concur with the common reader; for by the common
> sense of readers uncorrupted with literary prejudices, after all the

refinements of subtlety and the dogmatism of learning, must be finally decided all claim to poetical honours. (Quoted in Greene, *Samuel
Johnson* 768)

Who was Johnson's common reader? And what did this reader
have in common with today's readers? First, not everyone read
in the eighteenth century and not everyone reads now. As Harold Bloom points out, "there is no distinction between the uncommon and the common reader: to be a reader is to be uncommon. Reading is a frightfully elitist activity" (58). Nonetheless, of
all the great critics, Johnson is probably the least elitist. Unques-
tionably, he is less elitist and far less specific in his expectations
for his readers than, say, the great Victorian popular critics like
Macaulay, Carlyle, and Ruskin who assumed a large, leisured,
well-read, comfortably middle-class readership. He is also less
elitist than Allan Bloom who expects four years of college education to "civilize" and "complete" (339) the seventeen-year-olds who
enter the prestigious schools he is willing to discuss. Bloom lives,
at least in the pages of *The Closing of the American Mind*, in a
fantasy world that would amuse the less judgmental editor of
Cave's *Gentleman's Magazine*. Bloom deplores the ignorance of
the average college-educated computer scientist:

> [He is] cut off from the liberal learning that simpler folk used to ab-
> sorb from a variety of traditional sources. It is not evident to me that
> someone whose regular reading consists of *Time*, *Playboy* and *Scien-
> tific American* has any profounder wisdom about the world than the
> rural schoolboy of yore with his McGuffey's reader. When a young-
> ster like Lincoln sought to educate himself, the immediately avail-
> able obvious things were the Bible, Shakespeare and Euclid. (59)

But while Johnson loved learning and assumed that the more one
had of it the better, he knew that learning must begin with interest and available accessible texts. He would have been delighted with a reader who immersed himself in the complexities
of the popular magazines Bloom dismisses.[13]

Johnson, for all his deserved reputation as a man of great learning, began his writing career working for Edward Cave's *Gentleman's Magazine*, and from that experience he developed a no-

tion of the readership he was addressing that informed all his later work.

The *Gentleman's Magazine* attempted "to reach literate individuals in all classes" and did not cater to a "literary elite" (Tracy 408). It included, in addition to news and features of general interest,

> lists of promotions and appointments in the church, the army, and the navy, obituaries[,] . . . lists of commodity prices in the London markets, advices regarding ship movements around the world, and advertisements offering for sale a wide range of wares from the most learned books and the most sophisticated plays down to sure cures for venereal disease and pacifiers for teething infants. (Tracy 408)

Johnson almost certainly expected less from his common reader than 1980s academics expect from their students. Literacy was new to much of Cave's readership, as was concern with experiences outside the home, the village, the farm, or the factory. The worlds of courtly and polite learning were as distant as Mars. If the ordinary person decided, having attained literacy, to read *anything*, Johnson respected that impulse and was ready to meet his reader on as broad and uncluttered a ground as possible, keeping in mind the responsibility—openly sneered at by many educators today—to entertain as well as instruct.

From various places in the *Lives*, the "Preface to Shakespeare," the preface to the *Dictionary*, and in his conversation, a profile of Johnson's common reader emerges: a person who is, first of all, unsophisticated, who has no allegiance to any literary/critical or ideological position:

> The common reader is one who would soon be out of his depth if he tried to read metaphysical poetry or Butler's *Hudibras*, one who does not know Latin, one who cannot understand the technical terms used in ship-building, hunting, musicology, tactics, or versification, and one who is bored by classical mythology. (Tracy 410)[14]

Johnson's reader read for enjoyment or to gain specific information and for no other reason. Hence, Johnson rated entertainment a vital aspect of those writings addressed to the general reader: "that book is good in vain which the reader throws away"

(*Lives* 1: 454). Essentially, the common reader comprised "that class of readers, who without vanity or criticism seek only their own amusement" (*Lives* 1: 302). Even Johnson's famous criticisms of Milton are based on his sense of the general reader's response to the often slow-moving *Paradise Lost*, "one of those books which the reader admires and lays down, and forgets to take up again" (*Lives* 1: 410).

Johnson anticipates that modern moralist Doris Lessing in his respectful assumption that everyone loves to learn and, left to her or his devices, will learn and read the right things at the right time, according to some inner timetable.[15] Boswell relates the archetypal anecdote illustrating Johnson's assumption. In a boat floating down the Thames to Greenwich, they discussed education, Johnson affirming the relevance of a classical education. Boswell responded:

> "And yet . . . people will go through the world and do very well without [Latin and Greek]." "Why," said he, "that may be true where they could not possibly be of any use; for instance, this boy rows us as well without literature as if he could sing the song which Orpheus sung to the Argonauts, who were the first sailors in the world." He then said to the boy, "What would you give, Sir, to know about the Argonauts?" "Sir," said he, "I would give what I have." The reply pleased Mr. Johnson much, and we gave him a double fare. "Sir," said Mr. Johnson, "a desire of knowledge is the natural feeling of mankind; and every man who is not debauched would give all that he has to get knowledge." (*London Journal*, 329)

Whether Johnson was right or not is irrelevant. He assumed a thirst for knowledge; he assumed that attainment of knowledge was not easy and so should be as entertaining as possible; and he was willing to regard a probably illiterate barge boy as part of his potential readership. Johnson's imagined readers did not belong to a specific class but to "all classes." Johnson seems often to be thinking of members of

> the lower middle class, [of] the vulgar, a word that he defined in the *Dictionary* as "the common people." Clearly his periodical essays were written for readers far less genteel than those who read the

Tatler and *Spectator*, and in the *Idler*, in particular, he seems to have gone out of his way to bring shopkeepers, mercers, maids of all work, oilmen, and common soldiers within the orbit of his pen. (Tracy 411–412)

In chapter five, we will examine the role played by today's common readers and their journalistic and academic champions in the ongoing process of canon formation and reformation. As will quickly become apparent, by "common reader" we do not mean to designate a reader with the same social, economic, or educational background as Johnson's lower middle-class common reader. So perhaps we should take a moment now to articulate more precisely what we mean when we use the phrase, "the common reader."

3

The Common Reader Today

In eighteenth-century England, to be literate was to be uncommon. Now, despite the surprisingly high rate of functional illiteracy in the United States, most middle-class people take reading for granted. Yet neither Samuel Johnson nor we equate literacy with "reading." Nor does Harold Bloom, when he avers that "there is no distinction between the uncommon and the common reader: to be a reader is to be uncommon" (58). To "read," in this sense, is clearly more than to be able to understand the written instructions on a voter registration form or in a computer manual. While it is impossible to read unless one is literate, not all who are literate read.

Nor is it as easy now as it was in Samuel Johnson's day to define common readers demographically. Clarence Tracy believes that Johnson's imagined common reader belonged to the lower middle class, was a shopkeeper or soldier manifestly less genteel and less formally educated than the London gentlemen who read the *Tatler* and *Spectator*. Today's common readers may be found in all socioeconomic classes but are more likely to be middle-class. Whatever their class, most of them have spent 12 or more years reading books in a classroom, unlike the readers Johnson was addressing. Today's shopkeepers and soldiers are better educated and better off economically than Dr. Johnson's; they have more sources of enlightenment than the *Gentleman's Magazine*—not only the magazines Allan Bloom deplores, *Time*, *Playboy*, and *Scientific American*, but the *New York Times Book Review*, the *New Republic*, and the Book of the Month Club.

Richard Ohmann, whose definition of the common reader

we provisionally adopt in chapter five, focuses his attention on college-educated, urban, middle- and upper-class book buyers. Janice Radway singles out the mostly middle-class, nonacademic general readers who subscribe to the Book of the Month Club.[1] Later in this chapter we will look at a group of nine women in Washington, D.C., who formed a reading group in 1971 and will talk at greater length about the homemakers, artisans, and business people who attend reading programs in Vermont public libraries. What do these readers have in common?

For one thing, they are not "professional" readers. Unlike college professors, schoolteachers, literary critics, and book reviewers, they do not have to read unless they want to.[2] As we pointed out in chapter two, many Americans choose not to read books, turning for information and entertainment to other media such as film, video, and television. It is important to bear in mind, however, that television has not replaced books. Statistics that Lynne V. Cheney presents in *Humanities in America* show:

> In 1947 when less than one-half of one percent of U.S. households had television sets, 487 million books were sold. By 1985 when 98 percent of the homes in the United States had television, books sales were more than two *billion* — 400 percent of their 1947 level. (19, emphasis in the original)

Even allowing for the increase in U.S. population over those 38 years, these figures suggest, as Cheney concludes, that "people watch television *and* they read" (19, emphasis in the original).

What do they read? Are they weltering in the abysses of ignorance and psychosensual indulgence that Allan Bloom deplores? Do they profoundly require instruction in the basic units of culture, as E. D. Hirsch suggests? Are they in desperate need of a return to the verities of yesteryear recommended by *American Memory*? Do they read nothing but Danielle Steele, Louis L'Amour, and Agatha Christie? And if that is the case, is civilization tottering, as almost everyone seems to fear?

The undeniable popularity of such writers as Steele, L'Amour, and Christie suggests that today's common readers, like Dr. Johnson's, read for entertainment. But to assume that they are entertained only by romances, adventure tales, and mysteries is to ignore further data adduced by Lynne Cheney:

> The same bookstores that are selling the latest romance novels are also doing brisk business in Gabriel Garcia Marquez's *Love in the Time of Cholera*, Toni Morrison's *Beloved*, . . . and Richard Ellmann's biography of Oscar Wilde. Through bookstores and subscription, more than a million copies have been sold of volumes in The Library of America, a series containing the works of such authors as Melville, Whitman, Twain, Stowe, and Parkman. (3)

It is probably also a mistake to assume that people read what academics like to call "trash" in order to "escape from reality." As Janice A. Radway has compellingly demonstrated in *Reading the Romance*, many women use romance novels like Kathleen Woodiwiss's *The Flame and the Flower* and *Shanna* both to understand "their roles as wives and mothers" (87) and to rationalize those roles.

Richard Ohmann's reader looks to novels "for personal meaning,"[3] and Book of the Month Club members expect fiction to give them "practical advice about appropriate behavior in a changing world" (Radway, "Book-of-the-Month Club" 535). The "diverse crowd" of readers Lynne Cheney writes about in *Humanities in America* (1) are united only by their desire to gain "the insights that the humanities offer" (2). None of these common readers reads to "escape" reality but rather to understand and cope with it. What today's common readers, however more educationally, culturally, and economically heterogeneous than Dr. Johnson's, share with their eighteenth-century forebears is a belief that books matter, that they inform as well as entertain. If these nonacademic adults read some works that are part of the academic canon and others that are not, what motivates their choices?

If Dr. Johnson was right to insist that in literature the tests of time and continued popularity are everything, what does it mean that *Gone with the Wind* stays perpetually in print, while Elsa Morante's *History* was a mere blip on the radar screen tracking historical novels? Why do young people still read and love *Catcher*

in the Rye? Why do they like it better than *Huckleberry Finn*,
which all right-minded academics agree is the American bil-
dungsroman? For that matter, why do so many mothers, aunts,
and mentors pass along *Little Women* to their daughters, nieces,
and protégées? Why is that sentimental, didactic, wordy, moral-
istic girls' book, which is never taught in school or college or
graduate school, in print in at least seven paperback editions in
America and in countless foreign translations? Here is a book
that is not taught, is not respected by the literary/cultural establishment, but has nonetheless been a consistent best seller since it
was first published in 1868.[4]

Janet Sass's account of the reading group she participated in,
with eight other women, tells us a lot about the class and educational background of common readers, the value they attach to
books, and their experience with and subsequent attitude toward formal education. Here is Sass's profile of the group:

> We come from blue-collar and middle and upper-middle class back-
> grounds. We are married, single and gay. One of us is black, the rest
> white, ranging in age from 22 to 65. One woman has a Ph.D. in litera-
> ture; many of us have had some graduate training; all of us have B.A.s.
> Some of us are members of other women's groups. At this point in
> our lives, we are housewives, mothers, dropout graduate students,
> professionals, artists and part-time typists. In addition, we had two
> important things in common. We were all readers who believed in
> the power of literature. It went beyond our everyday experiences and
> defined the realm of human possiblity. Reading was a way to learn-
> ing about ourselves and to grow. Secondly, we all felt a need, no mat-
> ter how incoherently expressed, to interact with other women. (79–80)

These nine women signed up, in the fall of 1971, for a non-
credit course in Women and Literature sponsored by two Washington, D.C., women's groups, "with the traditional teacher, students and syllabi" (79). But they soon rebelled at their teacher's
choice of texts, beginning with Sinclair Lewis's *Main Street* ("after
four hours of discussion, [we] decided that Lewis had given Carol
Kennicott a raw deal" [79]), and took direction of their own reading and discussion. Because they believed literature was "a way
to learning about ourselves," they wanted to find women writers

"who could describe women's culture and consciousness, . . . offer some insight into the forces that had shaped our lives[,] and ways to overcome those forces" (80). They jettisoned Lewis and other male writers in favor of George Eliot, Doris Lessing, Simone de Beauvoir, Jane Addams, Maya Angelou, Sylvia Plath, and Margaret Mead. "It was exciting, electrifying," Sass reports:

> Discussion of women writers' books, because they described experiences common to us as women—pregnancy, child care, housework, marriage, loss of virginity—brought together our intellect and our feelings; made "book learning" relevant. . . . Our course is similar to consciousness-raising in that it helps us deal with our personal and political lives. Yet it differs from CR in that we are not exploring our problems and feelings directly but through literature, using the ideas and experiences of both group members and women writers as resources. (81–82)

"American Literature 201 was never like this" (80). Indeed, school had never been like this for these highly educated women ("We had nearly always read men writers in high school and college" [80]). They had been schooled not to demand that the books they read speak to their questions: "We now sensed a gap between what we were taught in school and the reality of our present lives" (81). More damagingly, they had been schooled not to trust themselves:

> In the traditional classroom, the teacher—whether male or female—is often an authority figure. This authority figure reinforces the woman student's passivity, lack of confidence and dependence on leaders. She turns to the teacher for knowledge, rather than developing critical skills and self-confidence in expressing her opinions. (83)

Perhaps their reading group meant so much to these women who wanted "to interact with other women" because "formal education has compartmentalized us" (81):

> The traditional classroom is . . . competitive and divisive with its emphasis on grades. Students and teacher often play one-upmanship games and try to impress each other with their knowledge; women are often intimidated by men students and those people with articulateness. These factors limit real communication. Competition may

be useful in certain situations, but learning depends on meaningful exchanges, not ego games. The traditional classroom doesn't teach people how to work together for common goals; it doesn't delineate when competition is appropriate behavior and when cooperation is. It divides feelings from intellect. Our classroom environment is very different from that described above. There are no authority figures and we try to maximize cooperation between members. We encourage people to care genuinely about each other and each others' ideas. We encourage reflection on personal experiences when that reflection is relevant to the point being discussed. We try to work together as a group. It's a give-and-take interaction between women rather than the lecture/test approach. (83)

Another extramural reading program serves to delineate not only today's common readers and the value they attach to the books they read but the failure of formal education to serve their needs. The Vermont Library Reading Project was initiated in 1978 as a pilot program for her community by Rutland, Vermont, librarian Pat Bates with a $9,800 grant from the Vermont Humanities Council. The reading series began modestly with modest expectations. The notion was to supply books on a theme, such as "Myths of Marriage" or "The Restless Spirit," to any library users who were interested and to publicize bimonthly evening meetings. At these, a humanities scholar would lecture on the book for about 40 minutes; then, after a break for coffee, cookies, and conversation, there would be 45 minutes or so of free-for-all group discussion, led as unobtrusively as possible by the scholar or, ideally, a volunteer from the group. This concept looked visionary in 1978. Victor Swenson, executive director of the Vermont Humanities Council, admits to skepticism in those early days about the public's response. "I'm not sure anyone reads anymore," Swenson remembers telling his staff. "Don't be surprised if it's not a success."[5]

The program was such a success that Pat Bates now works full-time for the National Endowment for the Humanities, supervising reading series programs in more than 30 states.[6] In 1985, the Vermont Library Reading Project became a separate entity, an offshoot of the state council. Administered by Sally Anderson, beginning with a federal grant of $200,000, the project keeps expanding and changing to meet new times and new interests.

In the last 11 years, all over the state, in big and little libraries in rich and poor, rural, urban and suburban settings, scholars have lectured on subjects as various as science fiction, crime literature, myths of marriage, restless spirits, the individual and the community, Canadian literature, and American biographies.

The women and men[7] who attend the Vermont Library Reading Project's series are primarily middle-class, most with at least a year or two of college, ranging in age from 25 to 70. Most of them work full- or part-time, most are married, most have children. Life for them is demanding; they do not have time on their hands. Often they describe having to find time to do the reading after getting home from work, making and serving dinner, putting the children to bed, doing the ironing and farm chores. They find the time, though, and they enrich book discussions with pertinent anecdotes from daily life, as well as with astute observations drawn from their often sophisticated understanding of politics, sociology, and psychology.

In the 11 years since the project was founded, it has attracted $600,000 in funds from the NEH, more than any other state. That, despite Vermont's population of only about half a million. Vermont has 251 communities large enough to have post offices, mostly rural towns and villages with small one- and two-room libraries close to half of which have offered at least one reading program; many plan two or three a year. In fact, townspeople have come to look forward to the discussions as part of the fabric of community life, replacing the dying tradition of the town meeting: "It recreates a sense of community that often is lost," Victor Swenson suggests. "We live in an immensely pluralistic culture where people have interests that differ widely. This program creates a common cultural area."[8]

The programs also provide intellectual challenge within a noncompetitive context. Horrace Strong, a Glover, Vermont, canoe builder, explained his enthusiasm: the reading series "forces me to read novels I would not read otherwise. I love the scholars that come. They bring out so much more you don't see."

And the scholars love to come. The many academics who are group leaders testify to the challenging atmosphere of the reading groups. Most who agree to do one talk sign on for more and more. While a small stipend is attached, few people would be willing to trek all over the state even in wretched weather for $150. It is the quality of interaction that attracts scholars. "I never say no," Pat Stuart of Norwich University in Northfield, Vermont, said. "When you're a college teacher, you have an audience of people who read because they have to. Here, people come because they love to read. Lots of times they think of things you haven't thought of."[9]

The Vermont series indicates—as do Janet Sass's account and our description of the founding of the *Doris Lessing Newsletter* and the Doris Lessing Society in chapter five—that common readers frequently long to be readers in common. Although reading itself is usually solitary, exchanging opinions and ideas about what one has read is an exciting enhancement. Teachers are familiar with the explosion of interest in a classroom when an actual discussion of a book occurs, and with the infrequent but delightful report from a student that "we left class and went to the student union and talked about the book for hours."

The Vermont Library Reading Project creates a situation that encourages the formation of communities of readers. People often attend because the evening at the library gives them a chance to put their week's reading into focus and perspective. Anticipating talking about a book makes reading it in the first place that much more stimulating.

So far as we can tell from attending and participating in this series over the past decade, many people—especially older people with some leisure time, but young and middle-aged people as well—want to continue learning. Such people, however, like those in Janet Sass's group, do not want a competitive situation that involves papers and exams. They *do* want a group leader, someone who is not quite a teacher in the conventional sense but who will supply background and biographical information, and some possible directions for group discussion. In Vermont, the discussion leader is asked to supply a list of questions to help get discussion going. Our experience indicates that these questions are the merest springboard. If the group wants to discuss, say, the incestuous nature of Maggie and Tom's relationship in *The Mill on the Floss*, no list of questions about historical period or types of symbolism will subvert the group's direction.

The common readers represented by Vermont readers have a freedom often denied college students and even academics: they read what they read because they decide they want to, and then they examine what they have read from personally relevant perspectives. Such freshness and immediacy can at its best form a constantly renewing circle between the community of readers and the academic participant. The academic brings her/his reading to the group; the group produces its often highly original reading(s); the group also benefits from the academic's research and more scholarly reading; both go back to their books having learned something new; and the academic becomes included in the community of readers. The inclusion of the academic is signified by her/his being invited back year after year to discuss different books, with the group becoming ever more challenging *and* friendly. This experience represents at its best an ideal of learning and reciprocity rarely achieved in the conventional hierarchical classroom.

Unfortunately, as Lynne V. Cheney emphasizes in *Humanities in America*, few college teachers can afford the luxury of conversing with the common reader:

> In trying to engage faculty members from some academic institutions, state councils and other groups often find themselves frustrated by a research-oriented culture that does not value what they do. . . . Young scholars, hoping for tenure, are particularly reluctant to become involved in public programming, not merely because it will take time that could be devoted to research and publication, but because it is not regarded by academic peers as activity which is sufficiently scholarly. . . . When work in public humanities projects is recognized, it is sometimes credited against "public service," a

category that may count for little in tenure, promotion, and salary decisions. Observed Anita May, Executive Director of the Oklahoma Foundation for the Humanities, "Working in public humanities is regarded as roughly the same as organizing a Girl Scout troop." (28)

Cheney finds it paradoxical that "at the same time that people outside the academy are increasingly turning to literary, historical, and philosophical study, are increasingly finding in the [humanities] a source of enrichment for themselves and their society" (5),[10] academics under competitive pressure to succeed professionally are increasingly withdrawing into specialization and esoterica:

> Almost thirty years ago, C. P. Snow expressed concern about the division between the "two cultures" of science and literature. At an [NEH] advisory group meeting in Washington, D.C., historian Gertrude Himmelfarb expressed concern about a newer chasm, equally deep and troubling. Scholarship in the humanities is frequently so arcane, she said, that now the "two cultures" are the academy and society. (10)

Responding for the academy, Barbara Herrnstein Smith, then president of the Modern Language Association, called Himmelfarb a "neoconservative history professor" who represents "a current, deeply disquieting tendency (among some academics as well as some government officials and journalists) to represent the university in this country as *at odds with* the community at large" ("President's Column" 3, emphasis in the original).

Nonetheless, despite Herrnstein Smith's optimism, there does seem to be division between the academy and the community. Using the Vermont Library Reading Project as a gauge, most of the humanists who participate as scholars are women; most are on the faculties of such institutions as Johnson and Castleton state colleges, Norwich University, Vermont College, Trinity College, and Saint Michael's College; or are teachers in middle and secondary public and private institutions; or are members of other professions who have humanities degrees and enjoy talking about books. A tiny minority of speakers are from the prestige institutions in the area: the University of Vermont, Middlebury

College, and Dartmouth College. Participation in the reading series does not count toward tenure and is the opposite of status-enhancing. Indeed, we are informed by colleagues that such participation is viewed in their departments as hopelessly middlebrow, as "mere" popularization, and as compromising scholarly standards of discourse. Even those who do not subscribe to these notions or who would like to see what participation in such a series is like, admit to embarrassment. Such information is, of course, informal and anecdotal, not statistical, but it is worth noting as a bellwether.

The relationship between the common reader and the academy is the subject of much of this book. Like Lynne Cheney, we often charge the academic establishment of disdaining, when it does not actively despise, common readers. But we are equally suspicious of the National Endowment for the Humanities's ostensible concern for their welfare. Our analysis of *American Memory* reveals what even a casual perusal of the NEH's 1988 report, *Humanities in America*, also shows: a fundamental mistrust of ordinary people's taste, revealed by such off-hand remarks as "Our society is . . . characterized by what may be kindly called triviality: badly written books, terrible television programs, mindless entertainments of every sort" that "exist because there is a demand for them" (*Humanities* 3). Cheney rejoices that "it is difficult to overestimate public audiences" after admitting that "there has always been concern that public programs would provide a watered-down version of the humanities, that they would be driven in this direction by a public less interested in real learning than in a thin imitation of it" (25). While on the one hand, she says public humanities programs, like the Vermont Library Reading Project, constitute "a kind of parallel school, one that has grown up outside established institutions of education," on the other she cautions that this "parallel school" is not an "alternative" to formal education because it "cannot provide the coherent plan of study, the overarching vision of connectedness, that our schools and colleges can" (27–28).

Leaving aside, for the moment, the question of whether an

"overarching vision of connectedness" is possible or desirable in an increasingly pluralistic, heterogenous society, Cheney's assumption that common readers will flounder in "unrestrained diversity" (27) unless directed by an omniscient professoriat is both insultingly paternalistic and willfully blind to the diverse needs of common readers.

As the pundits seek to shape educational policy today—asking how we are learning, what we are learning, why we are learning, and who is learning—they would do well to remember Dr. Johnson's respect for the common reader. Like his humble barge boy, the Vermont housewives and canoe builders who make time in their demanding schedules to read the often daunting books assigned for such series as "Perceptions of Japan," "Vermont and the New Nation," "Establishing America," and "The Community and Individual Rights"[11] "give what [they] have" to learn. Their sincerity, intelligence, and discernment deserve the tribute Dr. Johnson paid the barge boy, not the condescension of either the National Endowment for the Humanities or the academic establishment, to which we now turn our attention. In the next chapter, we will chart the vagaries over the past 100 years of the academy's attitude toward the common reader, whom it alternately woos and scorns.

4

Academic English
and the Common Reader

The pages of *Critical Inquiry* were enlivened in December 1983 by Stanley Fish's spirited defense of professionalism against journalists Peter S. Jay of the *Baltimore Sun* and Jonathan Yardley of the *Washington Post* and against fellow-professor Walter Jackson Bate.

Fish's point of departure was a recent column in which Jay had indicted professors of literature for abandoning "the study of life itself, as seen by writers of skill and vision," for "specialization" and "ephemera," thus making "their field so obscure, and its language so arcane, that no one can possibly understand it but themselves and a handful of other insiders" (Jay, quoted in Fish, "Profession" 349).

Yardley's attack was more specific, occasioned by the publication of a manuscript version of Virginia Woolf's first novel, *The Voyage Out*. He regarded this as "a byproduct of academic specialization," of interest only to Woolf scholars for whom "each new shred of information is grist for the mill that produces dissertations and offprints, and papers and seminars—the effluvia of English departments" (Yardley, quoted in Fish, "Profession" 351).

Fish read these strictures against academic specialization as thinly veiled attacks on "the profession of letters itself, with all its attendant machinery, periods, journals, newsletters, articles, monographs, panels, symposia, conventions, textbooks, bibliographies, departments, committees, recruiting, placement, promotion, prizes, and the like" (351). Indeed, he said, once you have identified the proper object of literary study with something so general as the study of life itself, it is hard to see why there would be any need for an army of specialists whose business it was to tell you about literature. Isn't everyone, after all, an expert in life itself, fully competent to read and understand the work of those who have taken life as their subject? (351–52)

Somewhat testily, Fish remarked upon "the ambivalence with which our society regards professionalism." The word "professional" is, in some cases, an honorific, inspiring confidence; in others—including, in Fish's representation of Jay and Yardley, academia—it designates "an activity in which a small and self-selected group conspires against the laity by claiming a superiority that is based finally on nothing more than an obfuscating jargon and the seized control of the machinery of production and distribution" (352).

Saddest of all to Fish (hence his essay's subtitle, "Fear and Self-Loathing in Literary Studies") was seeing critiques of "professionalism" being mounted from within the profession itself. He cited as one example an essay in which Walter Jackson Bate inveighed against a "new ersatz specialism" which had replaced "integrity and generality of vision" (Bate, quoted in Fish 353), and as another, Edward Said's attack on "the cult of expertise and professionalism" (Said, "Opponents" 9).

For the literary historian and sociologist, this conflict between specialists and generalists is suffused with an eerie quality of déjà vu, as is so much of the current debate about the canon. In "Professionalization and the Rewards of Literature: 1875–1900," Michael Warner outlines the conflict, at the founding moment in American academic English, between "philological scholarship" and an Arnoldian humanism he calls "literary culture," between German-educated philologists and "gentlemen amateurs" like Henry Wadsworth Longfellow and James Russell Lowell (1), between those who wanted "to organize their profession along the lines of the German graduate model" and "teach modern languages on a scientific model" (2) and those who invoked "humanism, platonism and Christianity" as "grounds for thinking of literature as the locus, in the college curriculum, of truth, the ideal, and the spiritual" and therefore "beyond the reach of mere specialists" (7).

What would seem, in Warner's analysis of the origins of academic English, to be a simple binary opposition turns out, in Gerald Graff's history of American academic literary studies from 1828 to the present, to be a dialectic between two opposed systems of value that, through a kind of institutional metempsychosis, assume different shapes from one generation to the next. "It is worth pondering," according to Graff,

> that the kind of scholarship we now think of as traditionally humanistic was regarded as a subversive innovation by the traditionalists of an earlier era. . . . It is also worth pondering that traditional humanists of the same era indicted research scholarship for many of the very same sins for which later traditionalists indicted the New Criticism and present day traditionalists indict literary theory: elevating esoteric, technocratic jargon over humanistic values, coming between literature itself and the student, turning literature into an elitist pastime for specialists. (*Professing* 4)

The dialectic Graff traces through 150 years of academic English in America is not, however, between professionals on the one hand and antiprofessionals on the other. If the German-trained philologists of the last quarter of the nineteenth century tried to "define the terms of professionalism in literary studies," so also did the "generalists" who favored the "ideal of liberal or general culture against that of narrowly specialized research." Granting that "in some ways" the generalists "epitomize[d] the viewpoint that Stanley Fish has recently called 'anti-professionalism,'" Graff insists that "they were not opposed to professionalism itself, but only to the narrow forms it had taken" (55).[1]

If the recurring debate within academic English has not been between professionalism and antiprofessionalism, what *has* it all been about? Fish, like the philologists before him, appears to be asserting that the study of literature is a "business" (351) best conducted by those "who know what they are doing" (352). The various Establishment opponents of this view have little in common, it would seem, save the belief that the common reader has the ability and the right to read literature without specialized training because, as Douglas Bush said in 1948, "literature deals with life" (quoted in Graff, *Professing* 186).[2]

But to know, at any particular moment in the institutional history of English studies, who was on which side of this war between the interests of a scholarly clerisy and those of an imagined body of lay readers is a ticklish business. For example, in 1948 Douglas Bush blamed New Criticism for dispossessing common readers of their literary bill of rights, and in 1983 Edward Said reiterated the charge:

> Until the advent of American and English New Criticism, the job of a critic was an appreciation of work as much for the general reader as for other critics. Functionalist criticism makes an extremely sharp break between the community of critics and the general public. The assumption is that to write a literary work and to write about one are specialized functions with no simple equivalent or cause in every day human experience. (*The World* 144)

Yet in another essay, Said thought it "strangely perverse" that the "legacy" of New Criticism should be "the private-clique consciousness embodied in a kind of critical writing that has virtually abandoned any attempt at reaching a large, if not a mass audience" because "in practice, New Criticism, for all its elitism, was strangely populist in intention":

> The idea behind the pedagogy, and of course the preaching, of [Cleanth] Brooks and Robert Penn Warren was that everyone properly instructed could feel, perhaps even act, like an educated gentleman. . . . The school deliberately and perhaps incongruously tried to create a wide community of responsive readers out of a very large, potentially unlimited, constituency of students and teachers of literature. ("Opponents" 10–12)

Terry Eagleton has noted a similar "ambivalence" about the English version of New Criticism represented by F. R. Leavis and *Scrutiny*, the journal he cofounded in 1932. While Leavis insisted "that there is no essential discontinuity between literature and social life," he did not "endorse a cult of genteel amateurism."

Criticism, for Leavis, was not "a mere matter of 'good sense,' but must engage modes of analysis and forms of specialized experience denied to the 'common reader'" (*Function* 72). *Scrutiny* both claimed "an authoritative title to judge all sectors of social life" and attempted to establish criticism "as a rigorously analytical discourse beyond the reach of both common reader and common-room wit" (74).

Both Said and Eagleton accuse the academy of delivering New Criticism into the hands of a clerical elite, thus depriving the common reader of its emancipatory potential. Said believes that "the tendency toward formalism in New Criticism was accentuated by the academy":

> For the fact is that a disciplined attention to language can only thrive in the rarefied atmosphere of the classroom. Linguistics and literary analysis are features of the modern school, not of the marketplace. Purifying the language of the tribe—whether as a project subsumed within modernism or as a hope kept alive by embattled New Criticisms surrounded by mass culture—always moved further from the really big existing tribes and closer toward emerging new ones, comprised of the acolytes of a reforming or even revolutionary creed who in the end seemed to care more about turning the new creed into an intensely separatist orthodoxy than about forming a large community of readers. ("Opponents" 12)

Similarly, Said charges academicization with turning the democratic impulses of F. R. Leavis into a "shrill withdrawal" from the world ("Opponents" 12), a charge amplified by Eagleton into a generalization about the consequences of institutionalizing English studies:

> The academicization of criticism provided it with an institutional basis and professional structure; but by the same token it signalled its final sequestration from the public realm. Criticism achieved security by committing political suicide; its moment of academic institutionalization is also the moment of its effective demise as a socially active force. (*Function* 65)

We seem to have returned to the terms of the debate characterized by Stanley Fish as a conflict between professionalism and antiprofessionalism, having aligned the former with a clerical coterie and the latter with the common reader. But there is a possibly unexamined contradiction at the heart of Said's and Eagleton's arguments that challenges this clear demarcation between lay good-guys and institutional bad-guys.

These two critics align themselves with an imagined dispossessed common reader. In fact, both Eagleton and Said are as firmly entrenched within the academic power structure as any two men can be, despite their ostensibly radical politics. As various articles in the *New York Times Magazine* make clear, and as their ease in finding voice in prestigious journals and with respected presses demonstrates, Said's and Eagleton's brands of populism and Marxism are accepted aspects of an American and British academy not noted for its egalitarianism. The battle between the professionals and the so-called antiprofessionals as we outline it here is waged entirely within the profession by strongly empowered members of the profession.

To return to New Criticism, then. As practiced on both sides of the Atlantic, it did not pass from a nonacademic phase to institutionalized ossification; close reading was, as Said admits, always a *pedagogical* tool, and the "populist," "democratic" motives he attributes to Brooks, Warren, and Leavis led them not out of the academy but, directly or indirectly, into academic reform.

F. R. Leavis began his academic career as a "freelance" tutor,[3] working under I. A. Richards at Cambridge in the early 1920s, when a generation of postwar scholars and students "made the new English School at Cambridge very different from the traditional academic establishment" (Mulhern 23). Amply documented by E. M. W. Tillyard, one of the school's "architects" (Eagleton, *Literary Theory* 30), as well as D. J. Palmer, Francis Mulhern, and Chris Baldick, the revolution in literary studies that took place at Cambridge in the decade after the armistice of 1918 was a direct consequence of and response to the economic, political, social, and cultural crisis caused by the Great War.

Mulhern suggests that this crisis manifested itself at Cambridge both ideologically and demographically. "The accumulated resources" of Britain's "inherited discourses" (religion, systematic philosophy, liberal economics, and sociology) were incapable of tackling the "new and taxing problems" created by the war, and

> the aggregate effect of the changing occupational structure of the economy . . . and the economic and political crises of the inter-war period, was to weaken the old intellectual bloc, whose inner cohesion and general authority had rested on its ties of kinship and privileged social intercourse with a confident ruling class. (312)

The men and women who fashioned the Cambridge English Tripos in 1917 and taught its students were, as Terry Eagleton pungently reminds us, a new breed of Oxbridge academics:

> F. R. Leavis was the son of a musical instruments dealer, Q. D. Roth [later Queenie Leavis] the daughter of a draper and hosier [and] I. A. Richards the son of a works manager in Cheshire. . . . English was to be fashioned not by the patrician dilettantes who occupied the early Chairs of Literature at the ancient universities, but by the offspring of the provincial petty bourgeoisie[,] . . . members of a social class entering the traditional Universities for the first time, able to identify and challenge the social assumptions which informed its literary judgements. (*Literary Theory* 30)

Thus, what had been the "belles lettres" of the aristocracy who had rooms at and took degrees from Cambridge became the "profession" of the petite bourgeoisie, descendents of the "shopkeepers, mercers, maids of all work, oilmen, and common soldiers" (Tracy 412) who comprised Samuel Johnson's common reader. Democratization and professionalization held hands at Cambridge in the 1920s.

The link between the Cambridge English School and American New Criticism was forged by I. A. Richards, who left Cambridge in 1931 to accept a visiting post at Harvard, which was regularized in 1943 (Graff, *Professing* 163). Richards brought with him a conviction that literature, a chief repository of cultural meaning and integrity, would fill the gap left vacant by the abdication of Britain's "inherited discourses."

American education suffered not because of the bankruptcy of inherited discourses but because of the young nation's lack of

the shared common culture such discourses might have provided. As in England, this lack was experienced most acutely in
the aftermath of war, that stern test of a nation's self-definition
and purpose. Educators responded to this crisis, after both world
wars, by setting up programs in general education, or "great
books" as they were more popularly called. Graff suggests that
"general education expressed a desire to restore common beliefs
and values, and the humanities were seen as central to this goal
by endowing the student with the sense of a common cultural
heritage" (*Professing* 162). John Erskine's General Honors course
at Columbia in the 1920s originated in an adult education course
he had developed for American soldiers in France, encouraging
them to read the classics as if they were contemporary—and
relevant—documents (Graff, *Professing* 132–33). In the 1930s,
Robert Hutchins, president of the University of Chicago, was
persuaded by a young philosophy professor who had worked
with Erskine, Mortimer J. Adler, to institute general education
on a large scale. But it was not until the end of World War II that
the idea caught the national imagination.

The 1945 Report of the Harvard Committee, *General Education in a Free Society*, was influential in spreading the idea of
general education from a few elite universities to secondary and
post-secondary schools nationwide. I. A. Richards served on the
committee that drafted this report, and "practical criticism" was
offered as the best pedagogical instrument for disseminating
general education. Close reading would give students

> access to the unified cultural tradition that was felt to be latent in
> the great literary texts beneath or above the merely fragmentary and
> incoherent flux of history and historical knowledge. Through the
> new pedagogy of explication, it was felt, tradition and cultural unity
> could thus be inculcated without providing elaborate historical con-
> texts. (Graff, *Professing* 163)

As in England, then, practical criticism appeared to offer a
way to democratize the academy from within, while still up-
holding the university and its faculty as the privileged sources
of knowledge. Practical criticism provided a vastly enlarged range

of students—veterans and first-generation Americans as well as sons and daughters of the working class and scions of wealthy capitalists—with equal access to a "common culture."

Therefore, to align professionalism with a clerical coterie in opposition to the interests of the common reader is not only to oversimplify but seriously to misrepresent the intentions and the pedagogical practice of New Critics on both sides of the Atlantic. But it is equally erroneous to assume that New Criticism championed the innate rights and intelligence of common readers. (Again, notions of oscillation and process are more useful and appropriate than concepts such as dialectic and progress.)

For "there is no Common Reader," Leavis announced in 1933; "the tradition is dead" ("How to Teach" 107). So Leavis set out to create him. In a 1930 pamphlet introduced by an epigraph from Matthew Arnold's *Culture and Anarchy*, Leavis revealed the elitism that underlay his later proposals for educational reform, *Education and the University* (1943) and *English Literature in our Time and the University* (the 1967 Clark Lectures):

> In any period it is upon a very small minority that the discerning appreciation of art and literature depends: it is . . . only a few who are capable of unprompted, first-hand judgment. They are still a small minority, though a larger one, who are capable of endorsing such first-hand judgment by genuine personal response. . . . The minority capable not only of appreciating Dante, Shakespeare, Donne, Baudelaire, Conrad (to take major instances) but of recognizing their latest successors constitute the consciousness of the race (or of a branch of it) at a given time. . . . Upon this minority depends our power of profiting by the finest human experience of the past; they keep alive the subtlest and most perishable parts of tradition. Upon them depend the implicit standards that order the finer living of an age, the sense that this is worth more than that, this rather than that is the direction in which to go, that the centre is here rather than there. ("Mass Civilization" 143–45)

Leavis's hypothetical "English School" was designed to produce "a mind equipped to carry on for itself; trained to work in the conditions in which it will have to work if it is to carry on at all; having sufficient knowledge, experience, self-reliance and staying power for undertaking, and persisting in, sustained inquiries" (*Education* 60). Modeled on the Cambridge Tripos, in Part I it would train students to read, analyzing selected poems at length in order to develop students' "perception, judgment and analytic skill" (69). "An elite" (42) selected from among these students for their "pertinacity and staying power" (34) would proceed to take Part II of the Tripos, "a study of the Seventeenth Century—the Seventeenth Century, not merely in literature, but as a whole; the Seventeenth Century as a key phase, or passage, in the history of the civilization" (48). The successful graduate of this course of study, having written a paper "on the process of change by which the England of the Seventeenth Century turned into the England of today" (60), would be thereby demonstrably equipped with

> a mind that will approach the problems of modern civilization with an understanding of their origins, a maturity of outlook, and, not a nostalgic addiction to the past, but a sense of human possibilities, difficult of achievement, that traditional cultures bear witness to and that it would be disastrous, in a breach of continuity, to lose sight of for good. (56)

Somewhat polemically, Terry Eagleton asks why the Scrutineers, who believed that by studying the Great Tradition they were "addressing questions of fundamental value—questions which were of vital relevance to the lives of men and women wasted in fruitless labour in the factories of industrial capitalism," should at the same time have dissociated themselves from "such men and women, who might be a little slow to recognize how a poetic enjambement enacted a movement of physical balancing" (*Literary Theory* 35). Without attempting to answer that question comprehensively, we acknowledge the paradox, which emerges again and again throughout the history of academic English.

One often unmentioned component, however, of the unacknowledged struggle between the pedagogical clerisy and the laity is the significance of print technology. In the eighteenth century Samuel Johnson was able to standardize both the lan-

guage and the literary canon because print technology was sufficiently advanced to change books from a clerical and aristocratic privilege to commodities widely available to the middle
and even working classes. When books and manuscripts were
handmade esoterica, obviously only persons with means and
education possessed them.

Interestingly, close reading itself is an offshoot of this new
technology: only with the text in front of one can the student or
pedagogue be attentive to every nuance of etymology, allusion,
and metaphor. Hence, the insistence on the common reader's inability to comprehend texts may be viewed as an (unexamined)
attempt by academics of whatever ostensible political stamp to
retain aristocratic hegemony.

It is easy to demonstrate that self-professed clerics like the
German-trained philologists who founded the Modern Language
Association scorned the common reader. Addressing the 1885
meeting of the MLA, Theodore Hunt deplored the then current
assumption "that English literature is a subject for the desultory
reader in his leisure hours rather than an intellectual study for
serious workers" (quoted in Warner 4). But it is equally important
to acknowledge that even Arnoldian humanists like Erskine in
the United States and Leavis in England, who believed that literature needed no "screen of historical and critical apparatus to
make it available to students or general readers" (Erskine, quoted
in Graff, *Professing* 86), still distinguished between "the cultured
classes" and "the vulgarity of the masses" (Graff, *Professing* 83).
General education and practical criticism appear more democratic than the arcane pursuits of research philologists, but they
were never truly populist.

Nor is the most recent educational initiative on behalf of the
common reader, the plan to promote "cultural literacy" propounded
by E. D. Hirsch and sanctioned by William Bennett and many
prominent educators. For great books, Hirsch substitutes a grand
list of dates, names, events, titles, and aphorisms Americans
"know" or "need to know." (As the editor of the *ADE [Association
of Departments of English] Bulletin* pointed out, "the title of the

list itself, 'What Americans Know,' becomes transformed in the
subtitle of the book [Hirsch's *Cultural Literacy*] to *What Every
American Needs to Know*" ["From the Editor" 4].) But his avowed
intention is the same as those of John Erskine, Robert Hutchins,
and other earlier advocates of general education, to provide all
students access to our shared cultural legacy as Americans.[4]

Like the architects of general education, the proponents of
cultural literacy employ emancipatory rhetoric: "The antidote to
growing specialization is to reinvigorate the unspecialized domain of literate discourse, where all can meet on common ground"
(Hirsch 31) like doughboys in French trenches engaged in a "free-
for-all discussion" of "the best sellers of ancient times" (Graff, *Professing* 134, quoting Erskine). It is generous and democratic: "We
have a duty to those who lack cultural literacy to determine and
disclose its contents" (Hirsch 26) because "cultural literacy constitutes the only sure avenue of opportunity for disadvantaged
children, the only reliable way of combating the social deter-
minism that now condemns them to remain in the same social
and educational condition as their parents" (Hirsch xiii). Or is it?

"The basic goal of education," according to Hirsch, is "the transmission to children of the specific information shared by the
adults of the group or polis":

> Plato rightly believed that it is natural for children to learn an adult
> culture, but too confidently assumed that philosophy could devise
> the one best culture. (Nonetheless, we should concede to Plato that
> within our culture we have an obligation to choose and promote our
> best traditions.) (xvi)

A generous concession. Who is this "we" who decides what's
"best," who "determine[s] and disclose[s]" the "contents" of cultural
literacy? Not the Amish:

> It is for the Amish to decide what Amish traditions are, but it is for
> all of us [excluding the Amish, of course] to decide collectively what
> our American traditions are, to decide what "American" means on
> the other side of the hyphen in Italo-American or AsianAmerican. (98)-

And not African Americans, because cultural literacy is encoded
in "standard written English" (3).

"To be truly literate," Hirsch explains, "citizens must be able to grasp the meaning of any piece of writing addressed to the general reader. . . . Books and newspapers assume a 'common reader,' that is, a person who knows the things known by other literate persons in the culture" (12–13). Since, as we have already noted, there is no single, unitary "common reader" in today's pluralistic, multilingual America, Hirsch is here indulging in myopic nostalgia for a world that has never existed except, perhaps, on the BBC's *Masterpiece Theater* and in the spate of British Empire films of the last decade. Hirsch's notion of cultural literacy seems overdetermined by Anglophilia. It embodies and evokes a world in which culture was unitary. This fantasy world is small and has a small population of racially similar people. It has one cultural center, one language, a long, relatively stable history, a dominant and widely accepted religion, a strong central government, and little immigration (with, concomitantly, lots of emigration of nonconforming elements).[5]

There is, moreover, a pernicious circularity built into Hirsch's apparently democratic appeal to the common reader. Only culturally literate persons can read prose addressed to Hirsch's "common reader." Only they, therefore, can "posit"—to use his word (135)—who the "common reader" is. Constructing a national vocabulary or "list" from material they know, these culturally literate common readers then declare as "ours" (and therefore necessary to inculcate through universal public education) a partial version of the actual national whole. The culturally illiterate are not involved in constructing the list and are not asked to verify and validate it. They are just to be taught it, which is probably why the Amish withdraw their children from public schools at the age of 14.[6]

The academic establishment from Cambridge (Leavis) to Harvard (Richards) to Virginia (Hirsch) to Chicago (Bloom) has, historically, distrusted when it has not actively despised the common reader, who is represented in professors' classrooms by the students they teach. Allan Bloom, in *The Closing of the American Mind*, scornfully describes today's students:

Lack of education simply results in students' seeking for enlightenment wherever it is readily available, without being able to distinguish between the sublime and trash, insight and propaganda. For
the most part students turn to the movies, ready prey to interested
moralisms such as the depiction of Gandhi or Thomas More ... or
to insinuating flattery of their secret aspirations and vices, giving
them a sense of significance. ... The distance from the contemporary and its high seriousness that students most need in order not to
indulge their petty desires and to discover what is most serious about
themselves cannot be found in the cinema. (64)

Even someone as sympathetic to students as Jim Merod, who
dignifies them as "intellectuals in process" (128), occasionally ex-
hibits the pedagogue's (inevitable?) mild condescension:

But the question that should trouble critics and teachers is ... how
to engage the dormant curiosity and sleeping critical instincts that
really do come alive (however imperfectly) when people are shown
their own stakes and inherent interests. This is the context in which
intellectual identities can be formed and set in motion. (141)

From the beginning, professors of literature in this country
have subscribed to what Brazilian educator Paolo Freire terms
"the 'banking' concept of education" in which "knowledge is a
gift bestowed by those who consider themselves knowledgeable
upon those whom they consider to know nothing." In this model,
students are "containers" or "receptacles," to be "filled" by the
teacher: "The more completely he fills the receptacles, the better
a teacher he is. The more meekly the receptacles permit themselves to be filled, the better students they are" (58).

By contrast, Freire developed and practiced what he called
"problem-posing education," which "consists in acts of cognition,
not transferrals of information":

Through dialogue, the teacher-of-the-students and the students-of-
the-teacher cease to exist and a new term emerges: teacher-student
with students-teachers. The teacher is no longer merely the-one-
who-teaches, but one who is himself taught in dialogue with the
students, who in turn while being taught also teach. They become
jointly responsible for a process in which all grow. In this process,
arguments based on "authority" are no longer valid; in order to func-

tion, authority must be *on the side of* freedom, not *against* it. Here, no one teaches another, nor is anyone self-taught. Men teach each other, mediated by the world, by the cognizable objects which in banking education are "owned" by the teacher. (67, emphases in the original)

In sum, "banking education treats students as objects of assistance; problem-posing education makes them critical thinkers" (71) by entering into "dialogue" with them. Freire defines dialogue as "the encounter between men, mediated by the world, in order to name the world" (76), and points out that it can take place only when both parties to the conversation are deemed fully and equally human and intelligent. Hence, his insistence that the teachers love their students, have faith in them, and remain humble about their own knowledge:

> How can I dialogue if I always project ignorance onto others and never perceive my own? How can I dialogue if I regard myself as a case apart from other men—mere "its" in whom I cannot recognize other "I"s? How can I dialogue if I consider myself a member of the in-group of "pure" men, the owners of truth and knowledge, for whom all non-members are "these people" or "the great unwashed?" How can I dialogue if I start from the premise that naming the world is the task of an elite? . . . How can I dialogue if I am afraid of being displaced? (78–79)

Freire developed his radical pedagogy to empower the illiterate South American peasants he so profoundly respected so that they might lay claim to their rights and redress social injustice. His *Pedagogy of the Oppressed*, published in the United States toward the end of the tumultuous 1960s, struck disaffected, radical American academics as uncannily pertinent to their project of reaching out to the oppressed and marginalized in this country. In particular, despite Freire's (or his translator's) unredeemed use of the generic "he," to many feminists "much of what Paulo Freire [had] written about the adult literacy process as a possibility of action for freedom seem[ed] to be applicable to women's studies" (Foster 6).

The women in the Washington, D.C., reading group we considered in chapter three testified that formal education had failed them in two ways. By erasing most women writers from history, it had denied them the validity of their experience. And by emphasizing the professor's authority and their own ignorance, it had reinforced their passivity and dependence. In "Toward a Woman-Centered University," Adrienne Rich named these as "two ways in which a woman's integrity is likely to be undermined by the process of university education. . . . In terms of the *content* of her education, there is no discipline that does not obscure or devalue the history and experience of women as a group" (134). But "the content of courses and programs is only the more concrete form of undermining experienced by the woman student":

> More invisible, less amenable to change by committee proposal or fiat, is the hierarchal image, the structure of relationships, even the style of discourse, including assumptions about theory and practice, ends and means, process and goal. (136)

Rich proposed changes in both the content and style of education to meet the needs of women, recommending a "reorganization of knowledge . . . that can help us know our foremothers, evaluate our present historical, political, and personal situation, and take ourselves seriously as agents in the creation of a more balanced culture" (141). And she called for a pedagogy that would be "more dialogic, more exploratory, less given to pseudo-objectivity, than the traditional mode," one that would be—above all—"antihierarchical" (143, 145).

Adrienne Rich developed her notion of feminist pedagogy through teaching in a program designed for the oppressed, the SEEK Program developed at the City College of New York in the late 1960s to extend higher education to poor and minority students. When she went to Douglass College in 1976, she "came to perceive stunning parallels" between "the so-called disadvantaged students at City" and women students ("Taking Women Students Seriously" 239).

Florence Howe developed her pioneering women's studies course at Goucher College after teaching in a freedom school and says that "it was not difficult to move from the Mississippi experience to teaching women. . . . In Mississippi, the starting place was the lives of black high school students, mostly poor; at Goucher, the starting place was the lives of white college women, mostly middle-class" ("Introduction" 1).

However they got there, from the freedom schools of the Deep South, the ghettos of Manhattan, or their suburban consciousness-raising groups, the women (and a few men) who taught the first women's studies courses in the late 1960s and early 1970s were committed to a pedagogy that affirmed and empowered students. In their introduction to *Female Studies IV*, Elaine Showalter and Carol Ohmann describe some of the features of the ideal feminist classroom:

> In terms of teaching techniques and the atmosphere of the class-room, radical approaches to women's studies include collectivism, both in teaching and research; breakdown of the professional bar-riers between teacher and students; elimination of student competi-tion in the form of domination of discussion and/or grades; and en-couragement and acceptance of the personal and experiential. (vii)

Ira Shor, reporting on his experience teaching women's studies in a community college, elaborated:

> To reconstruct consciousness, a classroom has to be casual, unthreat-ening and personal. The material in question has to evolve into and through students' own experience or else it will never evoke their energy or transform their ideology. Students must create during class debate as much as is brought to them at the outset, so that they do not feel overwhelmed by texts, reading lists and artifacts pre-sented to them. Education for them (and for us) has been an enor-mous and mysterious body of knowledge outside our needs and our experience. This classroom *gestalt* has to be broken as a stark an-nouncement that the immediate inside and outside of a student's life are necessary starting points for class discussion. . . . In this setting, English education does not place standard usage or great literature above student biography, but uses language as a means for provoking a student's conscious sense of self. That seems to be a starting point for transforming needs and expectations. (59)

If the women in Janet Sass's reading group had experienced such a classroom, would they have felt so disaffected by formal education? Barbara Scott Winkler interviewed 35 undergraduates at the University of Minnesota, the University of Missouri–Columbia, San Francisco State University, and Wellesley College to determine "how their involvement in Women's Studies affected them." She learned that students valued the information and "new, critical way of thinking" courses provided. Even more frequently, they asserted that women's studies "validated them as perceivers and knowers." She quotes one student's definition of a feminist classroom as "anti-elitist," as "restor[ing] authority to the mind that's questioning and learning" (29).

The *1989 Women's Studies Program Directory* published by the National Women's Studies Association (NWSA) lists 525 women's studies programs in the United States and Puerto Rico. At few of these colleges and universities is a course in women's studies required for graduation, however; and it would be naive to believe that all women's studies teachers succeed in creating the ideal feminist classroom we have depicted. But women's studies teachers are not the only practitioners of Paolo Freire's "pedagogy of the oppressed." In African-American and Hispanic studies programs and in innumerable classrooms across the nation, radical teachers like, for example, Jim Merod, acknowledge the authenticity of their students' experience and structure courses that validate their intelligence and curiosity. The Vermont reading series and similar relatively populist and nonhierarchical NEH and locally organized and funded "lifetime learning" programs embody something like Freire's noninstitutionalized co-learning model of education. As such, they continue the ideal established by Samuel Johnson two centuries ago, an ideal that assumes that "desire of knowledge is the natural feeling of mankind; and every man who is not debauched would give all that he has to get knowledge" (*London Journal* 329).

Perhaps this ideal has continued uninterrupted, if often imperceptible, throughout the history of academic English studies. Our reading of that history, however, suggests that there is something unprecedented about the present moment in American higher education. Over the last two decades, there have been a number of disparate but often complementary forces working from within the academy to call its hegemonic self-assurance and sense of superiority to the common reader into question. The profession of letters has been opened, often against its will, to previously disenfranchised constituencies with strong ties to common readers: not only women but African Americans, Asian Americans, Hispanic Americans, Native Americans, gays, lesbians, and working-class scholars as well. At the same time, new theoretical discourses like deconstruction and new historicism have challenged the bland assumption of "humanists" like Bloom, Cheney, Hirsch, Bate—and before them Bush, Hutchins, Richards, and Leavis—that there are "truths that pass beyond time and circumstance; truths that, transcending accidents of class, race, and gender speak to us all" (Cheney 14).

We can now examine in greater detail the complexities of the contemporary manifestation of what we have characterized as an oscillation between the common reader and a cultural/academic elite. We first turn our attention, in chapter five, to the power exerted by the common reader, when supplemented by certain elements within the cultural hegemony, in determining what is, at a given historical moment, "canonical." We focus in particular on the factors that have operated to move two popular contemporary women writers, Doris Lessing and Alice Walker, into the academic canon, arguing that in their cases certain previously marginalized members of the literary profession—African Americans and women—used their newly acquired confidence and authority to validate the common reader's high opinion of these authors.

In chapters six and seven, we attempt first to measure the actual impact feminist scholarship, so often sympathetic to the needs of the common reader, has had on the literary establishment and then to describe more precisely the challenge feminism offers to the profession of letters as, according to our analysis in this chapter, it has been traditionally practiced.

5

The Power
of the Common Reader
The Case of Doris Lessing

As we immodestly announced in the first chapter, we won an award in 1987 for a collection of essays on Doris Lessing we edited. The Northeast Modern Language Association (NEMLA)/ Ohio University Press Prize was awarded to *Doris Lessing: The Alchemy of Survival* almost a year to the day after the Modern Language Association's Committee on Teaching and Related Activities had invited us to submit a manuscript for *Approaches to Teaching Lessing's The Golden Notebook* for their series Approaches to Teaching World Literature. The implications of the coincidence began to strike us only when a friend wrote to congratulate us: "Wonderful news—publication (with prize!) of your collected essays on Lessing. Bravo. Between this book and the MLA publication you are leading the way for Lessing's canonization (in the secular sense, I mean)" (Rubenstein postcard).

In one peculiarly secular sense suggested by the acronyms MLA and NEMLA, our two projects do signal Lessing's canonization, her absorption into the massive institution of professional literary study in this country. At its conventions and in its publications, the Modern Language Association and its regional offspring (like NEMLA) establish the acceptable parameters of scholarly and critical discourse and the roster of authors and books deemed worth studying. If a paper on Author X is read at one of the MLA's annual conventions—better yet, if papers on Author X are read repeatedly, at NEMLA and SAMLA (the South Atlantic Modern Language Association) and MMLA (the Midwest Modern Language Association) as well as at MLA—then, by implication, it is okay to include Author X on your syllabus for English 101 or Comparative Literature 474. And if the MLA's Committee on Teaching and Related Professional Activities approves Author X for inclusion in its Approaches to Teaching World Literature series, the message is explicit: this author (or text) not only can but ought to be taught.

But a kind of circularity is built into this form of canonization. The MLA's "Guidelines for Editors of Series Volumes" for Approaches to Teaching World Literature say:

> The principal objective of the series is to collect within each volume different points of view on teaching a specific literary work, a literary tradition, or a writer widely taught at the undergraduate level. . . . The series is intended to serve nonspecialists as well as specialists, inexperienced as well as experienced teachers, graduate students who wish to learn effective ways of teaching as well as senior professors who wish to compare their own approaches with the approaches of colleagues in other schools.

Evidence that a work or writer is "widely taught" makes that work or writer eligible for inclusion in a series that aims to teach the "nonspecialist," the "inexperienced," and the neophyte how, and by implication what, to teach "effectively."

We came to realize fairly quickly that we had not led the way for Lessing's canonization, but had merely documented, to the MLA's satisfaction, that Lessing had already achieved de facto canonical status. We now want to examine in some detail the process by which she did so, hoping that "the case of Doris Lessing" will tell us something not only about the way a living author's works enter the academic canon but about canon formation in general.

The statistics tell one (fairly simple) story, and we begin with them in order to complicate the story later on. The history of Lessing's reception in the United States from 1950 when her first novel, *The Grass is Singing*, was published by Crowell to 1988, when Knopf brought out her nineteenth, *The Fifth Child*, conforms in general to the map Richard Ohmann has drawn of the route a contemporary novel or novelist follows from bestsellerdom to candidacy for inclusion in the academic canon.[1] The first step towards eventual canonization is commercial success, according to Ohmann. What makes a book a best seller? Ohmann consulted a variety of opinion research polls and concluded that a book's success depends on its being bought, read, and recommended by a fairly small but highly influential group of people, "of better-than-average education (most had finished college), relatively well-to-do, many of them professionals, in middle life, upwardly mobile, living near New York or oriented, especially through the *New York Times*, to New York cultural life" ("Shaping" 379).[2] Why do such people buy one book and not another? Ohmann suggested that literary agents and editors at major publishing houses "earned their keep by spotting (and pushing) novels that looked like best-sellers." Within this "closed circle of marketing and consumption," he noted in particular the "extraordinary role" of the *New York Times*:

> The *New York Times Book Review* had about a million and a half readers, several times the audience of any other literary periodical. Among them were most bookstore managers, deciding what to stock, and librarians, deciding what to buy, not to mention the well-to-do, well-educated east-coasters who led in establishing hardback best-sellers. The single most important boost a novel could get was a prominent review in the Sunday *New York Times*—better a favorable one than an unfavorable one, but better an unfavorable one than none at all. (380)

Because of the *Times*'s incredible influence on a book's sales—and hence on its chances of becoming a best seller—the publicity departments of most trade publishing houses "direct much of their prepublication effort toward persuading the *Book Review*'s editors that a particular novel" is important. Ohmann measured "the power of this suasion" by correlating advertisements and reviews and discovered "that the largest advertisers got disproportionately large amounts of review space." In 1968, Random House (including Knopf and Pantheon) ran 74 pages of ads and garnered 58 pages of reviews. Dutton, which took out 16 pages of ads, got 4 pages of reviews (381).

The first three of Lessing's books to appear in the United States

(*The Grass Is Singing*, 1950; *This Was the Old Chief's Country*, 1952; and *The Habit of Loving*, 1957) were published by T. Y. Crowell, a small house. Only *The Grass Is Singing* was reviewed in the Sunday *New York Times*. Things looked up when Lessing moved to Simon and Schuster in 1961 with the documentary *In Pursuit of the English*, which was reviewed very favorably in the *New York Times Book Review* by Malcolm Bradbury. During the years Lessing published with Simon and Schuster (1961–68), all her books were reviewed in the Sunday *Times*, often by "name" reviewers or critics like Bradbury. And after she moved to Knopf with *The Four-Gated City* in 1969, her niche in the influential book review was secure. From 1971 and *A Briefing for a Descent into Hell* through 1982 and the fourth novel in the Canopus series (*The Making of the Representative for Planet 8*), every novel Lessing published with Knopf was reviewed on the front page of the *New York Times Book Review*. Most of them received second, some third and even fourth, reviews. From 1950 to 1985, Lessing's books were reviewed 37 times in the *Times* book review section, and 29 of those reviews occurred after Lessing had signed up with Knopf, one of the biggest New York publishing houses, and one of the biggest buyers of advertising space in the *New York Times Book Review*, according to Ohmann's figures. Her editor at Knopf, until he left for the *New Yorker*, was Robert Gottlieb, arguably the most highly regarded editor in New York during recent years.[3] Yet according to Ohmann, commercial success is not enough to assure a novel's progress to precanonical status; his favorite example of a best seller that was never regarded as serious literature is Erich Segal's *Love Story*. What then determines which novels are accorded literary, as well as entertainment, value?

Ohmann says that here too the *New York Times Book Review* plays an important role, in "distinguishing between ephemeral popular novels and those to be taken seriously." He notes that "there was a marked difference in impact between, say, Martin Levin's favorable but mildly condescending (and brief) review of *Love Story* and the kind of front-page review by an Alfred Kazin or an Irving Howe that asked readers to regard a new novel as literature" (382). Even before Lessing regularly preempted space on the front page of the *New York Times Book Review*, her books were taken seriously by reviewers whose credentials as cultural authorities were impeccable. Malcolm Bradbury, for one, described her as "an impressive social novelist." And when Walter Allen compared Lessing to George Eliot, no professor of English needed to apologize for enjoying *Children of Violence*.

Citing a study of America's "cultural elite," Ohmann lists seven "top intellectual journals" that, together with the *New York Times Book Review*, "constitute the American equivalent of an Oxbridge establishment, and have served as one of the main gatekeepers for new talent and new ideas" (383). Reviews such as Lessing regularly received in the *New York Times* virtually guaranteed that she would be taken up by the other seven "gatekeeper" journals, the *New York Review of Books*, the *New Republic*, the *New Yorker*, *Commentary*, the *Saturday Review*, the *Partisan Review*, and *Harper's*. And taken up she was, with fervor. From 1950 to 1985, almost 100 reviews of Lessing's books appeared in these journals if we include, as Ohmann does, the *New York Times Book Review* among them. All eight of them reviewed *The Summer Before the Dark* in 1973; the first two Martha Quest novels were reviewed in six gatekeepers, as was the fifth, *The Four-Gated City*. And *Memoirs of a Survivor* received notice by five.

But it is the quality of these reviews rather than their sheer quantity that attests to Lessing's "precanonization" by the cultural establishment. There were only four gatekeeper reviews of the relatively early *Golden Notebook*, for example, yet Irving Howe's review of that novel in the *New Republic* may be the single most significant paving stone on *The Golden Notebook*'s road to the academy.[4] "By any final reckoning," he wrote magisterially, "*The Golden Notebook* is a work of high seriousness. . . . This novel will be discussed repeatedly in the years to come. It is the most absorbing and exciting piece of new fiction I have read in a decade: it moves with the beat of our time, and it is true" (181).

Other cultural authorities—critics and novelists—joined Howe in singling out Lessing's work for serious attention: Granville Hicks, Stanley Kauffman, Mary Ellmann, Joyce Carol Oates, Margaret Drabble, Joan Didion, Roger Sale, Alison Lurie, Elizabeth Hardwick, Doris Grumbach, Erica Jong, Maureen Howard, Ursula Le Guin, Malcolm Cowley, Gore Vidal, John Leonard.

According to Ohmann, "if a novel was certified in the court of the prestigious journals, it was likely to draw the attention of academic critics in more specialized and academic journals like *Contemporary Literature* and by this route make its way into college curricula" (384). But among the gatekeepers' stable of reviewers is a large body of academicians, simultaneously testifying to the role of these journals in vesting an author or book with precanonical status and blurring the very distinction between precanonical and canonical.[5] When, as in the case of Doris Lessing, the same critic wrote about her work both in gatekeeper journals and in scholarly publications, the "step" between adoption by the New York literary establishment and entry into the academic canon was virtually elided. In 1964, for example, Walter Allen not only reviewed *Martha Quest* and *A Proper Marriage* for the *New York Times Book Review* but discussed Lessing's fiction in both his own *The Modern Novel in Britain and the United States* and a collection of essays, *On Contemporary Literature*, edited by Richard Kostelanetz. He may or may not have included a work by Lessing in one of his courses at New York University, but he certainly directed Ellen W. Brooks's 1971 dissertation, "Fragmentation and Integration: A Study of Doris Lessing's Fiction."

And while Bernard Bergonzi reviewed *Martha Quest* and *A Proper Marriage* for the *New York Review of Books* five years before including Lessing in his *Situation of the Novel*, James Gindin devoted a chapter of his *Postwar British Fiction* to Lessing *before* reviewing *A Man and Two Women* for the *Saturday Review*. Academic interest in Lessing was, in fact, evident even before she became lionized by the New York cultural establishment. It was only after publication of *The Golden Notebook* in

1962 that gatekeeper journals regularly devoted space to serious discussion of Lessing's books, even the most ephemeral of them.[6] But if Gindin's book was published in 1962, it was surely drafted before then as, conceivably, was Frederick Karl's 1963 edition of *A Reader's Guide to the Contemporary English Novel*, which devotes several pages to Lessing. And it was the experience of teaching *The Golden Notebook* in his graduate course in Contemporary British Fiction at the University of Oregon in the late 1960s that generated Joseph Hynes's 1973 article in the *Iowa Review* about "The Construction of *The Golden Notebook*."[7]

In general, however, Doris Lessing's academic reputation rose in tandem with her commercial success, dating from 1962 and peaking in 1973, when all eight gatekeeper journals reviewed *The Summer Before the Dark* and the academy staked *its* claim to Lessing with a special issue of *Contemporary Literature* devoted to her work. By 1985, major university presses had published five books on Lessing, and over 300 articles on her work had appeared in a gamut of journals from *Critique* to *Publications of the Modern Language Association* (*PMLA*). Her fiction was taught in college courses as early as 1965.[8] The next year, the first American doctoral dissertation on Doris Lessing was submitted; by 1985, 52 academics had entered the profession with a dissertation on Doris Lessing in hand. Statistically speaking, Lessing was undeniably canonical.

Statistics are useful (they helped us persuade the MLA Committee on Teaching and Related Activities to authorize preparation of a volume on *The Golden Notebook* for the Approaches to Teaching World Literature series), but the story they tell isn't very subtle. Richard Ohmann's model of the path a novel travels from popular success to academic respectability is also useful; its chief virtue is its emphasis on the material base of the canonizing process, the inseparability of cultural formation and market forces. But, like statistics, a purely economic model of canon formation is too mechanical to measure the equally powerful if less quantifiable reasons why some novels achieve both popular acclaim and the imprimatur of the academy.

Ohmann is surely right to contend that the reading public does not "freely" choose its favorites from the total number of novels written in a given year but rather from the small proportion of those novels published and promoted by a powerful circle of agents, editors, advertisers, and journals (380). But as he also observes, the most successful of these commercial promoters are those with their fingers on the pulse of "the common reader," that educated, urban, middle- and upper-middle-class book buyer Ohmann claims is so crucial to a novel's eventual status as a best seller and, beyond that, as a potential work of "literature."

According to a study conducted by one of Ohmann's colleagues, the common reader looks to novels for "personal meaning, for some kind of map to the moral landscape," out of a need to "reinforce or to celebrate beliefs already held, or, when shaken by events, to provide support in some personal crisis."[9] Margaret Drabble has said it more succinctly: "Most of us read books with this question in our mind: What does this say about my life" ("Revelations")? Just so did Samuel Johnson's common reader turn to books in the eighteenth century. Plus ça change, plus c'est la même chose.

If the *New York Times Book Review* and the other gatekeepers are in tune with the needs and desires of the common reader, if only to exploit them in order to sell books, what aspects of Doris Lessing's books do they emphasize in order to suggest that these novels are relevant to their readers' lives? To confine this question within reasonable bounds, we have narrowed it to reviews of *The Golden Notebook*, Lessing's most popular book and the one now most securely lodged in the canon.[10]

The Golden Notebook was reviewed by three gatekeeper journals shortly after it was published—the *New Republic*, the *New York Times Book Review*, and the *Saturday Review*. In 1963, the *New Yorker* also reviewed it. Though the four reviewers singled out different aspects of the novel for particular praise or qualification, some generalizations can be made. All of them claimed that *The Golden Notebook* merited serious attention because it authentically represented contemporary reality in all its chaotic

complexity. If the book had a flaw, it was its cumbersome structure; its more than compensatory virtue was its humanism.

But the most noteworthy aspect of *The Golden Notebook*, the
reviewers agreed, was its depiction of what Granville Hicks called
the "complexities of a free woman." Irving Howe elaborated:
"Anna Wulf is sufficiently representative of a certain kind of
modern woman to persuade us that her troubles have a relevance beyond their immediate setting" (177–78). The "center" of
the book, for Howe, consisted of conversations between Anna
and Molly in the "Free Women" sections:

> When they discuss their failures in love, their problems as divorced
> women with children to raise, their disillusionments as former Com-
> munists who would still like to needle the Establishment, their in-
> ability to talk with the passionless and apolitical young, their con-
> tempt for the new gentility of intellectual London, their difficulties
> in reconciling the image they hold of a self-sufficient human being
> with the needs they feel as anything but self-sufficient women —
> when these conversations between Anna and Molly recur through-
> out the book, one turns to them with the delight of encountering
> something real and fresh. (178–79)

Reviews like these might suggest that *The Golden Notebook* was
assumed to appeal to one particular species of the genus "common reader," women of the well-educated, middle-class, professional, urban book-buying public. But although the novel was
claimed in retrospect by the Women's Movement of the late 1960s,
when it was published at the beginning of the decade it spoke
with equal urgency to men and women. "If we are not Nora,"
Florence Howe wrote in the *Nation*, "if we have not slammed a
door, we live with or next to someone who has. This is why
women (and men in self-defense) are reading Doris Lessing" ("Free
Women"). Some men may have read in self-defense, or out of
curiosity such as Irving Howe confessed,[11] but some of them
wrote about and taught her because they recognized Anna's problems as their own: men too suffer failures in love, political disillu-
sionment, contempt for the younger generation, and nostalgia
for the presumed order of the past.

The first American PhD candidates brave enough to write dissertations on Lessing when, in the words of one of them, "there was no serious scholarly material at all" on her work (Carey letter), were men, John Carey and Paul Schlueter. Both were impelled to write about Lessing, despite reservations by some senior professors in their departments, because she seemed to speak directly to them as human beings, not because she was of "scholarly" interest. When he read *The Golden Notebook*, John Carey knew "immediately" that "this was a writer I wanted to know more about." Looking back over the more than 20 years that have passed since he completed his dissertation on Lessing, the first in the United States, Carey reflects that "*The Golden Notebook* had a profound effect on my life and influenced me in a number of personal ways." He adds, as if it followed naturally from this confession of Lessing's personal importance to him, "I have never been much for MLAs and the formal apparatus of academia" (Carey letter).

Paul Schlueter, who completed the second U.S. dissertation on Lessing four years after Carey's, was also first attracted to *The Golden Notebook* for personal reasons. "I was amazed at how much it spoke to me and my own situation," he recalls, "nearing the pressure point . . . in my first marriage" (Schlueter letter). Unlike Carey, however, Schlueter used his MLA membership to provide an opportunity for others similarly affected by Lessing's fiction to meet and discuss her work. In 1971 he successfully petitioned the MLA for permission to hold a seminar on "The Fiction of Doris Lessing" at the December convention in New York.[12] More than 40 people attended.

Schlueter's petition was approved by the MLA's Program Committee because the "Little Bourgeois Cultural Revolution of MLA 1968" (Kampf and Lauter 34) had significantly altered at least some of "the formal apparatus of academia" to respond to the demands of radicals, women, African Americans and other minorities for more representation in the governance structure of the MLA. Paul Lauter and Louis Kampf recall, with relish, how a fairly small band of political activists turned the sedate lobby

of New York's Americana Hotel into a facsimile of the 1968 Democratic convention in Chicago, with riot-squad police hauling professors off to jail for hanging up a poster that said "The Tygers
of Wrath are Wiser than the Horses of Instruction."

What the disruptive professors wanted was more than token
representation of minority groups on the governing boards of
the MLA; they also wanted to force the literary profession to reexamine its ideology, to "explore the class biases, sexual biases,
and ethnic biases in the structure of literature departments as
well as in their operational definition, evaluation, and presentation of literature" (Franklin 94–95). "By the mid 1950s," Bruce
Franklin writes, "almost the entire body of literature created and
widely enjoyed by the peoples of America had been rejected [by
the academy] in favor of an infinitesimal canon of 'great' works
by literary 'masters,' mostly professional white gentlemen not
unlike those selecting them" (102).

The election of Louis Kampf as second vice-president of the
MLA at the conclusion of the 1968 convention signaled the ca-
pitulation by the governing structure of the MLA to the radicals'
demands for greater representation. This representation of previously marginalized interests, as we will see in chapter six, played
a significant role in opening up the convention program, after
1968, to authors, texts, and subjects previously spurned as "noncanonical," which in turn foreshadowed an opening of the canon
itself to them.

The delegates at the 1968 MLA convention also voted to establish a Commission on the Status of Women in the Profession,
and by 1970 the convention program began to register the impact women scholars would have not only on governance of the
organization but on what Bruce Franklin called the "operational
definition, evaluation, and presentation of literature." At a forum
on "The Status of Women in the Profession," Elaine Showalter
poignantly outlined the plight of the female undergraduate
English major studying a canon that presented the story of Oedipus as *the* human tragedy, and Carol Ohmann anatomized the

fate of Emily Brontë (and by implication all women authors) "in the hands of male critics."[13]

The next year, Paul Schlueter's seminar on Doris Lessing tacitly stated that stories told by and about women should command equal time in the canon of literature accorded academic attention with Oedipus's fantasy of sleeping with his mother. And while the lead-off speaker at the 1971 seminar on "The Fiction of Doris Lessing" was a man, the other papers were read by women, delivering a woman author from the hands of male critics.

The initial scholarship on Doris Lessing was written by men: James Gindin, Frederick Karl, Frederick P. W. McDowell, John Carey, Paul Schlueter. But after 1971, men as a class dropped out of Lessing scholarship. There were individual exceptions, of course: Frederick Karl's articles on *The Golden Notebook* and *The Four-Gated City*, John Carey's and Joseph Hynes's influential analyses of the structure of *The Golden Notebook*, Mark Spilka's comparative study of Lessing and Lawrence, Michael Magie's controversial essay on Lessing and Romanticism.[14] But from 1971 to 1986, 78% of the articles, 88% of the books, 93% of the MLA presentations, and 95% of the dissertations on Lessing in this country were written by women.

Many of them belonged to the Doris Lessing Society (DLS), established as an allied organization of the MLA in 1979,[15] and subscribed to the *Doris Lessing Newsletter* (DLN), founded in 1976 by Dee Seligman. Men too belong to the society and help publish as well as subscribe to the newsletter,[16] and neither the Doris Lessing Society nor its newsletter is explicitly feminist. Yet both have embodied one of the principles feminist scholarship shares with other radical critiques of the academy: to foster cooperation and collaboration rather than the competitiveness that characterizes traditional scholarship. As Dee Seligman wrote in an early issue of the newsletter:

> In this age of tremendous pressure to publish or perish, college and university faculty seek status-granting publications for their ideas.

However, the purpose of this *Newsletter* is to beat the system and to allow scholars to talk and share with one another, rather than to publish long critical articles which a very small number are interested in. Lessing readers have often been changed by what they have read, or certainly they are moved to see their lives in a different perspective. My own experience is that her readers want to share with one another that effect which Lessing has had on them and on their students.

Seligman's remarks link the desire for collaboration to the need to share with others the transformative, life-changing experience of reading Lessing, attested to earlier by pioneer Lessing scholars like John Carey and Paul Schlueter.

In associating Lessing's entry into the canon with the increasing presence and influence of women scholars within the academy over the past 20 years, therefore, we are not claiming that Lessing studies have been dominated by feminist critical approaches. They have not. Though statistically more women than men have written on Lessing, by no means have all of them employed the tools of feminist criticism to understand and elucidate her work. Women as well as men have approached Lessing's fiction from all available critical directions: Jungian/archetypal, Marxist, psychoanalytic, formalist, deconstructionist, reader-response.

Although chapters or sections on Lessing appear in some of the landmark books of feminist scholarship and criticism written over the past fifteen years—Patricia Meyer Spacks's *The Female Imagination* (1975), Sydney Janet Kaplan's *Feminine Consciousness in the Modern British Novel* (1975), Elaine Showalter's *A Literature of Their Own* (1977), Barbara Hill Rigney's *Madness and Sexual Politics in the Feminist Novel* (1978), Carol Christ's *Diving Deep and Surfacing* (1980), and Lee R. Edwards's *Psyche as Hero* (1984)—the bulk of Lessing scholarship has been published in "mainstream" rather than feminist journals. From 1965 to 1985, 85% of the articles published on Doris Lessing appeared in such journals as *PMLA, Contemporary Literature, Modern Fiction Studies, Critique,* and *Studies in the Novel* while only 15% were printed in *Signs, Frontiers, Women's Studies,* and *Regionalism and the Female Imagination.* To date, no feminist journal has devoted a special issue to Lessing, though two mainstream journals have, *Contemporary Literature* and *Modern Fiction Studies.*

What we mean to emphasize in associating Lessing's entry into the canon with women's increasing presence and influence in the academy, then, is that Lessing scholarship in this country participated in a larger historical phenomenon, the energetic attempt to reclaim literary studies by individuals and groups marginalized by both the governance structure of the Modern Language Association and the "canon" of literature inscribed in the syllabi, reading lists, and anthologies taught and studied in American universities in the middle decades of the twentieth century. Not only women but African Americans, Native Americans, Hispanics, and people of the working class claimed, in the revolutionary climate of the late 1960s, that a "liberal education" limited to stories of white male aristocrats was neither democratic nor universal. In seeking to open the canon to their stories, these groups were in effect returning the canon to its eighteenth-century roots, reaffirming the connections between text and context, stories and life. It was a moment in literary history when some professors read as common readers always have, asking "What does this book say about my life?"

The first American generation of Lessing scholars were, for the most part, unself-conscious about their participation in a cultural revolution. Those of us who, as graduate students or young professors in the 1960s and early 1970s, discovered Doris Lessing did so as other discriminating "common readers" did, by reading reviews of *The Golden Notebook* or *Children of Violence* in the *New York Times Book Review,* the *New Yorker* or the *New Republic.* Perhaps a friend recommended one or another of her novels at a dinner party or, if we were feminists, at a meeting of our consciousness-raising group. What we discovered, when we read *The Golden Notebook* or the Martha Quest novels, was a writer who, it seemed, knew us better than we knew ourselves, who—as *The Golden Notebook*'s Anna Wulf would say—"named" us and the welter of ambiguities in which we floundered. Disen-

chanted with politics-as-usual, confused by the sexual revolution, struggling to reconcile the conflicts we felt between public
responsiblity and private need, we identified with Martha Quest
and Anna Wulf and responded, uncritically at first, to the heu-
ristic pressure of Lessing's anatomy of their (and our) experience.

This, we felt, was what was lacking in our study and teaching
of literature which, to those of us who had cut our teeth on
Cleanth Brooks and Robert Penn Warren's *Introduction to Poetry,*
consisted of closely read "texts" hermetically sealed from the
mess we came home to every night. Doris Lessing "is the kind
of writer who changes people's lives," Margaret Drabble has said
("Cassandra" 50). She is a writer who certainly changed the direction of the professional lives of a significant number of academics. One woman we know scrapped the two chapters she had
written of a dissertation on "Time in the Works of James Joyce"
and begged her thesis advisor to let her supplant it with a study
of Lessing's *Children of Violence.* She was in the process of getting a divorce and struggling with the question of who should
have custody of the children, had been in therapy for four years,
was active in the movement against the Vietnam War. Martha
Quest *mattered* to her more than teasing out the ramifications
of Joseph Frank's "Spatial Form in Modern Literature" as they
might or might not pertain to *Ulysses.*

Writing to and for the common reader in the left-wing magazine *Ramparts,* Margaret Drabble called Doris Lessing both "personal" and "prophetic." She is personal not only because "she was
one of the first women to write truthfully about sex" ("Cassandra" 54), but because the shape of books like *Children of Violence*
and *The Golden Notebook* "is the shape of the exploration and
widening which is experience" ("Cassandra" 51). *The Golden
Notebook* "is a transforming work. . . . Intellectually, it is a masterpiece; but it has none of the aridity of an intellectual construction. It grows out of life" ("Cassandra" 52).

It was also, when it was published in 1962, a prophetic book.
"*The Golden Notebook,* with its insistence on freedom, its moments of aggression, its attacks on the masculine world . . . is in-

evitably a document in the history of [women's] liberation, but it was in a sense published too early, for its tone is not at all explanatory; it assumes its readers will know what is meant" ("Cassandra" 52–53).

By the time readers had caught up to Lessing, in the early 1970s, she had moved on. "The whole world is being shaken into a new pattern by the cataclysms we are living through," she wrote in her 1971 preface to *The Golden Notebook*; "probably by the time we are through, if we do get through at all, the aims of Women's Liberation will look very small and quaint" (*The Golden Notebook* viii–ix).

In the 1970s it was "the cataclysms we are living through" that absorbed Doris Lessing—impending nuclear holocaust, pollution of the ecosystem, a global epidemic of violence and terrorism. And she wrote about them with prophetic urgency in *The Four-Gated City, Briefing for a Descent into Hell, The Summer Before the Dark*, and *The Memoirs of a Survivor*. The common reader was, more often than not, discomfited. Having caught up with *The Golden Notebook*, readers resented Lessing for asking them to contemplate a world in which that book's essential humanism looked obsolete. Reviews of Lessing's novels of the 1970s are often querulous. Since *The Golden Notebook*, Melvin Maddock complained in his review of *Briefing*, "Lessing has been working through a sequence of disillusion toward a private religion of her own. . . . What she has forfeited—and the loss has to be enormous for any novelist—is the scale of humanity." Malcolm Cowley found *Memoirs* disappointing for similar reasons: "The whole book is visionary or prophetic, and it lacks, for the most part, the sharp observation of manners that helped to distinguish her earlier work. . . . [And] what shall we say about the end? . . . To this stubborn rationalist, it isn't an ending, really, but a cop-out." What Maddock and Cowley convey—and in this their reviews are typical—is a sense that Lessing has let them down, as individuals and as members of the human race. A critic or reviewer may be disappointed by a novel that doesn't live up aesthetically to its predecessors, but the common reader feels betrayed only by a writer who matters, personally, to her or his life.

The conviction that Lessing's fiction matters existentially also spills over frequently into academic criticism, disrupting the decorous conventions of "objective," "dispassionate" scholarship. Nancy Porter wrote of her "frustration" with Lessing's apparent rejection, in *The Four-Gated City* and *Briefing for a Descent into Hell*, of "direct political action" in favor of "madness and mutation":

> Having recovered in the images of time and place in [the first four volumes of] *Children of Violence* and *The Golden Notebook* large portions of my past, as a woman and as a child of violence, I would like to think that the recovery will be of use in determining the shape of the future. . . . We who have recovered our understanding through Lessing's understanding see possibilities she does not see, and we are disappointed that she does not share our sense of possible change with us and help us clarify our own vision now as she has in the past. (178–79)

Jean Bethke Elshtain was not so much disappointed as angry with Lessing for "repudiating history" (95). Clearly allying herself with those "ordinary folk who press ahead" with politics, for whom Lessing "lacks compassion" (98), Elshtain accuses Lessing of becoming "increasingly remote and abstract" (96), of "giving up on human beings," of "repudiating the fundamental wager of our time, that human beings must be allowed the choices of free persons" (114).

"How I hope her vision of the future will not come true!" wrote Sydney Janet Kaplan. "The clarity of her depiction of the dissolution of society, with its prediction of world-wide destruction and catastrophe makes many of her readers long to reject her prophesies, her rejection of the way most people live their lives" ("Passionate" 1).

But although the apocalyptic ending of *The Four-Gated City* made Frederick Karl uneasy too, he witheld outright criticism because he thought that "perhaps Lessing is serving the function reserved for the writer, which is to lead us, despite ourselves, into terrible areas of exploration" ("Four-Gaited Beast" 199).

The discomfort many readers experienced in reading Lessing's "apocalyptic" novels of the seventies, although it contrasts sharply with the shock of recognition with which they welcomed the early Martha Quest novels and *The Golden Notebook*, testifies to the prophetic quality of all her writing. "The most important point" about "the prophetic word," according to Gerald Bruns, is that it "is always addressed to the situation in which it is uttered, that is, to the moment at hand." Quoting a nineteenth-century Biblical scholar, he adds that "the element in which the prophets live is the storm of the world's history" (73).

We have been arguing that it is this immediacy, the sense that Lessing's novels are rooted in experiential reality, that drew common readers and academics disaffected with the hermetic sterility of the formalist canon to her work; that it therefore accounts both for her commercial success and for her entry, in the heady years following the 1968 MLA convention, into the academic canon. We now need to ponder what opening the canon to a prophetic writer like Lessing might mean.

Gerald Bruns uses the canonization of the Hebrew scriptures as a model for understanding the dynamics of literary canon formation.[17] The Hebrew scriptures were canonized into "Torah" (carrying the force of "law") during the reign of King Josiah. This written version of God's word was mediated through a priestly class, who served as its custodians and interpreters. Whatever might have been the religious motivation of the Deuteronomists for promulgating the Torah as the authoritative word of God, it served an "undeniable" political function: "to strengthen the monarchy and the priesthood by centralizing the court and the Temple cult in Jerusalem" (70). Extrapolating from history to hermeneutics, Bruns concludes that, from the "technical standpoint of literary or textual criticism," canonization signifies "an official closing and fixing of texts in a form that is declared to be authoritative (for whatever particular tradition) against all prior, competing, eccentric, and subsequent books and versions" (66).

Opposing the institutional authority of king, priest, and canon was the charismatic authority of the prophets. Unlike the priests, who claimed authority by citing Torah, the prophets derived their authority from their unmediated access to God:

> If you ask, Who speaks for Yahweh? the Deuteronomic and priestly answer is that the Torah of Moses, "the priestly Torah," contains the message of Yahweh to his people. By contrast, the authority of men like Elijah, Isaiah, and Jeremiah is equal to the unmediated authority of Moses. If you ask, Who speaks for Yahweh? the answer here is that Yahweh speaks directly through his prophets. (73)

And when he speaks, it is "in ways that are entirely unpredictable and which no one can control, neither king nor priest nor, indeed, the prophet himself." The prophetic word is always timely, addressed to the historical moment in which it is uttered; neither is it "part of a permanent record" nor does it "bind the future." Thus, "the prophetic word has something unwritable about it" (73).

Eventually, of course, the prophetic word *was* written, by Deuteronomic editors who, for example, turned the oral tradition of sayings attributed to the prophet Jeremiah into the Book of Jeremiah we now read in the Bible. Bruns asks, "What are we to make of the production and canonization of texts like the Book of Jeremiah" (74)? He gives two answers, equally plausible though apparently mutually exclusive.

On the one hand, we can see the priestly editors' critical revision of Jeremianic tradition as an attempt "to make sense of the prophetic message in order to understand and account for their own situation" (76). Thus, while "the Book of Jeremiah as a canonical text is not what Jeremiah said in his own historical moment," it still *functions* prophetically, speaking to the (newly contemporary) moment (77).

A "less benevolent" account sees "canonization [as] the priestly appropriation of prophetic authority by means of the superior forces of writing and textuality; or, in other words, writing [as] a way of getting rid of prophecy" (77). By "fixing" the prophetic word in writing, the Deuteronomic editors made it a matter of (past) history. They also kept it sacred by privatizing it within the ark of the covenant. The word became an object of veneration to be studied only in the synagogue, by men, assisted by the mediation of priests. As students of the sixteenth-century protestant reformation know, print technology robbed the text of its sacred, no less than its aristocratic, connotations and delivered it to the unruly lay population.

The analogy between the biblical and the academic literary canons is not strict. The Hebrew biblical canon, for instance, has been more or less fixed since the second century of the common era (Bruns 66), while the literary canon has been fluid from its inception. And the biblical canon is "binding," to use Bruns's term, in a way the literary canon never could be. You do not have to believe in *Hamlet*; you will simply be deemed culturally illiterate if you have not read it.

But if not exact, the analogy between the biblical and the literary canons is suggestive. In both cases, a "priestly class" certifies that certain texts are valuable. Why? What, in particular, are we to make of the canonization of a prophetic book like *The Golden Notebook*, of a prophetic writer like Doris Lessing? Is it an attempt to assure that future generations will try "to make sense of [her] prophetic message in order to understand and account for their own situation?" Or is it, as Alan Golding has charged in a slightly different context, an attempt to "detoxify" Lessing's message by dehistoricizing it, rendering it "culturally and intellectually harmless" (301)?

Bruns asks not only what the priests hoped to accomplish by incorporating the word of the prophet into the biblical canon but "What happens to the prophetic word when it is turned into a . . . canonical text" (74)? What does canonizing a text do to the relationship between that text and its readers? Does it encourage readers to ask of a book, "What does this say about my life?" Or does it, rather, signal that the book has been removed from history to a kind of museum where it can and should be studied more for its formal and aesthetic properties than for its contemporary relevance? Why *do* we read *Hamlet*? Why do we think we *should*? More to the immediate point, what happens to our relationship to *The Golden Notebook* when we are told we *ought* to read it—to be "well-read," or to pass a course?

Doris Lessing wrote in 1971 that she hoped *The Golden Notebook* would remain "alive and potent and fructifying" (*The Golden Notebook* xxii). Will it, now that it has entered the canon? Or will it become mummified?

When Lessing is confronted with a set of alternatives, she customarily retorts, "Why do you makc it 'or, or, or?' It could be 'and, and, and.'"[18] It is in that spirit, invoking Lessing as our model, that we suggest the following: canonizing Doris Lessing will both insulate some readers from her prophetic immediacy and impel others to reexamine their lives and question their priorities.

Citing Foucault, William E. Cain says that "ideological choices and exclusions are part of the business of building and arguing for a set of canonical works" (257). Arnold Krupat charges that "the canon, like all cultural production, is never an innocent selection of the best that has been thought and said; rather, it is the institutionalization of those particular verbal artifacts that appear best to convey and sustain the dominant social order" (310). That, we suggest, is the paranoid approach to canon formation. Canon formation is inescapably ideological, but the values of the "dominant social order" are constantly challenged by subversive elements within it, such as the insurgent force within the academy of radicals like those who fomented the "bourgeois cultural revolution" at the 1968 MLA convention and first-generation Lessing scholars determined to validate study of her work because it *mattered*.

Skeptics would argue that the dominant ideology is powerful enough to tame any insurgency, to neutralize its potential threat by co-opting it. Looking back in 1976 to the 1968 MLA "revolution," Richard Ohmann wondered how effective it was in the long run. Noting that Louis Kampf himself wrote that the "MLA's power lies in its strong stomach, in its capacity to digest almost everything," Ohmann commented wryly, "Well, the MLA did digest Louis Kampf and the rest of us cohorts, without more than a mild stomach-ache, and with few important changes in the professorial body politic" (*English in America* 50).

More recently, Elaine Showalter has charged that "feminist

criticism in general has moved inexorably, book by book, back into standard critical time":

> In 1974, *Daniel Deronda* . . . was read in radical feminist circles as a guide to living. . . . Since the late 1970s, though, feminist readings of *Daniel Deronda* show the impact of deconstruction . . . [and] the theories of Lacan and Foucault. ("Women's Time" 40–41)

"As Gayatri Spivak has warned," she concluded, "we must be wary of the 'recuperation of the critical energies of feminism into the ruling ideology of Departments of English' and the possibility that this integration 'might involve compromises . . . that might not let a feminism survive'" (42).

Since the academy declared its interest in Doris Lessing, a number of essays have been written emphasizing the formal, aesthetic qualities of her fiction, or situating her work in one literary historical context or another. Yet for every article on "referential language and fictional form" in *The Golden Notebook*,[19] you can find another describing Lessing's challenge to the social and political status quo. Ultimately, however, the question of whether Doris Lessing has been "detoxified" and "dehistoricized" by canonization cannot be answered by even the most thorough-going content analysis of scholarly books and articles published on her work. For what we need to know is not what the professors do with a text but what the effect on the common reader is of declaring a text canonical.

Any answer to this question must be provisional and suggestive, based on anecdote and personal experience rather than statistics. All we can assert with confidence is the volatility of the reader. Once a work has been certified for study—for whatever reason—it becomes a wild card. One professor may add *The Golden Notebook* to his or her syllabus for a course in modern British fiction hoping thereby to jolt students into critical awareness of the interconnections between art and social forces; another may include it in a graduate seminar on metafictions intending to ignore the issues it raises and to focus instead on the intricacy of its form and its generic relationship to *Tristram*

Shandy or *The Counterfeiters*. But what the professor intends is not necessarily what the student experiences.

Consider, for example, Roberta Rubenstein's account of teaching *The Golden Notebook* in an introductory course in women's studies in the mid-1980s. She chose that novel because, for her, it is "one of the most profound explorations of a woman's complex consciousness that exists in fiction" ("Women's Studies" 72). Yet her students, encountering *The Golden Notebook* in the context of the course, automatically read it as a historical document, like *The Second Sex*. Distanced from the book by expectations set up by the rest of the course syllabus ("different theoretical or descriptive approaches to the social construction of gender" [72]), the students "tended to see Lessing's novel as 'dated,' Anna Wulf's dilemmas as part of past history" (73). But even in that environment of expectation, *The Golden Notebook* spoke to some students with the immediacy of living literature. "The best students grasped that Anna Wulf's inner crisis mirrors a world in chaos then and, although the superficial lineaments of chaos may have changed somewhat, no less so today. The dilemmas that Anna confronts . . . [ultimately] spoke to them as well, resonating with questions they recognized as part of their own reality" (76).

This story makes a number of statements about "what happens to the prophetic word when it is turned into a canonical text." First, what happens can be neither predicted nor engineered by the canonizer; second, the context in which one discovers a book exerts an influence on how it will be read; and finally, some individual readers will escape this influence to meet the text on their own.

But because it is a short story, comprising one semester in the undergraduate career of one generation of students, Rubenstein's account only begins to suggest the long-term effects of canonizing a book. "Remember," Doris Lessing has written, "that the book which bores you when you are twenty or thirty will open doors for you when you are forty or fifty" (*The Golden Notebook* xviii). Some of the twenty-year-old women in Rubenstein's class may have been bored by *The Golden Notebook*, but they were told—because it was on the syllabus—that it was an "important" book. Its prophetic urgency exists, *in potentia*, in their (sub)conscious, from which it may emerge, when they are forty or fifty, to open doors. If, on the one hand, the canon can and has served "to convey and sustain the dominant social order" (Krupat 310), it can and has functioned as culture's subconscious, a repository of books that have spoken with prophetic immediacy in the past and may again, at some unpredictable moment in the future.[20]

A brief glance at the case of another popular writer, Alice Walker, supports our view that the canonization of a contemporary, popular, and politically relevant writer can be read both as evidence that the canon is volatile, constantly subject to revision, and that it operates to recuperate and neutralize radical challenge to the cultural status quo.

Like Lessing, Walker enjoyed both popular and critical acclaim from the publication of her first novel, *The Third Life of Grange Copeland*, in 1971. "Name" reviewers (Paul Theroux, Josephine Hendin, Robert Coles, Marge Piercy, Greil Marcus) paid attention to her in such gatekeepers as the *Saturday Review*, the *New Yorker*, the *Atlantic Monthly* and the *New York Times Book Review*. Her third novel, *The Color Purple*, hit the top of the charts when it was published in 1982. Mel Watkins, writing in the *New York Times Book Review*, found it "indelibly affective," and P. S. Prescott, in *Newsweek*, called it "an American novel of permanent importance." In 1983 *The Color Purple* won both the National Book Award and the Pulitzer Prize for fiction, and in 1985 Steven Spielberg, with considerable help from Whoopi Goldberg, made Miss Celie as affecting—and as well known—as E. T.

Walker's steady, uncomplicated rise to popular celebrity was paralleled by an equally steady though less meteoric ascent into the canon. In 1985, George Stade noted in the *Partisan Review* that even as Steven Spielberg was planning his movie, PhD candidates were writing dissertations on Walker (266). But scholars had begun paying attention to Alice Walker long before *The Color Purple* made her a household name. Trudier Harris published an article on "Violence in *The Third Life of Grange Cope-*

land" in the *College Language Association Journal* in 1975. By 1982, there were a dozen more articles on Walker in scholarly journals and at least two doctoral dissertations.

If white feminist scholars made Doris Lessing their own because she seemed to speak of and to their experience, black scholars (especially black feminists) took up Alice Walker because she articulated, eloquently and self-consciously, a black feminist position.[21]

Walker's first publication was an essay on the Civil Rights Movement which won the $300 first prize in the annual *American Scholar* essay contest. In the year *The Third Life of Grange Copeland* appeared, Walker also published one essay on her experience working with a Headstart program in Mississippi and another on her "heritage" as a "black writer in the South" (*In Search* 15–32). She continued throughout the early seventies to write about civil rights and her African-American heritage in the *New York Times* and *Redbook* as well as more arcane publications like the *Sarah Lawrence Alumni Magazine* (*In Search* 139–41, 146–57, 33–41). In 1973, the year she published her second book of poetry, *Revolutionary Petunias*, and her first collection of short stories, *In Love & Trouble: Stories of Black Women*, she told John O'Brien that she was "preoccupied with the spiritual survival, the survival *whole* of my people," above all "committed to exploring the oppressions, the insanities, the loyalties, and the triumphs of black women" (*In Search* 250–51). The next year she made her debut as a contributing editor to *Ms.* magazine with "In Search of Our Mothers' Gardens," an African-American version of Virginia Woolf's manifesto for the woman writer, *A Room of One's Own.*

By the time Trudier Harris wrote her pioneering scholarly essay on *The Third Life of Grange Copeland*, Alice Walker's identity had been constructed, in part by herself, not only as a representative contemporary black woman but as the heir of a specifically African-American literary tradition that was, in the early 1970s, just beginning to be claimed.

A number of scholars were more than willing both to unearth and study the tradition of black writers Alice Walker championed and to place her within it. The first scholarship published on Walker came from African-Americanists and black feminists. Trudier Harris (1975) treated *Grange Copeland* as African-American sociology written from an impeccably black perspective. Darwin Turner (1976) reviewed her poetry with Ishmael Reed's because he thought the two of them "define[d] the dimensions of black poetry today" (218). Chester Fontenot (1977) identified the peculiar dimensions of her achievement as a black writer by invoking W. E. B. Du Bois's notion of "double consciousness," and Trudier Harris (1977) compared African-American folklore elements in *In Love and Trouble* to nineteenth-century traditions represented by Charles Chesnutt and studied by Zora Neale Hurston. Two of these articles appeared in journals devoted to African-American studies—*Black American Literature Forum* and *Journal of Afro-American Issues*—while all of them situated Alice Walker in a black or African-American context.

Written in 1976, Mary Helen Washington's "Essay on Alice Walker" set the tone for numerous later articles. For Washington, who had written a doctoral dissertation on black women writers and was later to edit two anthologies of short stories written by black women, it was "clear that the special identifying mark of [Walker's] writing is her concern for the lives of black women" (133).

In 1979 Washington's essay was published in *Sturdy Black Bridges: Visions of Black Women in Literature,* one of the earliest anthologies to combine feminist and African-American concerns. As such, it was widely adopted for use in a variety of courses in African-American and women's studies programs, where Washington's presentation of Alice Walker as "apologist and spokeswoman for black women" (134) was widely disseminated.[22]

The volume of critical and scholarly articles on Alice Walker increased dramatically after *The Color Purple* won both the Pulitzer Prize and the National Book Award in 1983. Criticism of Walker after *The Color Purple* changes qualitatively as well as quantitatively. Identified before simply as "a black writer" (Harris, Turner, Fontenot) or "a prolific and imaginative artist" (the

editors of *Sturdy Black Bridges*), after 1983 she becomes "one of
America's finest novelists" (Christian 1984), author of "ten major
literary works, eight of which are poetry and fiction master-
pieces" (Parker-Smith). Walker's status as a "major writer" is implicitly verified by articles that situate her work in the context
of southern literature (Davis), feminist revisions of literary history (Washington 1984), or recent developments in narrative tech-
nique (Fifer). What distinguishes these articles from earlier efforts
to focus on the formal aspects of Walker's work, such as Peter
Erickson's and Deborah E. McDowell's, is that her color and her
sex are no longer ignored in favor of her "universal" themes or
"artistic maturity." It may be that, her stature "legitimated" by the
Pulitzer and National Book awards, Walker can now be used by
critics to liberate black women's writing from the critical ghettos
of African-American or black feminist special interests and claim
for it a place in some larger cultural, generic, or theoretical
context.

We are suggesting that Alice Walker's "canonization," in the
vulgar sense implied by George Stade's calling *The Color Purple*
a "sacred text,"[23] has enabled some scholars to reformulate the
literary "canon," altering it to admit the undenied and undeniable
blackness and femaleness also present in her best-selling, prize-
winning novel. One article, in particular, will illustrate our point.

In an article in the *Southern Review* arrestingly illustrated by
photographs of quilts and African-American quilters, Houston
A. Baker, Jr., and Charlotte Pierce-Baker claim that, as "represen-
tations of the stories of the vernacular natives who make up the
ninety-nine percent of the American population unendowed with
money and control," quilts "in their patched and many-colored
glory offer not a counter to tradition but, in fact, an instance of
the only legitimate tradition of 'the people' that exists." Baker
and Pierce-Baker are not writing an essay on the patchwork quilt
as a native art form. Rather, they use the quilt "as a trope for
understanding black women's creativity in the United States" (714)
which, by analogy, offers "not a counter to tradition" but a "legitimate" expression of creativity which belongs in any purport-

edly accurate or complete picture of "the American tradition." Indeed, the authors claim, "southern black women have not only produced quilts of stunning beauty, they have also crafted books of monumental significance" (713). Such writers as Harriet Brent Jacobs, Zora Neale Hurston, and Margaret Walker form "an ancestral line elegantly shared by Alice Walker" (714), whose story "Everyday Use" provides both an illustration of women's creative heritage and the "trope" by which Baker and Pierce-Baker propose to insert an indigenous black "vernacular" tradition into the American canon. In other words, Baker and Pierce-Baker capitalize on Alice Walker's current popularity and "respectability" to propose a radical reformulation of the American canon.[24]

The "case of Alice Walker" we have constructed amounts to a model of canonical "integration." The entry first of Alice Walker, the individual black woman writer, and then, through her, a category of writers (black women) into the existing canon results in the canon's reformulation. It is, of course, equally possible to argue that Walker and the black women writers she represents have been co-opted by the hegemony, "assimilated" into "southern" or "American" or "postmodernist" canons, their nappy hair hotcombed into bland respectability by such essays as Elizabeth Fifer's on the "masterful achievement" of *The Color Purple*'s "narrative strategies" (157–58).

Susan Willis has observed that the Saxon College episodes in Walker's novel *Meridian* underscore the university's "function" as "a social institution whose primary role is to assimilate bright young black women, who might otherwise be dangerously marginal, to dominant white culture." This is not, Willis says, "a cosmetic transformation, but one that separates the individual from her class and community and forever inscribes her within the bourgeois world" whose interests are "served" by the university (34).

Alice Walker herself has said she is suspicious of canonization by "racist, sexist and colorist capitalist society." The white establishment "doesn't care about art that is crucial to our [that is, the black] community because it doesn't care about our com-

munity," she told Claudia Tate in 1983 (183). Thirteen years earlier she had revealed that her ambition was "to write poetry that
is understood by [my] people, not by the Queen of England" ("The
Black Writer" 18). For that reason, she told Tate, she and other
black women writers "instinctively feel a need to connect with
their reading audience. . . . None of us will survive except in very
distorted ways if we have to depend on white publishers and white
readers forever. And white critics" (182).

Why then, a year before she published *Meridian*, with its critique of the hegemonic function of the university, did Walker agree
to address members of the (largely white) academic literary establishment assembled in San Francisco for the annual convention
of the Modern Language Association? The title of the forum at
which Walker spoke, "Visions of Power in Minority Literature,"
and its sponsor, the MLA Commission on Minority Groups and
the Study of Language and Literature, suggest an answer. Organized a few years after the MLA Commission on the Status of
Women, the Commission on Minority Groups (like the Gay and
Lesbian caucus for the Modern Languages, which was organized
in 1974) was an attempt to use the revolutionary impulse of the
"Little Bourgeois Revolution of 1968" to transform and democratize the institutional structure of the Modern Language Association, insisting that women, minorities, gays, and lesbians
be represented in the association's governance structure. More
importantly, through the forums, workshops, and panels they
sponsored at the annual convention, these commissions and
caucuses insisted that their concerns and scholarly interests *not*
be merely "assimilated" into some hypothetical "mainstream"
canon. Their demand was, rather, that the canon—like the MLA
itself—redefine itself, like the film version of "The Wizard of Oz"
when it moved from black-and-white Kansas to Technicolor Oz.

Walker's talk, and the forum at which it was given, participate
in a larger phenomenon that helps account for the dramatic
increase over the past decade or so of scholarly attention to "noncanonical" writers. Walker, like Adrienne Rich, Tillie Olsen, Margaret Atwood, and Toni Morrison, not only benefited from ges-

tures within the academy toward canon reformation but helped produce them by speaking with and to scholars at the annual MLA conventions, often specifically about revising literary history to include the previously silenced and invisible and the common readers to and for whom they wrote. As spokespersons for common readers and "lost traditions," contemporary women writers implicitly nominate themselves champions of those readers and heirs to those traditions, validating scholarly research on their own work at the same time, and by the same token, as they advocate the cause of their foremothers and readers.

This dialogue between women writers and the academy joined a dialogue between common readers and the academy, initiated in large part by feminist scholars, going on within the literary profession and exemplified by "the case of Doris Lessing." The ensuing colloquy seemed to many to mark a revolutionary moment in the history of canon formation and reformation.

Nonetheless, Walker's cooperation with the Establishment contains ambiguity and hints of co-optation. The film of *The Color Purple*, for example, prettifies and sanitizes the novel's anarchic and feminist elements. Inexplicably, the screenplay valorizes father-daughter rather than woman-woman relationships, changing the focus and meaning of the plot substantially. Such alterations illustrate the problematic nature for the outsider of trying to work within an essentially antipathetic power structure.[25]

We have occasional moments when we wonder, with other skeptics, whether feminist scholarship can retain its revolutionary edge, its political commitment to common readers, as and if it truly enters the "mainstream" of academia represented, in large part, by the Modern Language Association. But for the most part, we believe it is—to borrow the title of a recent anthology of feminist literary criticism—"making a difference."[26] In chapter seven, we attempt to spell out what that difference is, and in an afterword we discuss the complications inherent in making a difference by examining the double-pronged challenge to the academy of feminist canon revision and the accompanying theory and practice of feminist criticism.

Our real concern is not that feminist scholarship will renounce its fundamental allegiance to living readers and their felt needs, but that we and other feminists may be deluding ourselves about the extent to which we have inserted ourselves and our agendas into the literary establishment. In the next chapter, we take a hard look at some statistics that temper premature euphoria about the impact feminist scholarship has had on the academy.

6

Playing the Numbers
The Impact of Feminist Scholarship
on the Academy

In 1969, one year after the "Little Bourgeois Cultural Revolution of MLA 1968" had eventuated in the establishment of a Commission on the Status of Women in the Profession, 33 of the 211 papers listed in the program of the annual Modern Language Association convention (roughly 15%) were by women. By 1987, 886 of the 1,895 listed papers (more than 45%) were by women.

These figures suggest, first, that the MLA's annual convention has metamorphosed in scarcely two decades from a collegial assembly whose members were assumed to share common interests and attend plenary "general sessions," filling in the time between them with more specialized "seminars," to a behemoth intellectual supermarket, with as many as 45 sessions competing in any hour for the delegates' attendance.[1] They also suggest that the annual convention has become less "gentlemanly" not only in its pace but in its composition. That almost half the participants in the 1987 convention of the Modern Language Association were women reinforces other statistics suggesting that the profession of letters is becoming "feminized."

This impression was given powerful support by Elizabeth Kolbert's December 1987 article, "Literary Feminism Comes of Age," in the widely read and culturally influential *New York Times Magazine*. "On one level," Kolbert explained, "the profession is simply becoming more female-dominated." In 1986,

five years after women first edged by men to earn the majority of doctorates in English and American literature, women earned 59% of the Ph.D.s in the field, according to the National Research Council. . . . The latest figures available from the Modern Language Associa-

tion indicate that in tenure-track appointments in literature departments, women are roughly on a par with men. (112)

Annette Kolodny, commenting on Kolbert's article in the *Chronicle of Higher Education,* noted that "to be sure, a disproportion-
ate number of those women are employed at two- and four-year
colleges, rather than at research universities, and are clustered
at the lower end of both the rank and salary scales." But she con-
ceded that, "even so, the fact remains that women have become
numerically significant in literature departments" ("Respectability").

If the claim that women scholars are more visible and active
in the profession now than they were at the end of the 1960s
rests primarily on their role in the Modern Language Association, it can certainly be supported by the data. If we measure
women's active role in the organization by papers delivered at
the annual convention, we can see a dramatic rise in women's
participation in the MLA from 1969 to 1987. In 1969, women
delivered only 15% of the papers. By 1975, that percentage had
nearly doubled, and in 1980 women presented over a third (35.9%)
of convention papers. By 1985 it was 40%, and in 1987, the year
Kolbert reported on the convention, women gave nearly half the
papers (45.6%). A longitudinal study of the composition of the
MLA's Executive Council and Delegate Assembly reveals that
women's participation has increased proportionally in the association's governance structure. Reporting for the Commission
on the Status of Women in the Profession to the business meeting of the Modern Language Association in December 1969,
Florence Howe pointed out the disparity at that time between
women's membership in the organization and their role in its
governance:

> Anyone may calculate, with a little patience and arithmetic, the pro-
> portion of women who belong to the association—upwards of 25%,
> and the proportion who have served on the Executive Council, for
> example since 1945—less than 1%. ("A Report" 647)

Between 1970 and 1987, by comparison, although the gendered
composition of the council varied from year to year, on average

women constituted nearly half (44%) of its membership. In 1972, one year after the Delegate Assembly was established, the list of its members published in the September (directory) issue of *Publications of the Modern Language Association (PMLA)* revealed that less than a third (31.7%) were women. By 1987, there were almost as many women as men representing their constituencies at the Delegate Assembly (the peak year, till then, was 1986, when 49.7% of the delegates were women). The list of past presidents of the MLA in the September 1987 *PMLA* suggests that this is one organization where women executives have shattered the glass ceiling. Of its 97 presidents since the MLA was founded in 1883, only 10 have been women, but in the last two decades the presidency has virtually alternated between the sexes: since 1967, men have held the office 12 times, women 8. And in 1985, the MLA appointed its first woman executive director, Phyllis Franklin.

But as the title of her article—"Literary Feminism Comes of Age"—reveals, Elizabeth Kolbert was not only noting that there are more women in the profession now than fifteen years ago but contending that, in part at least because of their increased participation, "feminist literary criticism, once a sort of illicit half sister in the academic world, has assumed a respectable place in the family order" (110). In other words, Kolbert claims not only that there are more women in the profession now than fifteen years ago but that they have had a measurable influence on deciding which authors and topics are studied, that, in large part because of these women, feminist scholarship has changed both the constitution and the scholarly agenda of the Modern Language Association. (This is to assume, of course, both that the MLA is the professional organization of literary scholars, and that its agenda epitomizes that of the profession at large. As we will suggest later in this chapter, the latter may not be the case.)

Kolbert also seems to assume that most if not all feminist scholars are engaged in what Elaine Showalter has named "gynocriticism," the study of women writers. "The strongest evidence of feminism's impact on the academy," Kolbert writes, "comes from the increased representation of female writers on college syllabi and dissertation lists and at academic conferences":

> The program of the Modern Language Association's annual convention, a sort of barometer of prevailing literary trends, clearly shows this influence. In 1970, the convention had one forum on women and literature and just one seminar devoted to a female author. . . . This year's MLA convention . . . includes dozens of seminars on female writers. (114)

It is true that women writers have been increasingly represented at the MLA convention over the past two decades, as we discovered. Consulting convention programs from 1969 through 1987, we tabulated papers whose titles indicated that their focus, at least in part, was on a woman writer. We then counted division, discussion-group, and MLA-sponsored meetings whose titles indicated that they focused on individual women writers or on a class or group of women writers. Next, we grouped together allied organization meetings and special sessions (called "seminars" before 1976) and tabulated those whose topics focused on or featured women writers. And finally, we counted forums that highlighted women writers.

We cannot claim that our figures indicate *exactly* the representation of women writers at MLA conventions for the past 20 years. Not all papers listed in the program are actually delivered, while some that don't make it into the program are (because some are completed after the deadline for submitting program copy, because a panelist is added at the last minute, etc.). A paper's title or a panel's stated topic may not accurately reveal its contents, so we may have overlooked some that did focus on women writers and wrongly assumed a gynocentric focus in other instances. And from 1977 through 1982, the program did not list papers read at special sessions, but only listed names of scholars scheduled to give them. So for those five years, we counted only papers delivered at division, discussion-group, MLA-sponsored, and allied organization meetings. Nevertheless, our figures—summarized in table 1—indicate more accurately than Elizabeth Kolbert's generalizations the extent to which feminism has had an "impact on the academy," if that impact can accurately be assessed by discussion of women writers at that "barometer of prevailing literary trends," the MLA convention.

But we do not believe that the number of MLA sessions or papers on women writers provides a meaningful index of feminism's "impact on the academy" or even of the degree to which feminist scholarship has altered the canon. As Lillian Robinson points out:

> There are women authors, and much of the scholarship and criticism devoted to them—and to the best known of them in particular—concentrates on aspects of their work unrelated to their own gender or to questions of gender in their writing. There is certainly a feminist way—or rather several—of understanding Jane Austen's irony or George Eliot's religion or Virginia Woolf's metaphors. But the vast bulk of critical prose annually devoted to such topics tends, more often than not, to do the thing "straight," that is, gender-blind. ("Feminist Criticism" 143)

We could not determine from the title alone whether a paper about a woman writer was feminist in orientation. "Writing (Wo)-Man: Isak Dinesen and the Poetics of Displacement" sounds feminist, but does "The Woman Who Would Be King: Isak Dinesen in and out of Adventure Tropes"? What about "Isak Dinesen in and out of the Place with No Name"? We tried, at first, to distinguish between papers that sounded as if they were, to borrow Robinson's phrase, "merely on women" and those that sounded "feminist." "The Aristotelian View of *Pride and Prejudice*" exemplifies the former, "merely on women," category; "From Rape Victim to Artist: Eudora Welty's Creation of Female Voice in *The Golden Apples*" is a clear example of the latter. But we finally decided, as did Lillian Robinson and her colleagues in measuring the impact of feminist scholarship on their respective disciplines in *Feminist Scholarship: Kindling in the Groves of Academe*, that any increased attention to women authors may be one index or, to use Robinson's word, one "by-product" (144) of

Table 1   Representation of Women Writers
at MLA Conventions, 1969–87

	Papers on Women Writers		Division/ Discussion Group Mtgs. on Women Writers		Seminars/ Special Sessions/ Allied Organization Mtgs. on Women Writers		Forums on Women Writers	
	No.	%	No.	%	No.	%	No.	%
1969	3	1.4	0	0.0	1	1.4	0	0.0
1970	2	0.9	0	0.0	1	1.5	0	0.0
1971	6	2.4	0	0.0	4	4.7	1	16.6
1972	4	1.5	0	0.0	4	3.3	1	25.0
1973	7	2.5	1	0.9	7	4.4	0	0.0
1974	48	11.1	0	0.0	14	6.9	0	0.0
1975	74	9.4	3	2.1	21	6.1	1	20.0
1976	77	7.5	3	1.5	22	5.3	0	0.0
1977	67	9.9	3	1.2	27	6.4	2	28.5
1978	33	5.6	4	1.9	34	7.8	0	0.0
1979	72	10.3	10	4.3	37	8.7	0	0.0
1980	62	8.4	3	1.3	24	8.0	0	0.0
1981	71	8.5	3	1.1	28	7.0	1	16.6
1982	84	8.9	5	1.9	35	8.2	1	16.6
1983	164	10.5	8	2.8	28	7.0	1	20.0
1984	211	12.3	2	0.7	19	5.2	0	0.0
1985	204	11.8	10	3.5	32	8.9	1	20.0
1986	238	12.2	10	5.4	28	6.8	0	0.0
1987	257	13.5	5	1.7	28	7.7	0	0.0

feminist scholarship, since feminist critics were initially responsible for calling the profession's attention to more than the one woman writer traditionally considered "great," Jane Austen, who was the only female author on Columbia University's great books list in 1988.

But even if an increase in the attention accorded women writers is due at least in part to the efforts of feminist scholars, is it the *only* register of their effect on the profession? The study of women writers is one area of literary scholarship in which feminists have been active. But some feminists have devoted their energies to exposing the sexism and misogyny of such canonical texts as *Paradise Lost* and *The Sun Also Rises*, while others engage in "strategies of rereading" that enable them to "approach traditional texts not as the mystifying (and self-limiting) 'best' that has been thought and said in the world but as a *visible* past against which we can teach our students to imagine a different future" (Froula 171, her emphasis).[2] Other feminists are primarily interested in literary history or theory rather than textual analysis, while still others work principally on institutional reform and equity issues. All of these feminist activities, not just gynocriticism, are represented at the annual convention of the Modern Language Association.

In fact, the first public display of feminist activism within the Modern Language Association was the 1970 forum on "Women in the Profession," whose associated workshops included "Know Your Rights: University Women and the Law" and "The Job Market for Women." In any given year, the meetings arranged by the MLA Commission on the Status of Women are likely to include both "professional" and "literary" topics. In 1977, to choose a year at random, the commission considered both "Women and Part-Time Work" and "Women Writers of the Harlem Renaissance." Feminist scholarship is no less evident in a panel on "Feminist Criticism of Shakespeare" or "Feminist Aesthetics in Twentieth-Century Literature and Visual Art" than it is in a session devoted to "Four Women Writers and Their Journals."

Therefore, counting papers or sessions on women writers

will give only a partial sense of the effect of feminism on the
MLA's scholarly agenda. If we add to papers on women those
papers whose titles suggest a feminist analytical approach (e.g.,
"The Daughter's *Jouissance* and Phallic Law in Shakespeare's
Plays") or raise "political," often extratextual, questions (e.g., "Feminist Publishing: Ethical and Legal Issues"), we will probably
form a more accurate assessment of the extent of feminist scholarship's impact on the academy. Table 2 traces that impact from
1969 to 1987 as it can be measured by papers on women writers,
by papers whose titles indicate feminist scholarship ("Southern
Women's Literature: A Process of Discovery") or critical orientation ("Chaucer's Dorigen: Marriage Model or Male Fantasy?"),
and by papers on feminist issues such as pay equity.[3]

This tabulation of papers *does* suggest that feminist scholarship has become increasingly visible at the MLA convention
over the past two decades. But it also calls into question another
of Elizabeth Kolbert's unstated assumptions, that many if not all
of the women in the Modern Language Association are engaged
in feminist scholarship. Nearly half (46%) of the registrants at
the 1987 convention were women, but only a quarter of the papers read that year were on women writers or indicated, by their
titles, other feminist concerns. Analysis of that or any year's convention program indicates that women give various kinds of
papers: on women writers, men writers, literary history, literary
theory, rhetoric, composition, linguistics, foreign study—in short,
that women scholars are actively involved in the entire range of
interests that find their professional home in the Modern Language Association.

Of course there is no reason why one's scholarship should be
determined by one's sex. There is no reason why a woman should
be drawn more to Margaret Laurence than to Tom Stoppard, to
submit a paper to a panel on "The Politics of the Writings of
Women of Color" rather than to one, scheduled for the same
hour, on "Experimental and Exotic Study-Abroad Programs."
Nor is there any self-evident reason why only women should do
"feminist" work, although from time to time it is asserted that

Table 2   Papers Registering Feminist Scholarship
Delivered at MLA Conventions, 1969–87

	Papers on Women Writers		Papers on Feminist Issues, or Indicating Feminist Scholarship or Critical Orientation		Combined "Feminist" Papers	
	No.	%	No.	%	No.	%
1969	3	1.4	0	0.0	3	1.4
1970	2	0.9	7	3.3	9	4.3
1971	6	2.4	10	4.1	16	6.5
1972	4	1.5	7	2.7	11	4.3
1973	7	2.5	10	3.6	17	6.2
1974	49	11.3	5	1.1	54	12.5
1975	68	8.7	24	3.0	92	11.7
1976	77	7.5	81	7.9	153	14.9
1977	67	9.9	42	6.2	109	16.1
1978	33	5.6	46	7.9	79	13.6
1979	72	10.3	54	7.7	125	18.1
1980	62	8.4	39	5.2	101	13.6
1981	71	8.5	46	5.5	117	14.1
1982	84	8.9	57	6.0	141	15.0
1983	164	10.5	84	5.4	249	15.9
1984	211	12.3	152	8.9	363	21.2
1985	204	11.8	169	9.8	373	21.6
1986	238	12.2	167	8.6	405	20.9
1987	257	13.5	226	11.9	481	25.3

"men's relation to feminism is an impossible one" (Heath 1).[4] Indeed, of the 481 papers at the 1987 convention we have labeled "feminist," 114 or 23.7% were by men.

Does this mean, as Elizabeth Kolbert quotes Yale's Peter Brooks as saying, that "anyone worth his [sic] salt in literary criticism today has to become something of a feminist" (110)? Selective reading can lead to that impression. Wayne Booth, Jonathan Culler, Terry Eagleton, Frank Lentricchia, Lawrence Lipking—some of this generation's leading male critics—have not only called feminist criticism "one of the most significant and broadly-based critical movements of recent years" (Culler, *On Deconstruction* 42), but have also attempted to practice it.[5] This, plus the general increase of scholarly attention to women writers and feminist criticism, leads on the one hand to feminist euphoria and on the other to bitter accusations that men are "taking over" feminist criticism. Sometimes the same commentator expresses both sentiments. At the conclusion of one article, Elaine Showalter hazards the suggestion that "it may well turn out that in the critical histories of the future, these years will not be remembered as the Age of Structuralism or the Age of Deconstruction, but as the Age of Feminism" ("Women's Time" 42), while midway through another article she observes, more tartly, that "there is more than a hint in some recent critical writing that it's time for men to step in and show the girls how to do it" ("Cross-Dressing" 119).[6] In an essay entitled "Engorging the Patriarchy," Nina Auerbach notes that "some, though not all," of the men now practicing feminist criticism "have written of their conversion as if feminism were an act of grace freely given to them: lauding their own illumination, they fail to cite the names of any actual, female feminist critics" (156).

The numbers we have compiled, however, support neither the conclusion that feminist scholarship has irrevocably altered the way the profession as a whole reads and writes about literature nor the anxiety expressed by some women about male scholars taking over feminist criticism. Assuming that our method provides a reasonable assessment of the number of feminist papers, if a quarter of the feminist papers read at the 1987 MLA convention were by men, *all* of the feminist papers constituted only a quarter of the total number of papers presented. This means that most of the men (89%) and more than half of the women (58%) at the 1987 convention read papers whose titles do not indicate a focus on women writers or feminist concerns. It also means that, while not all women scholars in the Modern Language Association are doing feminist work, most of the feminist work is being done by women.

Much of that work may go on behind the scenes of the MLA convention, in the committees that constitute what might be called the critical filter through which topics, papers, and speakers must pass in order to gain public exposure at the convention. One need not engage in feminist scholarship in order to do important work on its behalf.[7]

The September 1987 issue of *PMLA* lists the following six types of meetings held at the MLA annual convention: division, discussion-group, and American-literature section meetings; special sessions; meetings of allied organizations; and forums.[8] These categories were established in 1976; before then—for our purposes, between 1969 and 1975—what are now "divisions" and "discussion groups" were "sessions" and "groups," and today's "special sessions" were called "seminars." But then, as now, decisions about programming for the convention passed through distinct critical filters. For divisions and discussion groups, five-member executive committees elected by members of each division and discussion group assume responsibility for programming and organizing sessions at the convention. Special sessions originate from individual members' initiatives and are intended to add a "topical element" to the convention ("Procedures" 454). But, "since their number has grown dramatically in recent years, it has become necessary to develop procedures whereby members submit proposals to organize special sessions and the Program Committee selects the sessions to be held" (454). Thus, while any member of MLA may submit a proposal for a special session, it must pass through the critical filter of the Program Committee, appointed by the Executive Council of the MLA, and chaired by the executive director, before the session gains a place on the convention program. On the other hand, once allied organizations are recognized as such by the Program Committee, they are free to set their own topics, subject to no review or approval by the committee.[9]

What do these procedural matters have to do with the representation both of women scholars and of feminist scholarship at the annual MLA convention? Generally speaking, during the years we surveyed, women more frequently chaired and gave papers at special sessions than at meetings of divisions or discussion groups. Feminist topics and papers showed up more often in special sessions or programs arranged by allied organizations than at division or discussion-group meetings. This situation reflects what might be called the bicameral character of the convention, as the assignment of governance responsibility to an Executive Council and Delegate Assembly signals the bicameral nature of the MLA. Division programs not only are "the largest convention meetings in terms of scope and attendance" but claim to "represent major areas of membership interest" ("Procedures" 452). Special sessions often reveal concerns simmering beneath the bland surface of business as usual or herald new directions in theory, practice, or pedagogy; and a number of allied organizations represent radical or minority constituencies (e.g., the Gay and Lesbian, Graduate Student, Radical, and Women's caucuses). In 1969, for instance, one allied organization—the New University Conference—sponsored 13 of the 19 workshops at that year's convention. Their topics included "Women's Liberation" as well as "Class Bias and the Teaching of Literature" and "Black Literature and Black Studies." The first wave of feminist criticism washed onto the convention floor in special sessions on "Images of Women" in everything from the American and British novel to Yiddish literature. At least four allied organizations are exclusively dedicated to the study of women writers: the Ellen Glasgow, Doris Lessing, and Virginia Woolf societies and the Friends of George Sand. Feministas Unidas and Women in German, as their names indicate, also offer forums for the exchange of feminist scholarship and criticism.

Since special sessions must be approved by the MLA Program Committee, it seems noteworthy that, as women's representation on the Program Committee has increased, so have special sessions devoted to women writers or feminist topics. In 1969, there was only one seminar (1.4% of the total number of seminars) on a woman writer, Emily Dickinson, and there were no women on the Program Committee. In 1975, 8.5% of the seminars at the MLA convention were devoted to women writers or feminist topics, and of the total number of papers given that year we have identified as "feminist," 70.4% were delivered at seminars and 18.3% at meetings of allied organizations. In that year, women constituted 16.6% of the membership of the Program Committee. In 1987, when 55% of the membership of the Program Committee was female, 16% of the meetings arranged by allied organizations and 23% of the special sessions were on women writers or feminist topics. In that year, of the papers we have identified as "feminist," 19.1% were delivered at meetings of allied organizations and 50.3% at special sessions.

These percentages also indicate that in 1987, 13.2% of division– and discussion-group–sponsored sessions were devoted to either women writers or feminist topics and, of the papers we have identified as "feminist," 30.4% were delivered at division or discussion-group meetings. In 1975, by contrast, no section or group meetings focused on women writers or feminist topics, and if 88.7% of the "feminist" papers were read at seminars and allied organization meetings, clearly only 11.3% were delivered at section and group meetings.

What has been happening in the 1980s to bring feminist scholarship from the periphery into the mainstream of MLA convention business? At least part of the answer may lie in the changing constitution of the bodies responsible for deciding what topics and papers will be featured at meetings arranged by divisions and discussion groups—that is, their executive committees.

In 1969, when no section or group sessions focused on women

writers or feminist topics, only 7.3% of the section and group executives were women. By 1975, women were 21% of section and
group chairs and secretaries, and although none of the section
or group meetings focused on a woman writer or feminist topic,
11.2% of the feminist papers delivered that year were read at section or group sessions. By 1987, women and men were almost
equally represented on division and discussion group executive
committees (in 1987, 42.3% of the division and discussion group
executive committee members were women).

Thus, it would seem that, as more women gain access to
decision-making bodies in the Modern Language Association,
more feminist scholarship is disseminated and, implicity, sanctioned. Yet that seems too simple an answer to the question we
posed earlier: "What has been happening in the 1980s to bring
feminist scholarship from the periphery into the mainstream of
MLA convention business?"

The answer to that question is far from simple. A number of
factors we have already noted separately were, in fact, more or
less simulaneously at play, creating a climate more hospitable to
the growth and dissemination of feminist scholarship. First, during the period we have been examining—1970–86—an increasing
number of women entered the profession, measured both by
PhDs awarded (59% of the total in 1986) and membership in the
Modern Language Association.[10] Second, as we have seen, between 1970 and 1987 these women played an increasingly prominent role in the association, both on the floor of the annual convention and in the MLA's governance structure. Third, during the
same period, feminism fueled political activism (in the MLA as
elsewhere) and generated an increasingly respected and influential body of research and scholarship. In the 1980s, men as well
as women began to practice feminist criticism and, by the end
of the period we are examining, "gender studies" emerged as a
new and promising area of specialization. At the same time, many
institutions eliminated requirements that literature majors take
courses in early periods, thus increasing the likelihood that students would enroll in courses including women writers and en-

couraging faculty to develop courses to meet students' demands. And fourth, the annual MLA convention grew in both size and scope from 1970 to 1986, accommodating an ever-increasing variety of interests.

None of these factors, in isolation, can account for the movement of feminist scholarship from the fringes to the very center of the Modern Language Association's agenda. This became clear to us when we turned from the programs of the annual MLA convention to the publication of the association, *PMLA*, to test the hypothesis that, as more women gain access to decision-making bodies in the MLA, more feminist scholarship is disseminated and, implicitly, sanctioned.

PMLA, like the MLA convention, claims to represent all members of the organization and their interests. We analyzed the contents of *PMLA* from 1970 to 1987 to assess the extent to which a journal that takes itself seriously as representing the scholarly concerns of its 30,000 members is receptive to feminist topics and feminist theoretical perspectives. As in our analysis of MLA convention programs, we were curious to see what percentage of published contributors[11] to *PMLA* were women and whether that percentage has grown over the past 15 years. We were also eager to discover the degree to which feminist scholarship was manifested, whether its influence was significantly greater in 1987 than in 1970. Above all, we wanted to know whether the percentage of women contributors and feminist scholarship published in *PMLA* was correlated in any way to the representation of women on the bodies that largely determine what will be published in the journal, the editorial board and the advisory committee.

We began by tabulating the number of published women contributors and the representation of feminist scholarship in *PMLA* from 1970 to 1987. (To assess feminist scholarship, we used the same method and categories we employed in analyzing MLA convention programs, identifying articles on women writers — regardless of whether the articles were feminist in critical orientation — as well as articles not on women writers but that employed a feminist critical approach or discussed feminist theory.) We discovered that there was a measurable increase in the 1980s, both in the number of women contributors to the journal and in its publication of essays on women writers or feminist topics. Between 1970 and 1979, while the percentage of articles by women in any single issue of *PMLA* varied from 4.8% to 29%, on average women constituted one-fifth (20.7%) of published contributors. During those years, articles on women writers or feminist topics made up, on average, only 5% of the journal's contents (by issue, the percentage ranged from 0% to 11.1%). In the 1980s, by comparison, women contributed, on average, over a third (36.5%) of the articles published in *PMLA* (the lowest percentage of women contributors was 25%, the highest 45.8%). And articles on women writers or feminist topics rose to an average of 17.6% of the journal's contents (ranging from 8.6% to 26%).

When we added to these figures others that showed the gendered composition, over the years, of *PMLA*'s editorial board and advisory committees, we discovered corresponding increases in women's representation. In the 1970s, women's representation on *PMLA*'s editorial board ranged from 0% to 33.3%, averaging 16%; on the advisory committee, women constituted from 5.2% to 25% of the membership from year to year, averaging 13%. In the 1980s, on the other hand, there was only one year in which no woman served on the editorial board, and one year in which more than half the board members were women; on average, women comprised slightly over a quarter (27.7%) of the board's membership. And from 1980 to 1987, women members never constituted less than 25% of the advisory committee. Three times women outnumbered men, and the average rate of women's participation on the committee was 40.7%.

These gross statistics seem to support the hypothesis that, as more women gain access to *PMLA*'s decision-making bodies, more women publish their scholarship in *PMLA* and more feminist scholarship is disseminated by the journal. Gross statistics, though, like generalizations, tend to oversimplify. We believe factors other than the presence of women on *PMLA*'s editorial board and advisory committee should be considered in any attempt to account for the increase in published women contributors and feminist scholarship in *PMLA* over the past 15 years.

For instance, it is true that feminist scholarship has been increasingly well represented in *PMLA* during the 1980s (in fact it has risen in direct proportion to the representation of feminist scholarship at the annual MLA convention). This is all the more noteworthy because, when Joel Conarroe became editor of *PMLA* in 1979, the journal abandoned its policy of publishing up to 15 articles in each issue. Since 1980, no issue has contained more than 6 essays. When 1 or 2 or, as in the October 1984 issue, all 6 of these essays are feminist in their orientation, then feminist scholarship would seem, indeed, to have "come of age."

But can we say the increased representation of feminist scholarship in *PMLA* is due to women's increasing representation on its editorial board and advisory committee? When we compared the representation of women on the advisory committee in a given year with the representation of feminist scholarship in *PMLA* during the next year (allowing for the time lag between acceptance and publication of an article), we did not find a direct correlation between women's membership on the committee and the journal's rate of publishing feminist scholarship. In 1981, 16.6% of the articles published in *PMLA* were on women writers or manifested feminist scholarship; the preceding year, women comprised 25% of the advisory committee. In 1986, too, 16% of the articles in *PMLA* were on women writers or manifested feminist scholarship. But almost half the members of the preceding year's advisory committee (46.6%) were women. It may be that *PMLA* is publishing more feminist scholarship these days because feminist scholarship has gained increasing respectability in the profession at large (fully a quarter [26.3%] of the feminist articles published since 1980 in *PMLA* were written by men).

As we have seen, not only has *PMLA* published more feminist scholarship in the 1980s than previously, but the percentage of published women contributors has increased as well. Yet this probably has nothing to do with women's increased representation on the editorial board and advisory committee of *PMLA* because, in 1980, *PMLA* instituted the policy of author-anonymous reviewing. As Domna Stanton explains, "the practice of withholding the identity of the author from those who evaluate a manuscript submitted for publication" is intended "to ensure that our judgments of others' merits are as uncorrupted as possible by our unconscious biases" (67).[12] Reviewing the effects of the policy eight years after its institution, *PMLA*'s current editor, John W. Kronik, noted that "the profile of the average contributor to the journal has undergone a transformation: our pages now house more women, more colleagues from the junior ranks, and authors from a greater variety of institutions" (733).

"In a word," Stanton says, "author-anonymous reviewing may provide the relatively powerless in the academy with more equal access to the means of scholarly production" (69). But although junior faculty, faculty from less prestigious institutions, graduate students, and independent scholars have, since the institution of author-anonymous reviewing, gained greater access to the pages of *PMLA*, it was women in the MLA who argued for adoption of the policy. *PMLA* instituted author-anonymous reviewing "after a three-year debate initiated by the Modern Language Association's Commission on the Status of Women" (Stanton 67).

According to Kronik, that debate was "heated" (733) and continues to this day. Domna Stanton made "the case for author-anonymous reviewing policies" in a 1982 volume of essays sponsored by the MLA's Commission on the Status of Women, and Myra Jehlen and Maureen Quilligan defended it in a 1986 Guest Column in *PMLA*. William D. Schaefer, then executive director of the Modern Language Association, presented his case against the practice in the *MLA Newsletter* in 1978, and Stanley Fish first recorded his objections in 1979, then published his updated remarks in a *PMLA* Guest Column in 1988.

Fish concedes that author-anonymous submission (which he calls, derogatively, "blind submission") is designed "to prevent a reviewer from being influenced in his or her judgment of merit by the professional status of the author," but he argues that "merit is inseparable from the structure of the profession" and therefore that "there will always be those whose words are meritorious (that is, important, worth listening to, authoritative, illuminating) simply by virtue of the position they occupy in the institution" ("No Bias" 740–41). Fish conflates author and idea in a transparent effort to maintain the status quo that empowers him. "When Geoffrey Hartmann speaks on Wordsworth, is his just another voice," Fish asks, "or is it the voice of someone who is in great measure responsible for the Wordsworth we now have" (741)?

Jehlen and Quilligan assert that "the process through which person and work tend to collapse into one another in the authority of a single name is as old as the medieval formula for an *auctor*, 'As Tully saith . . . .'" When they served on *PMLA*'s editorial board, Jehlen and Quilligan found that "in the absence of names, the editorial analysis remained immersed in the reality of the pages' particulars" (771).

Just as instructive as the substance of this debate is the constituency of its opposing factions. Not only do women scholars defend author-anonymous submission, but journals with women editors—*Signs* (Catharine Stimpson), *Victorian Studies* (Martha Vicinus), and *German Quarterly* (Ruth Angress)—were among the first to initiate the policy (Stanton 67).[13] And it does not seem coincidental that, with the exception of Frances Yates, all of Fish's intrinsically meritorious authorities are white male senior scholars at major research institutions. Domna Stanton conjectures that, behind the strong resistance to author-anonymous reviewing among "senior literary scholars and editors" like Fish and Schaefer, "who are, almost all, white males,"

> lies a fear of exclusion, of being denied the relatively easy access to one another's journals that they now possess, of being reduced to the level of unknown assistant professors and subjected to the same scrutiny. Author-anonymous reviewing may well pose the threat of losing one of the few perquisites and privileges that a senior professor of literature enjoys in our society. A symbolic castration, it

> evokes the possibility of being robbed of a powerful weapon that se-
> nior scholars secretly believe is rightfully theirs. (69)

Stanton's analysis is a clear and useful position statement for a
woman within the power structure. Implicit in it is her own
(and, by extension, other feminist scholars') wish to reduce her
"exclusion" in order to obtain those "perquisites and privileges"
now enjoyed by Fish, Hartmann, and the Old Boys. Stanton's longing is understandable, but it also raises the question of whether
feminist scholarship is best served by attempts to gain a place
in the existing hegemony. Surely such a process will change the
hegemony; it may well, though, change the challengers even more.
Thus, the process of oscillation we have been charting must
never be confused with self-evident improvement. As women
enter the centers of power, their role as critical outsider is com-
promised. This compromise, as in the case of Alice Walker, may
seem puzzling, even counterproductive to those still outside.

In 1976, the American Philological Association's Committee
on the Status of Women and of Minority Groups reported that
"the percentage of papers written by women and accepted for
presentation at the association's annual convention almost *tripled*
(from 6.7% to 19.5%) within two years after author-anonymous
reviewing had been put into practice" (Stanton 73). Though not
so dramatic, there has been a noticeable increase in the publication of articles by women in the years since *PMLA* instituted
author-anonymous submission. All six essays in the October
1984 *PMLA* were by women. The editor, English Showalter, was
so struck by this unprecedented event that he devoted the Editor's
Column in the March 1985 issue to discussing the phenomenon:

> The October 1984 issue of *PMLA* has been in our readers' hands for
> several weeks and I have received a number of letters with lines like
> "One of my friends observed that this was the first all-female issue
> of *PMLA*. Had you been aware of that?" Yes; . . . I refrained from com-
> menting in October in order to let the all-female issue occur as a nor-
> mal event, for it *is* normal now. In fact, it is almost inevitable if women
> submit half the manuscripts, if women's essays are accepted at about
> the same rates that men's are, if *PMLA* publishes articles in the order

they are accepted or revised after acceptance, and if the number of articles in each issue is relatively small. All four conditions have been true for several years. (139, emphasis in the original)

Of course, as Showalter immediately acknowledged, over the years a number of issues of *PMLA* have been composed solely of essays by male scholars:

There was an all-male issue in January 1983, certainly not the first, but the first and still the only one since anonymous submission became our policy. Joel Conarroe commented: "You have probably noticed that all six contributors are male. Before our policy of anonymous submission went into effect this feature might have been interpreted as evidence of bias; since, however, the identity of every contributor is now withheld until a decision has been reached, the fact of a single-sex issue is purely coincidental. Some future *PMLA* may well be made up wholly of work by women scholars." Joel's prophecy has been fulfilled and the laws of probability dictate more such issues in the years to come, unless the editor intervenes. *PMLA* and the profession have progressed a long way toward equality of opportunity and fairness in procedure since that not-very-distant past when issues of *PMLA* with over a dozen articles were all male. (139)

Given the policy of anonymous submission, Showalter goes on to assert that *PMLA* now both offers equality of opportunity and "reflects the changing interests of our profession," specifically greater and greater interest in "women writers and gender studies" (139). In other words, he offers *PMLA* as evidence to support the claim made by Elizabeth Kolbert and others that, not only are there more women in the profession now than there were 15 years ago, but feminist scholars have had an appreciable influence on deciding which authors and topics are studied.

We are not so confident that *PMLA* is the bellwether of the profession. John Kronik sadly noted in the Editor's Column in October 1988 that *PMLA*'s "requirement of anonymity has had undesired side effects: for example, some of the more established members of the profession have unfortunately been reluctant to send their work to *PMLA*" (733). The (relative) "feminization" of the Modern Language Association and its journal may not mean that the literary profession has been revolutionized by feminist scholarship but rather that the gravitational center of professional literary scholarship has shifted. If Kronik is right and "well-established" members of the profession are publishing elsewhere than *PMLA*, can we assume that the journal of the Modern Language Association represents the profession as a whole?

When the authors of *Feminist Scholarship: Kindling in the Groves of Academe* wanted to determine "the extent to which feminist scholarship has influenced the academic disciplines," they analyzed what they believed to be "the most conservative core of academic research: the publications in leading scholarly journals" (DuBois, et al. 158). For each of their disciplines (anthropology, education, history, literature, and philosophy), they selected 10 leading journals, including the publication of each field's professional organization, and intentionally excluded journals devoted primarily to research on women or feminist scholarship such as *Signs* and *Feminist Studies* or—in the case of literature—*Tulsa Studies in Women's Literature*. They then studied "the patterns of publication of articles on the subject of women from 1966 through 1980" (160) in order to gauge the extent to which feminist scholarship had altered the discourse of each discipline over those 15 years.

We decided to follow their example and analyze six journals from 1970 to 1986, most of them recently founded (*ELH*, inaugurated in 1933, is the oldest of the lot): *Contemporary Literature, Critical Inquiry, Diacritics, English Literary History (ELH), New Literary History (NLH)*, and *Novel*.

We analyzed the content of these journals from 1970 to 1986 to assess the extent to which feminism has altered the definition of "serious" or "prestigious" scholarship, since publication in any of these journals "counts," although in some academic circles it counts more to publish in *New Literary History* than in *Contemporary Literature*. We hoped to discover the degree to which feminist scholarship was manifested, whether its influence was significantly greater in 1986 than in 1970 and whether it was more evident in some journals than in others. To tabulate that influence, we used the same method and categories we employed in analyzing MLA convention programs. That is, we counted as "feminist" any article whose title indicated that it focused on a woman writer or employed a feminist critical approach or discussed feminist theory. As in our survey of MLA convention programs, therefore, our conclusions are to some degree speculative, since an article's title may not accurately reflect its contents. Furthermore, what sounds "feminist" to one reader ("*The Rainbow*: Ursula's 'Liberation'") might sound anti- or post-feminist to another.[14]

Table 3 summarizes publication rates by women and on women writers and feminist topics in all six journals, considered as a group, from 1970 to 1986. The first column represents the total number of articles published in a given year. The second column gives the percentage of these articles written by women; the third column the percentage of articles, some but not all of them written by women, on women writers or feminist topics; and the fourth column the total percentage of articles written by women and on women writers or on feminist topics, whether written by men or by women. The total in column four gives a slightly inflated sense of women's representation in these journals from 1970 to 1986, since some articles have been counted twice: once as having been written by a woman and again as being on a woman writer or feminist topic.

Clearly, there has been some increase in the last 15 years in the representation both of published women contributors to these journals and of articles on women writers or feminist topics. But is this increase dramatic or significant? In the 1970s, slightly more than one-sixth of the articles published in these journals were by women; from 1980 to 1986 the percentage rose to one quarter of all the articles published. But in 1975 women accounted for more than a quarter of the delegates to the MLA convention, and by 1986 women were giving nearly half of the convention papers. The increase in articles on women writers or feminist topics in these journals is modest. If special issues on women writers or feminist topics were subtracted from these totals, the

Table 3   Publication Rates of Articles by Women
and on Women Writers or Feminist Topics
in Selected Journals, 1970–86

	Total No. of Articles	Percentage of Articles by Women	Percentage of Articles on Women Writers or Feminist Topics	Total Percentage of Articles by Women, on Women Writers or Feminist Topics
1970	115	14.7	3.4	20.0
1971	105	16.1	6.6	22.8
1972	136	12.5	8.0	20.5
1973[a]	129	21.7	10.0	31.7
1974	145	18.6	10.3	28.9
1975[a]	161	18.6	11.1	29.8
Average rate 1970–75		17.0	8.2	25.6
1976	156	17.9	4.4	22.4
1977	167	13.7	6.5	20.3
1978	163	19.6	5.5	25.1
1979	162	17.9	16.0	33.9
1980	170	18.2	4.7	22.9
Average rate 1976–80		17.4	7.4	24.9
1981[a]	171	21.0	11.6	32.7
1982[a]	170	24.7	8.8	33.5
1983[a]	164	25.6	13.4	39.0
1984	161	22.9	11.8	34.7
1985	159	24.5	10.0	34.5
1986[a]	156	26.2	14.7	41.0
Average rate 1981–86		24.1	11.7	35.9

NOTE: [a]During this year, at least one of the journals published a special
issue on a woman writer or feminist topic.

"impact" of feminist scholarship would be even less impressive. In 1986, when a fifth of the papers read at the MLA convention were on women writers or feminist topics, only 14.7% of the articles published in these journals focused on women writers or feminist topics (the second largest percentage for any year we surveyed), and this figure includes the winter 1986 issue of *Contemporary Literature*, which was entirely devoted to articles on H.D.

The picture becomes more interesting when the publication rates of these journals are differentiated. Table 4 lists, for each journal, the total number of articles published in each year from 1970 to 1986 and the percentage of those articles that were on women writers or feminist topics. We have added *PMLA* to the six other journals for purposes of comparison.

Contemporary Literature, Critical Inquiry, and *Diacritics* each published at least one special issue on a women writer or feminist topic during the 15-year period we surveyed; *ELH, NLH, Novel,* and *PMLA* did not, although *ELH* occasionally and *NLH* regularly published special issues. That may mean that *Contemporary Literature, Critical Inquiry,* and *Diacritics* were more receptive to feminist scholarship, or it may mean that the publication rates for the other four journals "mean more," since they are not skewed by the statistical bump a special issue always raises. As DuBois, et al., note, "the phenomenon of special issues speaks ambiguously to the question of the impact of feminism on scholarship":

> On the one hand, special issues can and often do indicate recognition of a topic of particular interest and importance, one for which published dialogue is most exciting when collected together. . . . On the other hand, special issues can also serve to isolate their subject from the rest of a field, suggesting that it is not sufficiently accepted to be dispersed among more standard research. Thus they may also indicate that the subject of women has been ghettoized within a discipline. (177)

DuBois and her collegues found evidence of both these effects in their comparison of journals in different disciplines. "In education, for example, after journals publish a special issue they

Table 4

Percentage of Articles on Women Writers or Feminist Topics in Selected Journals, 1970–86

	Con Lit		Crit I		Dia		ELH		NLH		Novel		PMLA		Total	
	%	N	%	N	%	N	%	N	%	N	%	N	%	N	%	N
1970	0.0%[a]	24	NP		NP		6.4%	31	0.0%	39	23.5%	17	4.0%	50	4.9%	161
1971	13.0	23	NP		NP		6.0	33	3.0	33	6.3	16	4.8	41	6.1	146
1972	22.7	22	NP		0.0	28	12.1	33	0.0	36	11.7	17	10.0	50	8.6	186
1973	38.4[b]	26	NP		5.0	20	0.0	30	0.0	36	11.7	17	8.3	36	9.6	165
1974	22.7	22	21.0	19	0.0	20	5.8	34	0.0	32	22.2	18	3.3	60	11.7	205
1975	17.6	17	10.8	37	30.4[b]	23	8.5	35	0.0	33	0.0	16	0.0	37	9.0	198
1976	5.2	19	0.0	34	8.3	24	0.0	32	0.0	32	26.6	15	5.5	36	4.6	192
1977	16.6	24	2.7	36	6.2	16	5.2	38	0.0	34	15.7	19	5.5	36	6.4	203
1978	9.5	21	4.8	41	6.6	15	2.7	36	5.7	35	6.6	15	11.1	36	6.5	199

1979	40.0	15	16.2	37	18.1[b]	22	13.8	36	0.0	34	27.7	18	0.0	31	11.3	193
1980	9.0	22	6.9	43	0.0	14	2.5	40	2.7	37	7.1	14	12.5	24	5.6	194
1981	4.5	22	27.7[b]	36	0.0	18	8.8	45	5.4	37	23.0	13	16.6	24	12.3	195
1982	10.5	19	9.3	43	22.2[b]	18	2.3	43	2.9	34	23.0	13	21.7	23	10.3	193
1983	59.0[b]	22	7.6	34	5.8	17	5.4	37	0.0	35	21.4	14	8.6	23	12.8	187
1984	37.5	16	6.0	33	12.0	25	7.6	39	5.7	35	23.0	13	25.9	27	13.8	188
1985	22.2	18	20.6	29	0.0	17	2.5	40	2.6	38	23.5	17	17.3	23	10.9	182
1986	56.2[b]	16	6.6	30	11.7	17	12.5	40	0.0	39	21.4	14	16.0	25	13.8	181

NOTES: *Con Lit* = Contemporary Literature *Crit I* = Critical Inquiry *Dia* = Diacritics

N = Total number of articles published during the year

NP = Not published. *Diacritics* began publication in 1972, *Critical Inquiry* in 1974.

[a] While there was no article on a woman writer or feminist topic in *Contemporary Literature* in 1970, there was an interview with Gwendolyn Brooks, and there were review essays that featured works by Anaïs Nin and Doris Lessing.

[b] This includes at least one special issue on a woman writer or feminist topic.

virtually drop the subject from future issues. In literature, however, the appearance of special issues seems to stimulate more publication on the subject" (177). Our data indicate that this is not the case with all literary journals. After its 1981 special issue on "Writing and Sexual Difference" raised that year's percentage of articles on women writers or feminist topics to 27.7%, *Critical Inquiry* immediately returned to its more customary rate, which fluctuated between 0% and 20%, resting usually at around 9%.

Over the years, *Contemporary Literature* seems to have been consistently more receptive to articles on women writers and feminist topics than the other journals, with *Novel* a close second.[15] Between 1970 and 1986 *Contemporary Literature* devoted two special issues to women writers (Doris Lessing in 1973, H.D. in 1986) and one to *écriture féminine* (in 1983). In two years when it did not feature special issues on feminist topics or women writers, it had higher percentages of articles on these subjects (37.5% in 1984 and 40% in 1979) than its nearest competitor, *Novel*, whose top figure was 27.7% in 1979. More significantly, in no year between 1970 and 1986 did *Contemporary Literature* fail to publish at least one article on a woman writer or feminist topic, while *Novel* and *Critical Inquiry* omitted both in one year, *ELH* and *PMLA* in two, *Diacritics* in five, and *NLH* in ten.[16]

NLH is clearly the journal in our sample most resistant to feminist scholarship, which is surprising, given its publication in 1971—well before feminist scholarship had become generally respectable—of Lillian Robinson and Lise Vogel's mordant feminist critique of New Criticism, "Modernism and History." But for seven out of the next eight years, *NLH* published not a single article on either a woman writer or a feminist topic. In 1980, to be sure, the journal published Annette Kolodny's revolutionary "A Map for Rereading: Or, Gender and the Interpretation of Literary Texts," which provoked a number of responses and a reply by Kolodny, and in 1982 Mary Jacobus's equally provocative article, "Is There a Woman in This Text?" But in 1983, when *NLH* polled "representative scholars" to determine "what ought to be the aims and functions of literary theory at the present time," of the 37 responses the journal published only 3 were from women (Cohen 411). Not until 1987 did *NLH* devote a special issue to "Feminist Directions."[17]

What is most interesting about these journal statistics, given the steady increase in feminist scholarship represented by our survey of MLA convention programs during the same period, is the relative consistency of each journal's rate of publishing articles on women writers or feminist topics. *Contemporary Literature* and *Novel* have consistently high rates of publication, *ELH* and *NLH* consistently low rates. *Diacritics* and *Critical Inquiry* are generally on the low end of the scale, with occasional blips created by special issues.[18] Only *PMLA* appears to demonstrate a steady growth in its rate of publishing essays on women writers or feminist topics.

Several explanations of why *Contemporary Literature* and *Novel* publish more articles on women writers or feminist topics than do *Critical Inquiry*, *Diacritics*, *ELH*, and *NLH* suggest themselves. Both the novel in general and literature of the post–World War II period are noteworthy for distinguished women writers, and they were generally acknowledged as distinguished even before feminist scholarship began its task of reclaiming "lost" women writers. For the most part, the articles published in *Contemporary Literature* and *Novel* tend to focus on individual writers and/or texts. So, of course, do many of the articles published in *ELH*, but, given the historical scope of that journal's focus, many articles discuss literature written before the rise of the novel; during the years of our survey, hardly an issue came out without at least one essay on Chaucer, Spenser, Shakespeare, or Milton. *Critical Inquiry*, *Diacritics*, and *NLH*, however, less frequently publish articles on individual writers and texts (unless they are texts written by Jacques Lacan, René Girard, Jacques Derrida or Julia Kristeva). *Critical Inquiry*'s special issues typically interrogate "The Language of Images" or "Narrative" or "The Politics of Interpretation"—broad topics, inviting metacommentary. Whereas *Critical Inquiry* intersperses such special issues infrequently into a generally more eclectic format, *NLH* regularly focuses each issue on a single topic, such as "Ideology and Literature," "On Metaphor," "Literary Hermeneutics," or "The Sublime and the Beautiful: Reconsiderations." An editorial statement on the inside cover of the Spring 1977 *Diacritics* says that "the journal is concerned primarily with the problems of criticism." And while it goes on to assert that "the editors have adopted no formal policy governing the choice of books to be reviewed or critical perspectives to be explored," it is apparent, from even a casual persual of tables of contents over the years, that *Diacritics* is most interested in exploring whatever constitutes the current cutting edge of (usually continental) theory, not in providing a forum for practical criticism. The relative paucity of feminist articles in these three journals suggests, misleadingly, that feminists don't "do theory"—or at least not very often.

If the "market share" of each of these journals accounts, in part, for their differential receptiveness to articles on women writers or feminist topics, the constitution of their editorial boards and advisory committees does not. Our analysis of these journals does not suggest that there is a direct correlation between the representation of women on editorial and advisory boards and the rate of publication of essays by women or on women writers or feminist topics. *Contemporary Literature*, which has the highest, most consistent representation of feminist scholarship, and *Critical Inquiry*, whose representation of feminist scholarship is splotchy, have both had women coeditors or associate editors and substantial numbers of women on their advisory boards. Both *NLH*, the journal in our sample most resistant to feminist scholarship, and *Novel*, which ranks second to *Contemporary Literature* in its representation of feminist scholarship, did not add a woman to their advisory boards until the end of the 1970s.

We do, however, think it is not immaterial that, of all these journals, only *PMLA* has adopted the policy of author-anonymous submission, and that the rates of both published women contributors and feminist essays in *PMLA* have dramatically increased since 1980 when that policy went into effect. On the other hand, as we have pointed out, the other journals have—in keeping, one assumes, with their editorial policies—maintained fairly consistent rates of publication both of women contributors and of feminist essays.

Does it "count" more to publish in *New Literary History* than in *PMLA*? We don't know. Insinuating a skeptical note into Elizabeth Kolbert's rosy picture of literary feminism coming of age, Barbara Johnson observed that "the minute women start to rise in a field is concommitant with the demise of the overall prestige of the field" (Kolbert 117). Can that observation be extended from "field" to "journal"? Is it likely that the literary profession will differ from other professions that have opened their ranks to (some would say "been infiltrated by") women? Will *PMLA* become the journalistic equivalent of computer science's "pink ghetto"?

If it is true, as our comparison of some leading literary journals to *PMLA* and the MLA convention program would suggest, that the Modern Language Association is more responsive to women than other professional organizations, why is that the case? Are the factors we have identified as contributing to the increased representation of feminist scholarship in the MLA—an increase in number of women active in the profession, the rise of women to positions of institutional power, the growth and increasing prestige of feminist scholarship and gender studies, the adoption of author-anonymous submission policies—likely to hold true and extend even further? Or will the conservative backlash so evident in the media's representation of the current state of affairs in higher education lead to a halt in or even repeal of the MLA's 20-year program of expanding democratization? Additionally, is this expanding representation of women in the profession, however partial, a weakening co-optation or an empowering inclusion—or both?

We do not know the answers to these questions. But we believe that any attempt to answer them must begin by assessing the relationship of literary studies to power and male anxiety about power. What threat to masculinity does feminist scholarship, and the criticism and theory it has given birth to, pose?

7

Who Speaks for the Academy?
Discourses of Power

The last 25 years have been full of turmoil and ferment, much of it having to do with the claims of those who feel themselves to be disempowered, especially African Americans and women. It is customary to interpret the academic repercussions of this turbulent, fructive time as a (contained) response to the Civil Rights Movement, the years of Vietnam War protest, and the Women's Movement. Current academic debates and struggles over power, however, while certainly produced in and by the events of the last quarter century, also have much deeper historical roots.

Where does feminist criticism belong "in the republic of letters"? In "Women's Time, Women's Space: Writing the History of Feminist Criticism," Elaine Showalter suggests that we would have to "rewrite the history of modern criticism and its meta-histories of dynastic struggle and change" in order to answer that question (31).

Such a history might begin with the first major critical essay on poetry in English, "An Apology for Poetry," written in the early 1580s by Sir Philip Sidney:

> To all them that professing learning inveigh against Poetry may justly be objected, that they go very near to ungratefulness, to seek to deface that which, in the noblest nations and languages that are known, hath been the first light-giver to ignorance, and first nurse, whose milk by little and little enabled them to feed afterwards of tougher knowledges. And will they now play the hedgehog that, being received into the den, drove out his host, or rather the vipers, that with their birth killed their parents? Let learned Greece in any of her manifold sciences be able to show me one book before Mu-

saeus, Homer, and Hesiod, all three nothing else but poets. Nay, let any history be brought that can say any writers were there before them, if they were not men of the same skill, as Orpheus, Linus, and some other are named, who, having been the first of that country that made pens deliverers of their knowledge to their posterity, may justly challenge to be called their fathers in learning, for not only in time they had this priority (although in itself antiquity be venerable) but went before them, as causes to draw with their charming sweetness the wild untamed wits to an admiration of knowledge, so, as Amphion was said to move stones with his poetry to build Thebes, and Orpheus to be listened to by beasts—indeed stony and beastly people. (Sidney 83)[1]

This genealogy of poetic power begins with the mother/nurse and leads by a curiously inevitable illogic to threatened parent to pen-wielding fathers capable of taming and civilizing, thus providing a paradigm (which is monotonously repeated by later critics) of the way criticism attempts to supplant literature's maternal and nourishing function with a colonizing linguistic force that takes natural objects (stones/texts) and turns them into man-made cultural artifacts (Thebes/theory). What Sidney, whom Walter Jackson Bate calls "the first of the great English poet-critics" (77), doesn't mention is the occasion that provoked this spirited defense of poetry, the assertion in the frame narrative by the emperor's groom that horsemanship and war are the manliest accomplishments. Sidney, ruefully and self-consciously aware that "in these [his] not old years and idlest times, [he has] slipped into the title of a poet . . . [he knows not] by what mischance," is "provoked to say something . . . in the defense of that . . . unelected vocation" (83). Accepting the title "poet" calls Sidney's manhood into question. To reassert it, he elects the additional, more virile vocation of "critic." Throughout the "Apology," the poet and critic engage in an unconscious debate that is veiled for modern readers by Bate's igenuous hyphen.

For the critic Sidney, civilization is preferable to brute nature, as his alchemical metaphor makes clear:

Nature never set forth the earth in so rich tapestry as divers poets have done. . . . Her world is brazen, the poets only deliver a golden. (85)

For the alchemists, base metals could be sublimated into gold through spiritual intervention; for Sidney the critic, the poet transforms nature's brass into purest gold.

We have elided from this celebration of poetry's alchemical power Sidney the poet's paradoxically lyrical acknowledgment of nature's seductive allure (the "pleasant rivers, fruitful trees, sweet-smelling flowers, [or] whatsoever else may make the too much loved earth more lovely" [85]).[2] In order to articulate the power of poetry, the critic in Sidney has to subdue the poet in him, because the poet is allied to nature, as a later passage in the "Apology" makes clear.

Here, the critic Sidney conflates poetry, nature, and women in an attempt to explain why the Elizabethan establishment does not privilege poetry:

> First, that there being many other more fruitful knowledges, a man might better spend his time in them than in this. Secondly, that it is the mother of lies. Thirdly, that it is the nurse of abuse . . . with a siren's sweetness drawing the mind to the serpent's tale of sinful fancy. (97)

With elegant economy, Sidney catalogs "woman" in all her conventional Renaissance iconography: mother, nurse, siren, and (by metonymic association) Eve. He also implies that "a man might better spend his time" writing criticism than poetry because nonfemale reproduction may be preferable to (more "fruitful" than) natural maternity, entailing as the latter does seduction and mortality.

Sidney, a courtier and warrior, was fully aware of the Elizabethan conviction that "before poets did soften us, we were full of courage, given to martial exercises, the pillars of manlike liberty, and not lulled asleep" (97). To counter his own and his culture's fear (of castration), Sidney represents poetry in virile terms, as teaching and moving to "virtue" and as supremely "profitable."

Further, unlike later poet-critics, he is able to exalt poetry as more truthful than science: "Of all writers under the sun, the poet is the least liar. . . . The astronomer, with his cousin the geometrician, can hardly escape [lying], when they take upon them to measure the height of the stars" (97). Writing almost a century before the founding of the Royal Society (1662) and 30 years before Galileo's telescope discovered "craters on the moon, spots on the sun, moons around Jupiter, the phases of Venus, and the multitudes of stars in the Milky Way" (Merchant 129), Sidney can confidently empower poetry as a source of knowledge and truth because "science," as an empirically verifiable set of "truths" about nature, was in its barely perceptible infancy.

Indeed, even as late as 1668 John Dryden, poet laureate and founding member of the Royal Society, did not perceive a breach between the literary-critical and scientific enterprises. In "An Essay of Dramatic Poesy" he saw the second as facilitating the first. The narrative frame describes "a day wherein the two most mighty and best appointed fleets which any age had ever seen, disputed the command of the greater half of the globe, the commerce of nations, and the riches of the universe" (129). The official enterprise of the day (war) thus combined technology, capital, colonial power, and the exploitation of natural resources. Relying on the efficacy of this seventeenth-century military-industrial complex, the four debaters, complacently assuming a British victory, set off on a barge donated by Lisideius (the wealthy Sir Charles Sedley) to discuss at a safe distance the relative merits of the Ancients and the Moderns and the preeminence of British literature.

Like Sidney, Dryden associates poetry with nature. In the manner of those later critics who praised Emily Dickinson for her artless outpourings,[3] Neander (Dryden) characterizes Shakespeare as a naive avatar of poetic excellence, commending him as "the man who of all modern, and perhaps ancient, poets had the largest and most comprehensive soul. All the images of Nature were still present to him and he drew them, not laboriously, but luckily. . . . Those who accuse him to have wanted learning, give him the greater commendation: he was naturally learned; he needed not the spectacles of books to read Nature" (149). For Dryden the critic, there is a comfortable homology between humanistic learning and technology (books are "spectacles"); both are distinct from and capable of interpreting ("reading") nature as, by extension, criticism is distinct from and capable of interpreting poetry.

But while Neander and his friends discuss the Ancients, science and technology were gestating what Bacon called the "Masculine Birth of Time" which, as the war that frames the critics' debate symbolizes, would issue in a "blessed race of Heroes and Supermen" who would "hound," "conquer and subdue Nature," "shake her to her foundations," and "storm and occupy her castles and strongholds" (Keller, *Reflections* 54). By turning their backs on the battle, the critics implicitly, if unwittingly, concede that they are less "manly" than the scientists, and therefore less able to explain, much less "subdue," nature.

Lecturing "On Poesy or Art" in 1818, Samuel Taylor Coleridge, like Sidney, is concerned to assert the (virile) power of poetry. But unlike his Renaissance forbear, he can do so only by aligning it with science in its industrial-technological manifestation:

> Now Art . . . is the mediatress between, and reconciler of, nature and man. It is, therefore, the power of humanizing nature, of infusing the thoughts and passions of man into everything which is the object of his contemplation . . . and it *stamps* them into unity in the mould of a moral idea. (Bate 393, emphasis ours)

Unself-consciously, Coleridge employs a mechanical trope to legitimate poetry.

Matthew Arnold, far more self-aware, is also more ambivalent. For the most part, like Coleridge's friend and sometime collaborator William Wordsworth, he felt that "the idea of perfection as an *inward* condition of the mind and spirit is at variance with the mechanical and material civilization in esteem with us" ("Sweetness" 468, emphasis in the original). But he also insisted that culture, of which poetry is the highest expression, "is possessed by the scientific passion as well as by the passion of doing good" (467). By 1869, literary critics, recognizing the undisputed primacy of science, had begun tentatively but consciously to seek affinities with it.

When Arnold's heir, T. S. Eliot, wrote "Tradition and the In-

dividual Talent" in 1917 he was, as Walter Jackson Bate emphasizes, making "a general plea for increased objectivity in poetry"
(519). More specifically, Eliot elaborated his celebrated theory of
depersonalization by "inviting" his reader "to consider" a chemical
analogy: "It is in this depersonalization that art may be said to
approach the condition of science. I, therefore, invite you to consider, as a suggestive analogy, the action which takes place when
a bit of finely filiated platinum is introduced into a chamber con-
taining oxygen and sulphur dioxide" ("Tradition" 527).

Forty years later Northrop Frye invoked physics as a model
for literary criticism:

> Physics is an organized body of knowledge about nature, and a stu-
> dent of it says that he is learning physics, not that he is learning na-
> ture. Art, like nature, is the subject of a systematic study, and has to
> be distinguished from the study itself, which is criticism. . . . So
> while no one expects literature itself to behave like a science, there
> is surely no reason why criticism, as a systematic and organized
> study, should not be, at least partly, a science. (601)

In this brief passage, Frye not only allies criticism with science
but also distinguishes firmly between it and poetry. At the same
time, he allies art and nature; both become the objects of systematic study. Finally the process that began with Sidney is complete. In fact, we may now be in a position to understand why
Sidney is at such pains to transfer authority and author-ity from
the mother to the father; poetry must be severed from the natural, mortal (and feminine) world and allied with such supra-
natural, immortal (and masculine) endeavors as science and
philosophy. Science and criticism have become natural allies in
their mutual determination to master "nature," which by now includes poetry. And, as Elaine Showalter notes:

> Modern [masculinist] theory has been a defensive reaction against
> the feminization of the profession. Northrop Frye has been the frank-
> est in acknowledging the "dismal sexist symbology," which says that
> "the sciences, especially the physical sciences, are rugged, aggres-
> sive, out in the world doing things, and so symbolically male, whereas
> the literatures are narcissistic, intuitive, fanciful, staying at home

and making the home more beautiful, but not doing anything serious and therefore symbolically female." Frye's *Anatomy of Criticism* (1957) attempted to make the study of literature more serious and manly by structuring its principles scientifically like the laws of physics, biology, or mathematics. ("Women's Time" 41)

From at least 1957 on, in American colleges and universities, criticism increasingly attained the prestige assigned it by Frye, for reasons Frye would applaud: it became more "scientific." This is not to say that all critics and theorists now writing employ a scientific vocabulary or methodology. Rather, it is to acknowledge that contemporary critical theory appears to wield the power over art that physics appears to wield over nature. Critics from Sidney to Frye sought to master the seductive trio art/nature/woman. Contemporary theorists like Jonathan Culler, having to their own satisfaction, at least, succeeded, confidently privilege theory over art:

> To engage in the study of literature is not to produce yet another in-
> terpretation of *King Lear* but to advance one's understanding of the
> conventions and operations of an institution, a mode of discourse.
> ("Beyond" 323)

And Geoffrey Hartmann, who cautions that "the critical essay should not be considered a supplement to something else" (351), goes on to celebrate the triumph of "creative criticism":

> What to make of the "brilliance" of this phenomenon, which liberates
> the critical activity from its positive or reviewing function, from its
> subordination to the thing commented on. (346)

This "virile," "scientific" mode of critical discourse is strikingly evident in a recent special issue of *New Literary History*, entitled "Feminist Directions," which juxtaposes to it the "different voice" of feminist criticism, speaking out of a different social and scientific tradition.

The bulk of *NLH*'s special feminist issue is devoted to "Discussion" of a long essay by Ellen Messer-Davidow, "The Philosophical Bases of Feminist Literary Criticisms."

By "plac[ing] traditional and feminist literary criticisms on a

single plane of analysis," Messer-Davidow proposes to "show
how feminist literary criticisms can be differentiated from traditional ones and how they can be integrated theoretically with
the feminist criticisms proceeding in other fields" (65). The "plane
of analysis" or "framework" she establishes specifies as the "philosophical bases" of "diverse theories and practices" of scholarly
inquiry "their *subject, subject matters, methods of reasoning* and
epistemology" (66, emphases in the original). When feminist criticisms "borrow" from traditional literary criticism "its subject,
subject matters, methods of reasoning and epistemology," they
"borrow trouble," Messer-Davidow argues (69). She urges feminist
literary criticisms to recognize that they "have a subject of their
own ['not literature but the feminist study of ideas about sex
and gender that people express in literary and critical media'],
subject matters that are aspects of that subject, an enlarged
methodological repertoire, and a rehumanized epistemology" (77)
and that "what distinguishes feminist literary critics from feminists working in other fields . . . is mostly medium" (79). What
unites feminist literary critics and feminists working in other
fields is their subject ("the feminist study of ideas about sex and
gender") *and* their epistemology, which is "based on the assumption that we as diverse knowers must insert ourselves and our
perspectives into the domain of study and become, self-reflexively,
part of the investigation." This epistemology Messer-Davidow la-
bels "*perspectivism*, a feminist philosophy that counters objec-
tivism, which privileges objects, and subjectivism, which privileges subjects" (88–89). And she concludes that "feminist literary
criticisms and the feminist criticisms proceeding throughout
the humanities, social sciences, and natural sciences constitute
a single inquiry, [which] in league with the developing criticisms
of race, class, and affectional preference . . . promise a new research tradition" (90).

Nine scholars accepted the editor's invitation to respond to
Messer-Davidow's essay. The three men sport impressive creden-
tials in the list of contributors: Eugene Goodheart (Edytha Macy
Gross Professor of Humanities at Brandeis University, author of

The Failure of Criticism and *The Skeptic Disposition in Contemporary Literature*), Gerald Graff (John C. Shaffer Professor of Humanities and English at Northwestern University, author of *Professing Literature: An Institutional History*), and Cary Nelson (professor of English and founding director of the Unit for Criticism and Interpretative Theory at the University of Illinois, author of *Our Last First Poets* and editor of *Theory in the Classroom* and *Marxism and the Interpretation of Culture*). The women seem more diverse. Three are full professors (Joan Hartman, Ruth Hubbard, and Jane Tompkins), but only one is credited with a book of her own, Tompkins's *Sensational Designs*. Hartman "has written on Clarendon, Milton, and women's studies, and is an editor of *The Norton Reader*"; Hubbard "has written numerous articles and edited several collections." There are two associate professors (presumably tenured). Nellie McKay is credited with one book of her own (*Jean Toomer, Artist: A Study of His Literary Life and Work*) and another forthcoming ("on autobiographies of Afro-American women"), but Patricia Clark Smith is merely said to have written "with Paula Gunn Allen a chapter on American Indian women authors for *The Desert is No Lady: Southwestern Landscapes in Women's Writing and Art*, edited by Vera Norwood and Janice Monk."

Untenured are Amy Ling, assistant professor, with a book—or rather "chapbook"—of poems and paintings of her own and another (*Between Worlds: Women Writers of Chinese Ancestry in the U.S.*) in the works, and the author of the essay under discussion, Assistant Professor Ellen Messer-Davidow, who has co-edited two books (*Women in Print I* and *II*), is coediting another (*Critical Issues in Feminist Inquiry*), and is "completing" one of her own (from which the essay in *NLH* is taken), *The Philosophical Bases of Feminist Literary Criticisms.*[4]

This (conceivably boring) taxonomy of contributors to the "discussion" of Messer-Davidow's "theoretical essay" is intended to focus attention on several salient features of the difference between "masculinist" and "feminist" literary-theoretical discourses. (We are calling these modes of discourse "masculinist" and "feminist," although with no claim that one has to be male or female, respectively, to engage in either: "Everytime [we] say 'masculine' or 'feminine' or 'man' or 'woman,' please use as many quotation marks as you need to avoid taking these terms too literally" [Cixous 1].)

In this colloquy, male discussants occupy positions of (canonical) authority as comfortably as presumably they sit in their endowed chairs. They have authored (seldom if ever coauthored) books that magisterially write history (Graff), evaluate criticism (Goodheart), and analyze culture (Nelson). Female discussants, on the other hand, even those who have attained positions of academic security and respectability, have not laid claim to personal authority. The books they have authored or are in the process of writing bring others to writing (to adapt Tillie Olsen's memorable phrase)—Ling's "women writers of Chinese ancestry," McKay's Jean Toomer, Tompkins's fiction writers of 1790–1860. More often they have served as editors to bring others to writing (Hartman and Messer-Davidow, Hubbard) or have contributed to edited collections (Hartman, Smith). And one (Smith) coauthors.[5]

The discursive positions taken by male and female discussants contrast as strikingly as their positions in the academic and publishing establishments. The men begin their responses by briefly characterizing Messer-Davidow's argument in words that establish their distance from and superiority to it. Nelson: "Ellen Messer-Davidow's 'The Philosophical Bases of Feminist Literary Criticisms' is *one of a number* of overviews and syntheses of feminist scholarship that have appeared in recent years" (117). Graff: "*It is hard not to be sympathetic* with Ellen Messer-Davidow's arguments for a more contextual and theoretically self-reflective kind of literary and cultural studies" (135). Goodheart: "For Ellen Messer-Davidow, 'perspectivism' is a magical term that 'would bring together . . . the personal and cultural, subjective and objective.' . . . *I speak of it as a 'magical term,' because the process by which this is accomplished remains hidden to me*" (179, emphases in all these quotations ours).[6] Having put Messer-Davidow in her place, the men speedily mount their own hobby horses. Graff finds the idea of perspectivism "attractive" (135) because he wants literary theory to recognize the "historically constructed nature" of "textual production, reception, and cultural dissemination" (136). Despite his secure seat in the John C. Shaffer Chair of Humanities and English and his authoritative book on the institutional history of literary studies, Graff appears threatened by Messer-Davidow's suggestion that a perspectival stance is feminist. But he cloaks his anxiety with language that strongly suggests that Messer-Davidow doesn't quite know what she means to say: "Though she does not quite put it in these terms" (135), "[w]hat puzzles me, however, is how all this comes to be equated with feminism. . . . Messer-Davidow seems to have been pushed into this strange position" (136). "Curiously, it is where Messer-Davidow's argument is most borrowed that it is put forth as most exclusive" (138). And, most damningly, "Perhaps Messer-Davidow will object that her aim was to transcend . . . established political-gender distinctions, not to reinforce them. In that case, my response is that her overly dichotomized scheme has prevented her from doing so" (138). By the end of his response, Graff has firmly reestablished his authority by turning Ellen Messer-Davidow into a well-meaning but dumb graduate student.

Goodheart, like Graff, is bothered by Messer-Davidow's claim that perspectivism is a feminist epistemology. So he sets out to counter (what he says is) her claim by employing that renowned feminist critic, Jonathan Culler, to establish that feminist criticism "implies more than provocation or challenge or another perspective. It lays claim to a truth superior to the truth of 'masculinist' criticism. . . . [Feminists] wish to reverse the hierarchy of domination" (182). Thus Goodheart feels "coerced" by feminist theory (the title of his response is "Against Coercion") and, while Graff conceptualized Messer-Davidow as a graduate student, Goodheart asks her to be a lady:

> The increasing presence of women in the academic professions is the sociological basis of feminist criticism. Like any new ideological presence, theirs is bound to be at once aggressive and defensive, il-

luminating and misleading. They have something to teach and something to learn, and what they have to learn may come from their ad-
versaries as well as from within their own ranks. The success of
feminist criticism, that is, its constructive effect will depend upon
its willingness to shed its ideological character and content itself
with defining new forms of attention, coequal with and competitive
with other forms of attention, claiming no special privileges of victimization or oppression. (185)

While Graff and Goodheart are concerned, on the one hand,
to deny feminist theory originality and, on the other, to oblige
it to be respectful, Nelson's anxiety is that Messer-Davidow may
have pre-empted his authority as a feminist spokesperson. Characterizing her essay (wrongly) as an "overview" of feminist scholarship, he substitutes his own.

Although he grants that Messer-Davidow has added "a useful
and challenging polemical reduction to this debate" about feminist scholarship and theory, allowing that her "critique, even if
overstated, is thus pertinent" (118), Nelson finds "biases in this
ambitious paper" (119) which he proceeds to rectify. Suggesting
that she is "not adept" at using metaphorical language (121), Nelson concludes that (French) "feminist inquiries into language and
efforts at a more experimental writing style" are "unavailable" to
Messer-Davidow and, therefore, not given the weight in her essay
they deserve (122). So he donates three and a half pages of his
"response" to Messer-Davidow to a discussion of *écriture féminine*
and concludes by suggesting that "it might have been more true
to feminism if *New Literary History* had been able to publish
several such [overview] essays rather than giving such promi-
nence to one" (127). Apparently Nelson thinks he should have
been asked to contribute an "essay" rather than a "response."

Yet if Nelson wants to be recognized as a feminist spokesperson, he has rhetorical (and political) lessons to learn. "Women
don't trash women," lesbian-feminist singer Alix Dobkin said at
a London concert in 1980. Cary Nelson has a quibble with Ellen
Messer-Davidow which at least two women respondents share.
Yet the language in which he and they voice their complaint is
strikingly divergent. Both Nelson and Joan Hartman think that

Messer-Davidow, indicting masculinist literary theory for its dualistic hierarchization, substitutes a feminist dualistic hierarchy in its stead (Graff also makes this charge). But while Hartman sees Messer-Davidow's "feminist literary study as traditional literary study transposed" (110), she recognizes the "political imperatives" (109) for this transposition. Nelson, on the other hand, is relentless and judgmental, irritatingly more-feminist-than-thou: "The necessary paradox underlying Messer-Davidow's whole project, then, is that, while she spends a good part of her essay warning against the dangers inherent in any feminist effort to borrow from existing male scholarly traditions . . . her own project is in fact almost wholly in thrall to the very tradition she rejects" (121). "This binary model that pits logic against the dissolving world of sense data, feeling, and metaphor has a whole history in the West—a history that is articulated to the categories of male and female. It is at least arguable that Messer-Davidow's deepest loyalties are to the former rather than to the latter" (127).

Having determined that Messer-Davidow's "deepest loyalties" are to the male tradition of rationalism, Nelson is able to find "real value" in her essay, "despite [his] disgreement with it" (125). Because she is "working within the patriarchal tradition," she is "able to validate feminism" to "them," the patriarchs, in a way that "we" (feminists like Nelson) have not been able to. "We now have both a fine weapon to use against them and a text that has a chance of persuading them to think more deeply and self-critically about feminism's epistemology and its scholarly achievements. If feminism itself does not need this essay, the nonfeminist world undoubtedly does" (127).

What the male feminist puts down, the female feminist picks up, with gratitude. Amy Ling thinks that "if we as feminists can appropriate something useful for our purposes from what is already in the common storehouse, we make our new ideas more accessible to others who are not as far along as we" (154). Ling believes that "the value of Messer-Davidow's essay may be that [a male department] chair may eventually be persuaded by its theoretical analysis and its abstract language to admit the validity of a variety of perspectives. She at least employs the 'discourse' so respected in academia" (158).

In her response to Messer-Davidow's essay, Jane Tompkins identifies, employs, critiques, and finally dismisses this discourse as "the voice of a critic who wants to correct a mistake" in the essay. But, Tompkins says, there is another "voice" in her, that "of a person who wants to write about her feelings" and to talk not *about* Messer-Davidow's argument but *to* "Ellen" (169, emphasis in the original). "This is how I would reply to Ellen's essay if I were to do it in the professionally sanctioned way," Tompkins writes:

> The essay provides feminist critics with an overarching framework for thinking about what they do, both in relation to mainstream criticism and in relation to feminist work in other fields. It allows the reader to see women's studies as a whole, furnishing useful categories for organizing a confusing and miscellaneous array of materials. It also provides excellent summaries of a wide variety of books and essays that readers might not otherwise encounter. The enterprise is carried out without pointed attacks on other theorists, without creating a cumbersome new vocabulary, without exhibitionistic displays of intellect or esoteric learning. Its practical aim—to define a field within which debate can take place—is fulfilled by *New Literary History*'s decision to publish it, and to do so in a format which includes replies. (171)

Thus far, Tompkins's voice sounds uncannily like Graff's or Nelson's. But her "other" voice intrudes parenthetically to comment, giving her "professional voice" a self-consciousness entirely absent from the men's. "(Very nice, Jane. You sound so reasonable and generous. But, as anybody can tell, this is just the obligatory pat on the back before the stab in the entrails)" (171).

The "goal" of the "professional voice," Tompkins suggests, is "to beat the other person down" (172). Borrowing from Ursula Le Guin, Tompkins names it "the father tongue":

> The dialect of the father tongue that you and I learned best in college . . . only lectures. . . . Many believe this dialect—the expository and particularly scientific discourse—is the *highest* form of language, the true language, of which all other uses of words are primi-

tive vestiges. . . . And it is indeed a High Language. . . . Newton's *Principia* was written in it in Latin, . . . and Kant wrote German in it, and Marx, Darwin, Freud, Boas, Foucault, all the great scientists and social thinkers wrote it. It is the language of thought that seeks objectivity.

. . . The essential gesture of the father tongue is not reasoning, but distancing—making a gap, a space, between the subject or self and the object or other. . . . The father tongue is spoken from above. It goes one way. No answer is expected, or heard. (Le Guin, quoted by Tompkins 173, emphasis in the original)

Tompkins's "other voice" would speak what Le Guin calls "the mother tongue," which,

spoken or written, expects an answer. It is conversation, a word the root of which means "turning together." The mother tongue is language not as mere communication, but as relation, relationship. It connects. . . . Its power is not in dividing but in binding. (Le Guin, quoted by Tompkins 173-74)

Whether they employ what Messer-Davidow in her response to commentators calls "academic" or "personal" styles (191), all of the women discussants of her essay speak the mother tongue. Even when they disagree with her, they do not attempt to "beat down" Messer-Davidow but to "relate" to her in "conversation."

Unlike the men who, as we have seen, begin their responses by "objectively" summarizing or characterizing Messer-Davidow's argument, thus distancing themselves from it and her, the women begin by introducing themselves. As Messer-Davidow's collaborator, Hartman says they have "a context of shared concerns"; nevertheless she "has not come to terms" fully with her colleague's essay (105), perhaps—she suggests—because of the difference in their ages and, therefore, of their experiences in the academy (107). Ruth Hubbard introduces herself "as a biologist invited to comment on a paper about feminist criticism," grateful to Messer-Davidow (from whose essay she quotes as epigraph to her response) for allowing her to make "a more daring exploration of the ways our society goes about constructing sex and gender than scientists usually permit themselves" (129). Patricia Smith begins with a long personal anecdote that shows, dramatically, the need for the kind of "perspectivism" Messer-Davidow advocates. In similar fashion, both Amy Ling and Nellie McKay establish the "perspective" from which each speaks, as an Asian-American and an African-American woman scholar respectively. And Jane Tompkins introduces the "two voices inside me answering, answering to, Ellen's essay" (169).

We should here supplement our brief discussion of how the tones of their disagreement with Messer-Davidow distinguished Joan Hartman and Cary Nelson with a more detailed examination of Hartman's rhetorical strategy: her "conversational" (rather than "adversarial") response to her colleague's essay.

The principal difficulty Hartman has with Messer-Davidow's essay is that it proposes that "literary inquiry and feminist inquiry are 'fundamentally incompatible.'" Rather than seeking to poke a hole in Messer-Davidow's logic, Hartman carefully establishes the reasons why she does not *want* to "write off" literary inquiry (105). Hartman creates an approachable, kindly persona who talks about "literature as I experience it," about "my delight in the medium of literature," about the "investment" of her "self" she has made in "the profession of literary study" (106). She attempts to understand why Messer-Davidow should think literary inquiry and feminist inquiry are "incompatible" and concludes, provisionally, that it is because of her graduate training, which took place two decades after Hartman's. "New Criticism as I experienced it," says the older scholar, "did not determine and dehumanize inquiry as forcibly as Messer-Davidow characterizes it as doing" (107).

Having explained why she does not like Messer-Davidow's suggestion that we substitute "the feminist study of ideas about sex and gender that people express in literary and critical media" for the study of "literature"; having, in addition, attempted to understand why Messer-Davidow made the suggestion, Hartman concludes not by showing that Messer-Davidow is *wrong* but by attempting to *extend* her vision of a more humane, "feminist" inquiry to literary studies:

> I want to salvage for all literary study what I admire in Messer-Davidow's description of feminist inquiry, a rehumanized epistemology and an enlarged canon. . . . While I remain unregenerate in my commitment to a subject called literature, I want to redeem for it the humane inquiry that [Messer-Davidow] describes. (113, 115)

Quietly, without fanfare, Ruth Hubbard extends Messer-Davidow's notion of perspectivism to scientific inquiry, thus tacitly demonstrating and validating Messer-Davidow's argument that "feminist criticisms proceeding in . . . traditional disciplines and in women's studies constitute a single inquiry," that "what distinguishes feminist literary critics from feminists working in other fields . . . is mostly medium." And, as she builds on Messer-Davidow's argument, so she offers hers as "a large, uncharted territory for feminist scholars, indeed all women," to explore (133).

Nellie McKay extends Messer-Davidow's essay not so much by using it to map new territory as by filling it in with details from black and third-world feminist experience Messer-Davidow acknowledges but has not lived through firsthand. By so doing, McKay commends Messer-Davidow's enterprise:

> She has done a careful examination of the structures of traditional literary criticism, and has emerged with a philosophical position which is congruent with the approaches that others outside of the dominant group have used to validate their experiences as the subject of knowledge. . . . If feminist literary criticism moves seriously toward the philosophical position that Messer-Davidow outlines in her essay, it will become appreciably richer and more rewarding. (166–67)

Patricia Smith not only "explore[s some of] the implications of Messer-Davidow's project for the feminist criticism of American Indian literature" (145) but extends it and its implications to her friend and collaborator:

> All the time I have been responding to Ellen's essay, with its hopeful project for a feminist literary criticism that embraces "our diverse perspectives centered in selves diversified through cultural and per-

sonal experience," I have been thinking of my friend Paula Allen, who has done so much in the field of American Indian studies to call attention to the kinds of misconceptions remote authorities have put forth concerning Native American women, literatures, and cultures. (147–48)

Patricia Smith's friend, Paula Allen, is working on a novel that does not resemble "the latest John Updike." Yet Smith "fears" critics who will bring to *Raven's Road* "the same set of expectations and standards they would bring to *The Witches of Eastwick*." Her personal gratitude to Messer-Davidow for the ideal of "perspectivism" is explained by her "wish for Paula Allen" of a critic sensitive to the cultural specificity out of which she is writing her novel (147–48).

Smith reaches out to include her friend and colleague in Messer-Davidow's vision. More globally inclusive, Amy Ling recognizes that Messer-Davidow's project not only impels her to extend it to analyze and account for the experience of Asian-American women but teaches her, "paradoxically," that "the more we hear about the experiences of each particular group, the more we learn how much we share as a community of women and how often our commonalities cross cultural and racial barriers" (154). Concluding her response, Ling reaches out to include in the "community" (156) engaged in fomenting a cultural and ideological "revolution" not only herself and Messer-Davidow but Adrienne Rich, Judith Fetterley, Jane Tompkins, Elaine Showalter, Dale Spender, Catharine Stimpson, Elaine Hedges, Barbara Christian, Mary Helen Washington, and Deborah McDowell. "We may each be working in separate corners of the garden, but we are all working in the same garden" (159).

When given the opportunity to respond to the commentators on her essay, Ellen Messer-Davidow gave a succinct and elegant explanation for the differences between men and women discussants we have just documented. They participate in a sex/gender system:

> From an advantaged position [in that system], Eugene Goodheart fears that I "wish to reverse the hierarchy of domination." From my

disadvantaged place, I see domination *and* who dominates, sex/
gender categories *and* who defines them, the structure of literary
studies *and* who maintains it as implicated problems.

. . . Place in a gendered structure explains why Ling, McKay, and
Smith support perspectivism, while Goodheart regards it "as a magical term, because the process by which [it] is accomplished remains
hidden to me." The Asian-American, black, and Native American
literature that Ling, McKay, and Smith study have been shut out of
the discipline, just as Asian-Americans, blacks, Native Americans,
and women have been shut out of the academy. . . . The academic
decision-making that empowers Goodheart situates Ling, McKay,
and Smith in vulnerable places. When all around him confirm his
perspective, he must find my reality disconcerting. Understandably,
he tries to moderate the threat to his perspective and place by urging
feminism to aim for gentle persuasion, "genuine assent, a voluntary
change of mind" and to "shed its ideological character and content
itself with becoming [actually, Goodheart's word was 'defining'] new
forms of attention . . . claiming no special privileges of victimization
or oppression." ("Knowing" 191–92)

While we honor Messer-Davidow's attempt to "understand" Goodheart's (and Graff's and Nelson's) psychological need to put feminist theory in its place, we have been more concerned in these
pages to display the sharp contrast between feminist and masculinist discourse.

Juxtaposing the genealogy of mainstream masculinist literary
criticism from Sir Philip Sidney to Geoffrey Hartmann to a feminist alternative expressed in this special issue of *New Literary
History* permits at least tentative generalizations about the etiol-
ogy and significance of contemporary feminist literary theory.[7]

In *Metamorphosis*, Ernest Schachtel provides a description of
masculinist discourse in its most familiar form, the scientific:

Modern natural science has as its main goal prediction, i.e. the
power to manipulate objects in such a way that certain predicted
events will happen. . . . That is to say that his [the scientist's] view of
the object will be determined by the ends which he pursues in his
experimentation. . . . He may achieve a great deal in this way and
add important data to our knowledge, but to the extent to which he
remains within the framework of this perspective he will not perceive the object in its own right. (171)

Barbara McClintock, winner of the Nobel Prize for her work on genetic transposition and her prototype for a new scientific model, would agree:

> Much of the work done [by scientists] is done because one wants to impose an answer on it—they have the answer ready, and they [know what] they want the material to tell them, so anything it doesn't tell them, they don't really recognize as there, or they think it's a mistake and throw it out. (Quoted by Keller, *Feeling* 162)

McClintock's alternative method is to listen to the material, recognizing and respecting individual difference, which she distinguishes from division and separation. "Division severs connection and imposes distance; the recognition of difference provides a starting point for relatedness," says Evelyn Fox Keller, McClintock's biographer (163). The contrast between these two models of scientific inquiry replicates the contrast manifested in the *NLH* discussion of Messer-Davidow's essay and resembles the distinction the authors of *Women's Ways of Knowing* draw between "separate" and "connected" knowing.

Carol Gilligan uses these terms "to describe two different conceptions or experiences of the self, as essentially autonomous (separate from others) or as essentially in relationship (connected to others)" (Belenky, et al. 102). In *Women's Ways of Knowing*, Mary Belenky and her colleagues borrow these terms "to posit two contrasting epistemological orientations: a separate epistemology, based upon impersonal procedures for establishing truth, and a connected epistemology, in which truth emerges through care" (102). Like Evelyn Fox Keller, who resists the "temptation" to label Barbara McClintock's way of doing science "feminist" or even to claim that, because of its "emphasis on intuition, on feeling, on connection and relatedness," it is a uniquely female mode of inquiry (Keller, *Feeling* 173), Belenky and her colleagues do not claim that "connected" thinking is limited to women. "Separate and connected knowing are not gender-specific," they say:

> The two modes may be gender-related: It is possible that more women than men tip toward connected knowing, and more men

than women toward separate knowing. Some people, certainly, would argue that this is so, but we know of no hard data (to use a favorite separate-knowing term) bearing directly on the issue. (102–3)

The discussion of Ellen Messer-Davidow's essay in the special feminist issue of *New Literary History* we have analyzed does not, certainly, constitute "hard data." Nevertheless, it is at least suggestive that all the men discussants employed techniques characteristic of separate knowing while all the women used connected modes. "Separate knowing is essentially an adversarial form. . . . Presented with a proposition, separate knowers [like Graff, Goodheart, and Nelson] immediately look for something wrong—a loophole, a factual error, a logical contradiction, the omission of contrary evidence" (Belenky, et al. 106, 104). Connected knowers, on the other hand, try empathically "to understand" the other person's ideas by trying "to share the experience that has led the person to form the idea" (113), as Joan Hartman did in her response to Messer-Davidow's essay. Separate knowers, like male respondents to the essay, engage in "debate"; women enter "conversations" (114). Separate knowing, to return to Ursula Le Guin's distinction, speaks the father tongue; connected knowers prefer the mother tongue.[8]

While women can and do learn the father tongue, especially academic women, their apparent preference for the mother tongue springs naturally from women's psychological, social, and political experience in America over the last 200 years—as Nancy Chodorow, Carol Gilligan, and Sara Evans have convincingly documented. Female modes of relationship established in early infancy are reinforced throughout the life cycle. It is not then surprising that American women should have moved from church groups to temperance leagues to suffrage organizations to civil rights agitation to antiwar protest to a women's movement characterized by consciousness-raising groups, out of which came some of the first feminist reconsiderations of literature.

Contemporary feminist literary theory is the latest, most recent manifestation of "women's ways of knowing." While much literary theory today is written either by or in response to men,[9] there is also a formidable body of feminist theorizing that differs substantially from masculinist theorizing. In "Daughters of Anger/ Material Girls: Con/Textualizing Feminist Criticism," Jane Marcus names Sandra Gilbert and Susan Gubar, along with Elaine Showalter, as the "material girls" of feminist theory because their theory is not only grounded in readings of women's texts but—for our purposes, more significantly—because they have sought democratic connection rather than colonizing, pseudo-scientific obscurantism:

> [Their] reaching out to the mass of readers, however much one may quibble over the choice of texts, is characteristic of the political nature of American feminism and its struggle to change institutions. . . . The writing of [these] American critics is aimed democratically at a very large audience of "common readers," not a small academic coterie, in a political gesture to change hearts and minds. They have played the role Virginia Woolf ascribed to the political feminism of Ethel Smyth, as the "armoured tanks" who make it possible for foot soldiers to cross the narrow bridge of art.[10] (289)

Before these women were feminist theorists, they were feminist readers, and, as Patrocinio Schweickart has strikingly demonstrated, feminist reading differs markedly from masculinist reading. Schweickart's case for the difference between masculinist and feminist readings rests on a comparison between the model of reader-response proposed by Georges Poulet in "Criticism and the Experience of Interiority" and the paradigm of feminist reading illustrated by Adrienne Rich's essay, "Vesuvius at Home: The Power of Emily Dickinson." Both models present the reading experience as an intersubjective dialogue between reader and implied author, but the similarity stops there. The metaphors characterizing Rich's reading of Dickinson ("witness," "visit," "an insect, vibrating at the frames of windows, trying to connect") differ dramatically from those Poulet uses to describe his encounter with a text ("invaded," "annexed," "usurped," "dispossessed"). Schweickart concludes that "the metaphors of mastery and submission, of violation and control, so prominent in Poulet's essay, are entirely absent in Rich's essay" (53).[11] Extrapolating from her close analysis of Rich's reading practice, Schweickart concludes that "feminist readings ... are motivated by the need 'to connect,' to recuperate, or to formulate—they come to the same thing—the context, the tradition, that would link women writers to one another, to women readers and critics, and to the larger community of women" (48).

Schweickart distinguishes "gynocritical" readings, in which one woman reads another empathically, "connectedly," from "resistant" readings of androcentric texts, the sort Judith Fetterley performs with liberatory gusto in *The Resisting Reader*. Indeed, Schweickart believes that a woman *must* "take control of the reading experience" and resist male texts "to understand and therefore undermine the subjective predispositions that had rendered her vulnerable to its designs" (49, 51).

But she concludes her essay with the hope that the "community of feminist readers and writers" will expand ultimately "to include everyone" (56). We detect signs that this is beginning to happen. Feminist criticism has gained confidence and commanded increasing respect in the nearly two decades since Kate Millett empowered women to name and resist the misogyny of D. H. Lawrence, Norman Mailer, and Henry Miller. Now a generation of feminists whose reading skills were developed by gynocritics is beginning to reread male writers, no longer to resist but to reclaim them for women. Adrienne Munich, for example, contends that "the relation of women to literary culture can be discovered not only in women's fiction and poetry but in 'gynocriticism' of the ['malestream'] literary canon" (243). What she means by this is demonstrated by her reading of a passage from Cervantes's *Don Quixote,* in which she employs a gynocritical model adumbrated by Gilbert and Gubar in *The Madwoman in the Attic* as a "palimpsest":

> Women from Jane Austen and Mary Shelley to Emily Brontë and Emily Dickinson produced literary works that are in some sense palimpsestic, works whose surface designs conceal or obscure deeper, less accessible ... levels of meaning. (Gilbert and Gubar, *Madwoman* 73)

Applying this model to the Marcela episode in *Don Quixote* enables Munich to uncover the text's "subversive knowledge of the gendered arena of [its] production" (244). Her brilliant close reading is an instance of "connected knowing" at its best, attentive equally to the official (male) voice of the text and to its (female) "counter-text" (247). It authorizes Munich to conclude that, while Cervantes's text "finally closes off the radical possibilities it had admitted" (250), a feminist gynocritical reading such as the one she has just performed can liberate the woman "trying to escape into readability" who lurks "in the background of patriarchal texts" (257).

Christine Froula's reading of the "nativity scenes" in *Paradise Lost* similarly "liberates" not only the woman *in* the text but also the woman reader, not by "resisting" Milton but rather by listening attentively for the text's "less accessible" voice. She concludes that such "strategies of rereading" enable us to "approach traditional texts not as the mystifying (and self-limiting) 'best' that has been thought and said in the world but as a *visible* past against which we can teach our students to imagine a different future" (171, emphasis in the original). In other words, feminist criticism has the power to enlist even patriarchal texts in its emancipatory project.

So also, we believe, is feminist literary theory working to extend masculinist theory in ways its originators might find discomfiting. Neither adversarial nor slavishly dependent, feminist theorists like Gilbert and Gubar invoke Harold Bloom (in *Madwoman*) or Sigmund Freud (in their more recent book, *No Man's Land*) not to demolish them but to *cooperate* with them in an effort to construct a theory that will comprehend both men's *and* women's experience and reality.

In *Madwoman*, Gilbert and Gubar specifically emphasize not "what is wrong about Bloom's conceptualization of the dynamics of Western literary history, but . . . what is right (or at least suggestive) about his theory" (47). Bloom's model is "useful" to them because it helps them "distinguish the anxieties and achievements of female writers from those of male writers" (48). In "using" Bloom, however, Gilbert and Gubar permanently altered his theory; it is impossible, after *The Madwoman in the Attic*, for any self-respecting critic to invoke "the anxiety of influence" without mentioning both Bloom's male *and* Gilbert and Gubar's female paradigms.

It is probably too soon to assert confidently that Freud's model of female psychosexual development has been similarly transfigured by Gilbert and Gubar's adaptation of it in volume one of *No Man's Land*. But it is noteworthy that their intention in this book is to augment not only Freud and Bloom but their own earlier theoretical formulations:

> In the twentieth century ... Freudian concepts like the girl's "secondary Oedipus complex," as well as Freud-derived Bloomian paradigms like the "anxiety of influence" and our own "anxiety of authorship" must give way to a paradigm of ambivalent affiliation. (170)

To construct such a paradigm, they turn to Freud because, though "flawed," his model of the "family romance" in "useful" in implying a "range of reactions to (literary) parentage" (169). But, having applied their "Freud-derived" affiliation paradigm to twentieth-century women writers from Edith Wharton to Gertrude Stein, Gilbert and Gubar "enter an area uncharted by Freud," the "literary implications" of "female autonomy" (189). It is here, we suspect, that they will be seen to have permanently altered, through extending, the Freudian model.

Whether the "text" in question is a theoretical essay, a volume of poems, or a whole theoretical construct, in this chapter we have seen feminists reading it with courtesy, generosity, and a sense of relatedness. The "material girls" of feminist criticism and theory are thus, at their best, moving us back to the original matter/mater/mother of literary discourse, the text. They are healing the breach between "criticism" and "poetry" whose widening aperture we observed in our survey of mainstream literary theory from Sidney to Hartmann, conscious all the while that it mirrored the similar disjunction between "mind" and "matter," "man" and "nature" that feminist historians of science have traced from Bacon to Crick and Watson. In the process, as Jane Marcus reminds us, feminist critics empower and dignify the common reader. As yet, however, feminist scholarship has not transformed—though it has challenged—the academy.

Once again, our notions of oscillation and process are useful and cautionary. That is, feminist criticism has certainly challenged the academy. Equally, feminist criticism has been challenged by the academy. Further, to rephrase ourselves, lest we get misty-eyed and blindly optimistic, as yet the academy has not transformed feminist theory. The notion of oscillation, though, suggests that it very well may.

Increasingly over the past 10 years, this two-way challenge has manifested itself at universities and colleges all over the country, from Alverno College in Milwaukee to Yale University (Schmitz 98–122), in faculty development projects designed to transform the general curriculum by incorporating the findings and perspectives of feminist scholarship. As Peggy McIntosh, program director of the Wellesley College Center for Research on Women, explains, faculty development is necessary because feminist scholarship calls into question traditional "methods of organizing and imparting knowledge" and therefore "requires revision and correction and, in some cases, transformation of existing bodies of knowledge" and ways of teaching (Schmitz ix). Equally, incorporation of feminist scholarship into the curriculum requires adaptation to accepted modes of teaching, research, recognition, and dissemination.

In 1987, the architects of one of the first of these feminist curriculum integration projects—a cross-disciplinary program conducted at the University of Arizona from 1981 to 1985—published an article describing and evaluating their experience, focusing on the substantial resistance they encountered from at least half of the 45 participants who volunteered for the program. "Although the project made significant headway in modifying the liberal arts curriculum on our campus," they wrote, "it also served to reveal in stark detail the nature and depth of opposition to feminist scholarship" (Aiken, et al. 258). The most intransigent form of resistance they encountered was "an unwillingness or inability to perceive the implications of feminist critiques" of traditional scholarship that often "was reflected in rhetoric":

> One participant spoke repeatedly, for example, of how he planned to "shoehorn" a few women's issues into his otherwise untouched syllabus. His metaphor suggested that, given the small space he planned to allot to women, such "shoehorning" would necessitate the academic equivalent of *footbinding*. This preoccupation with "what to cut" . . . illustrates that without genuine commitment to the legitimacy of feminist scholarship and serious consideration of its epistemological implications, academics will probably achieve only the most minimal changes. (259–60, emphasis in the original)

But at least the man with the shoehorn was willing to admit that feminist scholarship challenged the adequacy of his existing syllabus. Not all academics would go so far.

In 1988, a woman teaching at a large urban university proposed a version of a standard departmental course in literature and science she called "Mother Nature and Scientific Man."[12] Drawing on such contemporary feminist critiques of science as Brian Easlea's *Fathering the Unthinkable*, Evelyn Fox Keller's *Reflections on Gender and Science*, and Carolyn Merchant's *The Death of Nature*, she proposed to examine the paradigms of science presented in Nathaniel Hawthorne's short story "The Birthmark" and Mary Shelley's *Frankenstein*, concentrating class discussion on several questions:

> Why do western, scientific cultures as well as primitive societies conceptualize nature as female? Why does science seek to "know" and "control" nature? Are these two questions connected, and if so, how?

The course was to conclude with two weeks' discussion of an eight-hour videotape of a conference held at the university earlier in the year, on the topic "Will Women Change Science and Technology or Will Science and Technology Change Women?"

Reviewing her proposal, the departmental curriculum committee unanimously commended the instructor for putting together a remarkably coherent syllabus. But during her annual review, her department chair expressed grave doubts about the course's legitimacy, which he later inserted in her personnel folder. He said he felt "strongly" about "not reducing the quality of our courses by including feminist issues or figures who are not first rate." He noted that five of the seven authors on the course's reading list were female and suggested that this "may not correspond to the best writings" since "most major authors have been male" and "the study of outstanding literature means studying male writers"; he also thought that topics like "nature as female," "the sexual anxiety fueling scientific research," and "feminist critiques of science" offered a "skewed representation of Literature and Science." He concluded his critique, curiously, by agreeing with the faculty member that the university should "move forward to revise the canon in the light of women's studies." But, he added, "please, not at the expense of excellence."

The academy's intransigence to change and its jealous regard for its own authority are hardly new phenomena. Having glimpsed the "difference" feminism might make in the academic point of view, we nonetheless hesitate to predict confidently that feminist scholarship will transform the academy and sensitize it to the needs and desires of the common reader. We also, more devoutly, hope that the academy will not transform and co-opt feminist scholarship as it attempts to bridge the gap between the academy and the common reader.

Afterword

We are compelled by the terms of our own argument, no less than by the force of the evidence we have examined in these chapters, to refuse to make any predictions. If, as our survey of literary history indicates, the process of canon formation and reformation is an organic and ongoing process, then even if—as we have also argued—there is something novel about the current confluence of the political interests of groups previously excluded from the academic/cultural hegemony and theoretical challenges to humanism and positivism, what we are now going through feels unprecedented only because we are so involved in our moment in history that we have not yet put it into perspective.

As chapters four and six demonstrate, the (predominantly male) canons have created a "canonical" profession that operates according to certain rules and procedures, that agrees on certain criteria for judging the merit of scholars and scholarship, as well as of literary texts. These rules and procedures, as we have shown throughout this book, are currently under more forceful attack than they have been for at least half a century.

As we examine, then, among other things, the relationships among this entrenched academic hegemony, feminist scholarship, and canon formation and reformation, we find a complex of problems. First, most obvious and most pervasive, the process of which canon revision is emblematic calls for a significant alteration in the traditional class system in the academy. Women and minorities are asking for changed status and for reclassification of literatures and subject areas previously disregarded and trivialized when they were considered at all. These new groups want power. They want: more positions, a larger share of tenured positions, more important roles in departmental politics, more courses and more say in curriculum decisions, more significance in professional organizations and journals, better publishing opportunities, more influence on critical theory.

The academic establishment as it is now constituted, and as we have discussed in chapter four and elsewhere, purports to speak multivocally while in fact its utterances are univocal, empowering a white male elite whose differences are more apparent than real. Edward Said and Terry Eagleton are the examples we cite of ostensibly radical voices that nonetheless enjoy all the privileges the academy can confer. When challenge comes from a group that is truly outside the class and power structure of the academy, as in Ellen Messer-Davidow's essay in *NLH*, broad and fierce hegemonic resistance is evident in the responses.

Our discussion in chapter six of male establishment indignation at the author-anonymous submission policy at *PMLA* is another pellucid illustration of how those in power strive to retain a comfortable status quo under such amusing rubrics as "maintaining standards."

Second in this complicated interrelationship, and connected to our first point, the substance of feminist approaches challenges the established organization of the curriculum. Women and minorities are asking not only for additions to the established curriculum but for adaptive excisions. Courses and whole fields of study that appear meaningless to establishment figures like, for example, Walter Jackson Bate, are looking for, and in some cases gaining, respectability—courses in minority and foreign literatures, popular culture, women's studies, and literary sociology. "Fringe" programs like African-American and women's studies are demanding legitimacy. The terms of study, too, are under attack. As an obvious example, feminist theory and pedagogy, as we show in chapter four and elsewhere, often privilege previously despised personal experience over so-called textual objectivity.

Even the discrete disciplines are under threat. Free-standing women's studies programs, for example, are by definition inter-disciplinary. Once such a program is in place at a college or university, the traditional disciplinary division of the curriculum must, in various instances, give way. First it must give way to an overarching concept of the inclusion of the outsider (the woman) in all aspects of the standard curriculum, thus upsetting conventional course structure. Second, the traditional disciplinary division must give way even more radically to include how the excluded (the woman) thinks and knows. Once the institution admits this much change, not only will its catalog list some interdisciplinary programs, some new courses, and some new material in old course descriptions, but epistemological and pedagogical models prevalent for decades will begin to change as well. Moreover, the list of faculty will probably include more women and minorities.

A third facet of the complex problematic introduced by shifting relationships among the entrenched academic hegemony, feminist scholarship, and canon formation and reformation is that the practice of feminist criticism calls into question accepted conventions of canonical professional discourse: language itself. Ursula Le Guin, defining canonical discourse as the "father tongue" and feminist discourse as the "mother tongue," states with customary clarity the threat feminist scholarship poses to traditional pedagogues. She rejects what she experiences as her own dismissal by the old learning and language:

> We are told by their deafness, by their stone ears, that our experience, the life experience of women, is not valuable to men — therefore not valuable to society, to humanity. (155)

Le Guin's tone is angry, insurrectionary, disrespectful, and representative. No wonder, given such anger and threat to entrenched power, there is such resistance, examined and unexamined, to feminism from the academic establishment as that adumbrated in the special issue of *NLH* we examined in chapter seven.

The battle over language, as waged between various common readers and the professions, is particularly interesting because

it so clearly goes beyond the boundaries of the academy. In doing so it throws into high relief the profound social, political,
and legal significance of issues that sometimes appear hermetic
to those outside the academy. In some cases the need for clear
language, some version of "the mother tongue," has reached the
level of legislation. About 20 states have passed plain-language
laws to protect ordinary people from obfuscational legalese. As
a result, many law firms now employ language consultants, often
women, often with PhDs in English. Such consultants meet with
predictable resistance. Richard Miller, language consultant to a
New York City law firm, reports that obscure language is an important part of the system:

> It is reinforced in law school with a vengeance. . . . And the hier-
> archy of the law firm militates in favor of turgid writing. When I
> challenged something a young lawyer had written, he complained,
> "But we want to sound like lawyers." They are afraid of what the
> supervising partners will think. I stress directness and simplicity. . . .
> I encourage them to say things in a way that any literate, intelligent
> person can understand. (Quoted by Stein)

Ordinary people, common readers, are demanding inclusion in
heretofore professional mysteries. As the young lawyer quoted
points out, and as any number of frightened members of the professoriat can substantiate, such inclusion threatens to undermine status as well as the status quo.

As a logical consequence of such challenges, people empowered by things-as-they-are fight back in many ways, some sketched
in this book. One way is to attempt to dismiss pressure for change
as coming from fringe and extremist groups. Unfortunately for
this ploy, feminist political and scholarly challenges to the masculinist academy encompass at least three strategies, and hence
are hard to dismiss as "merely" extremist, limited, isolationist,
or whatnot. Liberal strategy, for example, as we show in chapter
six, is to get feminist scholarship accepted as equal in merit to traditional scholarship, Le Guin's "language of the fathers." An early
manifestation of liberal strategy is embodied in remarks from the

American Association of University Women (AAUW) *Journal* cited by Ginny Foster in an article on "Women as Liberators":

> We need to show high school girls they can go to the universities on the *same basis as men*, that they have a chance for an intellectual life within the university or working life in private industry. . . . Women throughout society [should] *have the same choice about their roles that men have*. That really has to be the focus—equality. (Foster 7, emphases in the original)

Radical strategy, not explicitly treated in this book but implicit and an important option throughout, is separatist. It embodies itself in feminist journals, in journals like *Sinister Wisdom* that have no interest whatsoever in the academy, in such organizations as the National Women's Studies Association, and in some women's studies programs. Suspicious of liberal feminist demands for "equality" (which she rephrased as "give us our share of the poisoned pie"), Foster urged women's studies practitioners to "re-define education as 'cultural action for freedom,'" to "think of what women's studies *could* be, as opposed to the kind of thinking which asks how we can get women's studies into the existing educational system":

> If we must be illegitimate in terms of the university values, let us. If we must face not having status within a hierarchy, let us deny the hierarchy. They may think us "little darlings playing," but that may be an advantage, for in that way we will not be a threat. But let us be about our business of extricating ourselves from the dominant frame of reference, for reasons of *necessity* and for reasons of *utility*. (8, emphases in the original)

Early women's studies programs were often self-consciously separatist. In the early 1970s, women's studies faculty at Portland (Oregon) State University eschewed departmental status, asked for "no high-powered conferences, no research institutes, no battles for outside funding, no grantsmanship, no female faculty moving into administration, [had] little worry about men, no definition of professionalism," because they saw themselves as representing "the radical women's movement, using an institution where women congregate as a place for organizing and learning. Here women's studies is larger than an academic program, and continuous with a feminist movement for significant social change" (Hoffman 166). The Feminist Studies course at Goddard-Cambridge "dissolved itself rather than compromise its commitment to structural change in the education process" (Boxer 675–76).

What we might call integrationist strategy, analyzed in chapter seven, attempts to change the rules, procedures, and criteria of conducting professional business. It aims to transform the academy and, by extension, academic discourse, to accommodate both men's and women's ways of knowing and evaluating. Integrationist strategy manifests itself tactically as the faculty-development and curriculum-integration projects we allude to in chapter seven, theoretically as gender studies. As Elaine Showalter points out, many feminist scholars came in the 1980s to believe that "the study of gender relations involving both women and men . . . would ultimately have a more radically transformative impact on the disciplines than studies of women, which too easily could be ghettoized, leaving disciplinary structures and practices intact" ("Introduction" 2).

Quick reconsideration of "The Case of Doris Lessing" (chapter five) provides a concrete way of reviewing how feminist reformulation of the literary canon and feminist alternatives to the rhetoric and substance of the critical/professional canon combine and interact to challenge the status quo. Personal and passionate emotions were an important component of academic interest in Lessing. These emotions translated into a variety of conventional and unconventional manifestations. Desire to communicate with like-minded people, not simply or reductively professional ambition nor any version of scientific objectivity, encouraged formation of the *Doris Lessing Newsletter*, the Doris Lessing Society, preparation of PhD dissertations on Lessing, publication of books and articles, and presentations and seminars at the MLA and elsewhere.

Thus feminist scholarship and feminist criticism dismantle the facade of scientific detachment and scientific method assembled with great difficulty over so many years. Feminist scholarship and criticism recommend introducing the "merely" personal, the nonobjective, the relative into the world Northrop Frye hoped to make like physics. No wonder Ellen Messer-Davidow's radical and relativist notion of "perspectivism" acts like a red flag to male critics of various political allegiances.

This rapid review brings us full circle to our chapter on the American Dream as defined and mourned by the National Endowment for the Humanities. The nightmare that people like William Bennett, Lynne Cheney, E. D. Hirsch, and Allan Bloom fear will replace their particular American Dream is not just a changed English literature curriculum, or even a changed general education canon of great texts that they see adding up to the quintessence of western civilization. They envision an improbable and horrific gorgon of feminism in the academy, sporting snakes of pedagogy, scholarly approach, rhetoric, and critical theory that will turn to stone not merely the "ears" of the fathers, as in Le Guin's fantasy, but the entire body of the male academy. If feminism's gorgon, as projected by Bloom and company, triumphs in its confrontation with the academic establishment, the establishment is in danger of becoming a sort of mouldering Ozymandias. Substituted for the old ways, writ in stone, may be a terrifying new reality: bloody, mutable, fragile, permeable, subjective, and unscientific.

If this nightmare vision is accurate, what is most profoundly under attack, then, is just what Allan Bloom worries about: all ideals and universals. Feminist pedagogy, scholarship, and critical theory all deny that there are such things as universal standards of beauty or artistic merit. As a correlative, feminism unequivocally insists that all canon formation—including, especially, feminist canon formation—is ideological. Of course, as we have stressed continually, the threat from feminism is nowhere near as powerful as its opponents seem to think. Nor can feminism come intact through encounters and engagements with the establishment.

Given this context, it is easy to see why conservative critics and pedagogues are uneasy about feminist and minority challenges. As we demonstrate in chapter two, however, critics who identify themselves as radicals and Marxists also appear uneasy. Their distress returns us to the crucial question posed in that chapter: who owns culture? Who, indeed?

As this study shows, feminists, minorities, and common readers are not owners of culture—nor are they likely to be. These groups do, though, currently have enough education, interest, economic and political power, and access to publishing sources to make themselves heard as never before. They can no longer comfortably assume from the outsider's impoverished but privileged position that "*the master's tools will never dismantle the master's house*" (Lorde 112, emphasis in the original). White women and minorities can and do now use these tools; the question today is: do we want to use them to tear down the old edifice, to remodel the place, or just to redecorate? After all, we have begun to move into that house. Do we want a roof over our heads? Do we want *that* roof? Much of what we chart in this book is the oscillation engendered as these rambunctious new groups strive to find house room. No element will emerge from this process unscathed. Nor, though there will no doubt be lulls, will the process cease. Challenge is inevitable; cooperation is a necessity; co-optation is a danger.

We are left with unanswerable but exciting questions. What next? What are we going to do with the literary manifestations of gender differences while we wait for social change? If women and minorities get power in the academy, must we become more like the present hierarchy? Is academic discourse, even at its most feminist-influenced, its most "motherly," likely to reach the common reader? And if it does, can those who are sufficiently bilingual to speak both the mother and father tongues afford to nurture the common reader while the entrenched males carry on the real business of the academic profession? If white women and minorities acquire enough real power to begin to replace the present system, how do we protect ourselves from our own version of the hubris we are currently defining and condemning?

Endorsing, then, openendedness and questioning, oscillation rather than dialectic, reluctantly eschewing the myth of progress, we conclude with the hope that our moment is one of the more expansive and humane episodes in the process, complex and dynamic, by which humans make culture.

[1]   *The American Dream*

1. See also articles in *Profession 87* by Wayne Booth, Robert Scholes, and Cary Nelson that accuse "traditional" curricula of promoting cultural tunnel-vision. "We may ask ourselves," Nelson suggests,

> what it means to graduate students with a major in literature who have not had a single course in minority literature? When a curriculum requires a course in Shakespeare but not a course in black literature, what message does it give students about black or Hispanic people, what message about the cultural traditions that are valuable and those that are expendable? Are the students we graduate from such programs as likely to see divestment from South Africa as a crucial issue? Are the students we graduate from such programs as likely to see racial justice in their own country as important? The confidence that such values will be dependably if obliquely encouraged by the eternal truth of the literature we do require is an evasive fiction. ("Against English" 50)

2. For sounds of this rich polyphony see, for example, *This Bridge Called My Back: Writings by Radical Women of Color*, ed. Cherrie Moraga and Gloria Anzaldua, and *Reconstructing American Literature: Courses, Syllabi, Issues*, ed. Paul Lauter.

3. In the NEH's 1988 report, *Humanities in America*, Lynne V. Cheney insists that the humanities derive their value from "truths that pass beyond time and circumstance; truths that, transcending accidents of class, race, and gender, speak to us all" (14).

4. We could as easily, though less concisely, have begun by entering the discussion of E. D. Hirsch's *Cultural Literacy* taking place in such professional journals as *Academe* and the *ADE (Association of Departments of English) Bulletin*. Or we might have subjected to close reading an article in the *Wall Street Journal* of 2 February 1988, which begins with the assertion that "while businessmen have spent the past several

years frantically searching for excellence, many literature professors have been just as busy repudiating it" and concludes by accusing "revisionists" like Stanley Fish, Jane Tompkins, and Barbara Herrnstein Smith of both profiteering ("in many cases, the salaries that lured these professors [to Duke] were in the six figures") and of "compact[ing] the world's great literature to fit their coarse and ham-fisted political framework" (Brooks).

5. In addition to Von Hallberg's *Canons* see, for example, Kampf and Lauter's *Politics of Literature*, which reflects the 1960s tumult that demanded canon reformation. See also Fiedler and Baker.

6. Kolodny is citing Clifford Geertz, "Ideology as a Cultural System," *The Interpretation of Cultures: Selected Essays* (New York: Basic Books, 1973) 232.

7. "As marxist method is dialectical materialism, feminist method is consciousness raising: the collective critical reconstitution of the meaning of women's social experience, as women live through it" (MacKinnon 543).

8. See chapter six for a detailed account of that research.

9. E. D. Hirsch calls Hugh Blair, who was appointed first Regius Professor of Rhetoric and Belles Lettres at the University of Edinburgh in 1762, "the first definer of cultural literacy for the English national language" and claims that Blair's *Lectures on Rhetoric and Belles Lettres* (first published in 1783 and reprinted 130 times between then and 1911) were "as influential in fixing the cultural content of the language as Johnson's dictionary in fixing its forms" (84–85). But D. J. Palmer notes that, throughout the eighteenth century and well into the nineteenth, the study of "belles lettres" was not an academic discipline in the modern sense. Rather, "an understanding of polite literature" was intended simply to refine "the tastes of a gentleman" (11). In order to "realize the true potentialities of the subject," he maintains, "a School of English had to be created with the necessary authority . . . to give the lead to the rest of the country" (65). That necessary authority was established, according to Palmer, when the Oxford English School was founded in 1894.

Franklin E. Court claims that the course of lectures on English literature developed by the Reverend Thomas Dale, the first professor of English language and literature at University College, London University, was "the first bona fide course in English taught in a specifically English university" (796). But Dale's tenure at UCL was brief (1828–30) because, as Court acknowledges, "higher education in England in the 1820s and 1830s, even at the new progressively experimental university in the metropolis, was hesitant to endorse a program that dealt purposefully with attempts to popularize the study of English literature" (806).

Betsy Bowden moves the debate to the other side of the Atlantic by asserting that "English as an academic subject . . . was founded by Benjamin Franklin" and that the first professor of English at the academy that would eventually become the University of Pennsylvania was Ebenezer Kinnersley, appointed in 1753 (894).

10. Boxer was writing in 1982, but a report on *Women's Studies in the United States* prepared by Catharine R. Stimpson and Nina Kressner Cobb for the Ford Foundation in 1986 indicates that feminist scholarship continues to pose a "moral challenge" to the academy by demanding "that research work *for* women" (13).

[2] Dr. Johnson's Canon

1. In addition to Bertrand Bronson's lucid discussions of Johnson's ambivalence and complexity in *Johnson Agonistes*, W. B. C. Watkins's *Perilous Balance* and George Irwin's *Samuel Johnson: A Personality in Conflict* remain two of the best studies of the psychological states informing the writing. Donald Greene's *The Politics of Samuel Johnson* is still the best extended treatment of Johnson's complicated political views, while Robert DeMaria, Jr.'s recent *PMLA* article, "The Politics of Johnson's *Dictionary*," is a helpful addition to the ongoing explication.

2. True, Johnson, faithful to his times, approves universality as the great virtue of literature, and does indeed, as Tompkins argues, claim in the "Preface to Shakespeare" that, for the Bard, "'the effects of favour and competition,' 'the tradition of friendships,' the 'advantages' of 'local customs' and 'temporary opinions'" (Tompkins, *Sensational* 5) are no longer operative. But she quotes without contextualizing. Without impugning the brilliance and originality of Tompkins's examination in *Sensational Designs* of the cultural forces determining the formation of the American canon, we would like to note that her use of Johnson as the paradigmatic, implacable, arch-conservative of literary criticism is absurd, knee-jerk reductionism: Johnson initiated the now ossified canon; down with the canon, down with Johnson.

3. Gerald L. Bruns's "Canon and Power in the Hebrew Scriptures" provides further amplification of the relation between biblical and literary canon-making. See chapter five for additional commentary on this fruitful analogy.

4. In this respect, it is amusing to note the similarities in appearance of Lentricchia and Johnson. Johnson, of course, was notorious for his

sloppy, unconventional, ungentlemanly mode of dress, to which he adhered long after the excuse of poverty was no longer valid (see, e.g., Boswell, *The London Journal* 260, 267). Atlas describes Lentricchia's appearance at length, and the article includes a full-page color photo analogous
to one of Reynolds's portraits: "The photograph on the book jacket of
'Criticism and Social Change' shows a guy in a sports shirt, posed against
a graffiti-scarred wall—the 'Dirty Harry of contemporary critical theory,'
a reviewer in The Village Voice called him." (73) It is perhaps not too far-
fetched to suggest that both critics consciously disregard conventional
gentlemanly dress in order to make an implicit class statement.

5. See, for the most exhaustive discussion of this new readership,
Roy M. Wiles, *Serial Publication Before 1750* and *Freshest Advices: Early
Provincial Newspapers in England*.

6. Almost every page of Bloom's *The Closing of the American Mind*
reflects his anxiety about possible loss of status. The first words of his
preface are as good an example as any:

> This essay—a meditation on the state of our souls, particularly those
> of the young, and their education—is written from the perspective
> of a teacher. Such a perspective, although it has grave limitations and
> is accompanied by dangerous temptations, is a privileged one. The
> teacher, particularly the teacher dedicated to liberal education, must
> constantly try to look toward the goal of human completedness and
> back at the natures of his students here and now, ever seeking to
> understand the former and to assess the capacities of the latter to
> approach it. . . . The teacher is . . . guided by the awareness, or the
> divination, that there is a human nature, and that assisting its ful-
> fillment is his task. (19–20)

Bloom's assumptions are obvious and grandiose: the teacher can evaluate souls, can guide them to completion, indeed, has the role of priest-
cum-god.

7. See, for example, Terry Eagleton in *The Function of Criticism*, who
argues that the function of criticism is

> to contribute in a modest way to our very survival. For it is surely
> becoming apparent that without a more profound understanding of
> such symbolic processes, through which political power is deployed,
> reinforced, resisted, at times subverted, we shall be incapable of un-
> locking the most lethal power-struggles now confronting us. Modern
> criticism was born of a struggle against the absolutist state; unless
> its future is now defined as a struggle against the bourgeois state, it
> might have no future at all. (124)

8. Attitudes toward popular culture indicate that a central issue

influencing canon questioning from the left and right is the distrust both groups feel for what they see as likely to usurp the literary sphere: popular culture. Merod, for example, deplores "the mostly visual, truly anticommunal world of advertising and commercial *entertainment* controlled by giant corporate interests, [that] opposes but also surrounds the world of literacy, the world of books and critical *thinking*" (13, Merod's emphases). Allan Bloom devotes an entire chapter of *The Closing of the American Mind* to inveighing against the corruptive horrors of "this generation's . . . addition to [rock] music" (68), which "has the beat of sexual intercourse" (73), is "very big business" (77) and "ruins the imagination of young people and makes it very difficult for them to have a passionate relationship to the art and thought that are the substance of liberal education" (79).

9. Merod, too, uses the endemic language of battle. For example, he describes the text itself as a battlefield: "This rereading of the narrative field, of a text as itself a field of competing forces, becomes a reading or rereading of history too" (17).

10. Burney, *Journals and Letters* 7: 240n. For more information about this literary friendship that so clearly illustrates Johnson's open-minded eclecticism, see also Joyce Hemlow, *The History of Fanny Burney*, 110–11, and Chauncey Brewster Tinker's collection of Burney's writing about Johnson, *Dr. Johnson and Fanny Burney*.

11. See, for instance, Matthew Arnold, *Six Chief Lives* (*Complete Prose Works* 12: xii); and T. S. Eliot, "Johnson as Critic and Poet," *On Poetry and Poets*, 184–222. Walter Raleigh, one of the founders of the English literature course at Oxford University, in *Six Essays on Johnson*, describes Johnson's *Lives* as "a book of wisdom and experience, a treatise on the conduct of life, a commentary on human destiny" (26). M. J. C. Hodgart effuses in *Johnson and His Times* that Johnson's "greatest and most enduring work seems to me . . . to be his contribution to wisdom" (120).

12. Johnson's famous remark to Boswell about keeping a journal is an excellent example of the ambivalence and ambiguity pervading his critical stance, at once in favor of the neoclassical ideal of the universal, and at the same time fascinated by particularity. Boswell shows how Johnson typically manages to conflate the two, suggesting that the second leads to the first: "I told Mr. Johnson that I put down all sorts of little incidents in [my journal]. 'Sir,' said he, 'there is nothing too little for so little a creature as man. It is by studying little things that we attain the great knowledge of having as little misery and as much happiness as possible'" (Boswell, *London Journal* 305).

13. If Bloom's college student is in any way analogous with Johnson's

common reader, then Bloom's recommendations for general readers are wildly ambitious compared to Johnson's. Bloom insists that they read Plato, especially the *Republic*, then recognize the crisis facing modern life and the university: "an incoherence and incompatibility among the first principles" (346). From there, it appears dimly, Bloom's reader will go on to read whatever essential books lead to Truth and Wisdom and join a community of generous-minded souls like those who dine together in the *Symposium*. It is all vague and strange; strangest of all is the real popularity of this odd book with vast numbers of today's common readers. The large numbers of readers who lined up to buy Bloom's weird diatribe against them suggest that Johnson's reader is still out there, hungering for direction, largely ignorant of vast areas of knowledge, but deserving better than Bloom's elitist slap in the face.

E. D. Hirsch's book, *Cultural Literacy*, is the other recent best-selling book of wisdom that insults the common reader as Johnson never would. Why must Hirsch's readers know, for example, who Ludwig Wittgenstein and Tintoretto were? Why, for goodness' sake, must they know what a run-on sentence is?

14. The one area of knowledge Johnson would assume in his readership that contemporary academics cannot expect is biblical. Most of the newly literate in the eighteenth century began with the Bible, under the influence of Puritan encouragement to encounter sacred texts firsthand and not through the intermediary of a priest.

15. "There is only one way to read," Lessing believes. That is

> to browse in libraries and bookshops, picking up books that attract you, reading only those, dropping them when they bore you, skipping the parts that drag—and never, never reading anything because you feel you ought. . . . The book which bores you when you are twenty or thirty will open doors for you when you are forty or fifty, [so] don't read a book out of its right time for you. (*The Golden Notebook* xviii)

These words recall Virginia Woolf's to an earlier audience of students and would-be readers: "The only advice, indeed, that one person can give another about reading is to take no advice, to follow your own instincts, to use your own reason, to come to your own conclusions" ("How Should One Read" 235).

[3]   The Common Reader Today

1. Radway notes that, in 1958, "while eighty-three percent of [Book of the Month Club] members had a college education, only thirteen percent of the members were teachers of one sort or another." She allows

that "this may have changed recently with the Club's use of the *Oxford English Dictionary* as a Club premium, but the continuing difference between the Club's selections and those of the Reader's Subscription Book Club, associated with the *New York Review of Books*, the literary journal read by many American intellectuals, suggests that the Book of the Month Club still does not cater to this group" ("Book-of-the-Month Club" 519 n.10).

2. Thus college students—as students—are not common readers, because they read what their professors assign them. We are, however, interested in what students read, if they read, in their spare time.

3. Phillip H. Ennis, *Adult Book Reading in the United States*, National Opinion Research Center (U of Chicago, 1965) 25, quoted in Ohmann, "Shaping" 379.

4. One of us recently had occasion to talk about *Little Women* to a group of readers assembled to discuss a series of books gathered under the rubric "Not for Children Only," one of many such series sponsored by the Vermont Library Reading Project, which we will discuss in greater detail shortly. She forgot to ask the Reading Series to send her a copy of the book, so she went looking for one in Burlington, Vermont. The two copies owned by the University of Vermont Library were out, as were the copies owned by the (public) Free Library and kept in the children's section. The library at Saint Michael's College did not own a copy. The first two bookstores she tried carried the book in up to seven paperback editions, which they said they could not keep in stock, they sold so fast. Only the $15.95 hardback, illustrated Random House gift edition was in stock. She finally found a paperback copy at a third bookstore. When she expressed surprise about the book's elusiveness to the saleswoman in this store, she was told, "Well, it's a wonderful book. Little girls all want to read it; their mothers give it to them. In fact, I still read it occasionally myself."

5. Interview with Victor Swenson, May 1988.

6. See Cheney for a largely sympathetic account of these and other public humanities programs, which she says constitute "a kind of parallel school . . . that has grown up outside established institutions of education" (27).

7. For some unaccountable reason, attendance at these reading programs has been overwhelmingly female, no matter what the subject. Why? The assumption has been until recently that it was because novels have been the backbone of the series and that novels are notoriously soft literature, women's reading ("Novels? My wife reads that stuff"). Programs entitled "Myths in Marriage" and "The Madwoman in the Attic" also seemed particularly designed for women. But the predominantly female participation continues with only mild modification even with

series such as "Perceptions of Japan," "Vermont and the New Nation," and "Establishing America."

8. Interview with Swenson, June 1988.

9. We are grateful for this quotation to Eve Raimon, whose research on the Vermont Library Reading Project for *Vermont Life* contributed importantly to this chapter.

10. See *Humanities in America* 2–3 for statistics detailing increased public interest in the humanities.

11. The books for "The Community and Individual Rights" included Plato's *Republic*, Locke's *Treatise on Human Understanding*, Shakespeare's *Coriolanus*, Hawthorne's *Scarlet Letter*, Rousseau's *Social Contract*, and large chunks of Tocqueville's *Democracy in America*.

[4] Academic English

1. Graff's "dialectic" presupposes a simple dualism between opposing forces that ultimately reach a synthesis. His paradigm is clear and reassuring, but reductive. First, the dialectic of professionals pitted against antiprofessionals leaves no room for other participants. The struggle Graff sketches is joined entirely by Establishment forces fighting over, once again, who owns culture. Possible owners are the media, entrenched professional specialists, equally entrenched generalists, the Old School, the radicals. All of these groups are male, powerful, and representative of various aspects of ruling-class culture. Graff ignores disenfranchised, unempowered challenges to the academic power structure, many of whom have been vociferous since the late 1960s.

And—a second point following from this one—dialectic, as we argued in chapter one, has a predictable trajectory that obviates our less chartable notion of oscillation. Binary opposition does not effectively describe the complexity of any human process, certainly not of the curriculum/canon/theory/class/gender debates within and without the postmodern multiversity.

2. The anti-Establishment opponents of Fish have had little voice in the debate carried on in *Critical Inquiry*. They too, it would seem, look to common readers. Their common readers, though, are more heterogeneous, less predictable, and probably less docile than the happy recipients of culture envisioned by Bush and well-intentioned but potentially condescending liberals.

3. As Francis Mulhern explains, these were scholars unaffiliated with the university or any of its colleges, paid per capita by students who attended their courses (22).

4. Despite the mandatory inclusion of Homer among the great books

and on Hirsch's list, the idea of cultural literacy, like that of general education, is tied to nationalism. In a letter to the *New York Times*, Cyrus Veeser—citing several historians—reminded readers that "today's Western Civ classes are the offspring of a Government-sponsored propaganda course instituted during World War I . . . in an effort to produce what an editorial of the time in History Teachers Magazine called 'thinking bayonets.'" Graff calls Harvard Professor James Bryant Conant's appeal in 1948 to "common beliefs" and "a common set of values" a "rank expression of Cold War anti-Communism" (*Professing* 167). Hirsch concedes that multicultural study is "valuable" because "it inculcates tolerance and provides a perspective on our own traditions and values." But "it should not be allowed to supplant or interfere with our schools' responsibility to ensure our children's mastery of American literate culture" (18).

5. Many educators long for this or some other charming never-never land. Allan Bloom, for example, yearns for an even less likely world than mid-Victorian England. He aches to reestablish his dream of fifth-century B.C. Athens.

6. Since E. D. Hirsch lambasts John Dewey in *Cultural Literacy* for not showing "an adequate appreciation of the need for transmission of specific cultural information" (xvi), justice requires us here to quote Dewey's reservations about Hirsch's predecessor, Robert Hutchins:

> Dewey charged that Hutchins had "conveniently ignored" the problem "of who is to determine the definite truths that constitute the hierarchy" of learning. For there was "implicit in every assertion of fixed and eternal first truth the necessity for *some* human authority to decide, in this world of conflict, just what these truths are and how they shall be taught." (Graff, *Professing* 166, quoting Dewey; emphasis Dewey's)

[5]   *The Power of the Common Reader*

1. Ohmann uses the term "precanonical" to designate novels, and by extension authors, "that are active candidates for inclusion [in the canon], not those that will in fact be canonical at some later time" ("Shaping" 398).

2. This segment of the reading public constitutes Ohmann's "common readers," although he does not use that term. For reasons adumbrated in chapter three, we provisionally accept this characterization of the common reader, although we extend it to account for readers who are less well off or who live in the hinterlands. Of course, the *New York Times* and its Sunday *Book Review* are sold and read in Vermont as well as in Manhattan and New York's Westchester County.

3. Parenthetically, the combination of Bob Gottlieb, Knopf, and front-page reviews in the *New York Times Book Review* by big-name reviewers seems to have paved the way for Margaret Drabble's entry into the canon as well. In fact, much of what we discovered about Doris Lessing's route to canonization applies with uncanny precision to Margaret Drabble.

4. This hypothesis is strengthened, if not confirmed, by the inclusion of Howe's review in a recent anthology of mostly academic criticism of Lessing in a highly canonical publishing series, G. K. Hall's Critical Essays on Modern British Literature (Sprague and Tiger). A number of scholars and teachers we surveyed in preparing *Approaches to Teaching Lessing's The Golden Notebook* cited Howe's review as important background reading for the would-be teacher of the novel.

5. Benjamin De Mott, Robert Alter, Robert Tower, Malcolm Bradbury, James Gindin, Bernard Bergonzi and Lawrence Graver are all academics who reviewed Lessing for one or another of these journals.

6. The *Harper's* reviewer thought *Particularly Cats* "a delightful and remarkable *bonne bouché* from this often redoubtable writer" (Cook).

7. For an account of the classroom genesis of this article, see Hynes's essay, "A Sixties Book for All Seasons."

8. Short of polling every college teacher in the United States, we cannot say how many courses now include Lessing's books on their syllabi. But the survey we conducted in preparing the volume on *The Golden Notebook* for the MLA series on teaching world literature indicated that, in 1987, that novel was taught in major universities and community colleges, at the undergraduate and graduate level, in introductory courses in women's studies and graduate courses in postmodernism, in surveys of modern fiction, and in seminars in major authors.

9. Phillip H. Ennis, *Adult Book Reading in the United States*, National Opinion Research Center (Univ. of Chicago, 1965) 25, quoted in Ohmann 379. In her discussion of the editorial policies and practices of the Book of the Month Club, Janice Radway says it is "clear" that most of the works chosen for the category of "serious fiction" were selected because "BOMC editors seem to believe . . . that their readers purchase serious fiction because . . . they are seeking a model for contemporary living and even practical advice about appropriate behavior in a changing world" (535). For these editors and the "general readers" (aka "common readers") they serve, "the value of 'serious fiction' . . . is a function of its capacity to be used as a map which is, despite its status as a representation, a tool for enabling its reader to move about more effectively in the world to which it refers" ("The-Book-of-the-Month-Club" 537).

10. See the introduction to Kaplan and Rose, *Approaches*, for substantiation of this claim.

11. Irving Howe took an almost voyeuristic delight in eavesdropping on Anna's and Molly's conversations: "My own curiosity, as a masculine outsider, was enormous, for here, I felt, was the way intellectual women really talk to one another when they feel free and unobserved" (179).

12. In chapter six, we consider the utility of "seminars" and "special sessions" at MLA conventions in intruding the concerns of the common reader into academic discourse.

13. With other papers read at this forum, Showalter's and Ohmann's papers are published in a special issue of *College English* 32 (1971).

14. In addition to Karl's "Four-Gaited Beast of the Apocalypse," see his "Doris Lessing in the Sixties: The New Anatomy of Melancholy"; John L. Carey, "Art and Reality in *The Golden Notebook*"; Joseph Hynes, "The Construction of *The Golden Notebook*"; Mark Spilka, "Lessing and Lawrence: The Battle of the Sexes"; and Michael L. Magie, "Doris Lessing and Romanticism."

15. See chapter six for a discussion of the role of allied organizations within the MLA.

16. From 1982 to 1987, Pat C. Hoy II of the United States Military Academy served as treasurer to the DLS; over the years Paul Schlueter has served as general editor and associate editor of the newsletter and is now archivist of the DLS; Terrell Dixon of the University of Houston was the first vice-president of the DLS; and Alvin Sullivan of Southern Illinois University at Edwardsville has served on the Program Committee of the DLS and on the Editorial Board of the newsletter.

17. A number of scholars use the same model. See, for example, James Norhnberg, "On Literature and the Bible"; and Christine Froula, "When Eve Reads Milton." As we pointed out in chapter two, Alvin Kernan has argued that Samuel Johnson's canon-making occurred at a time of crisis analogous to the historical moments of biblical canon formation.

18. This, in fact, was her response to Susan Stamberg who, interviewing her for National Public Radio's *All Things Considered* on 25 April 1984, asked whether Lessing thought the writer's role was "to show us the world as it is, or the world as it should be, or the world as it might be" (Lessing, Interview 4).

19. See, for example, Caryn Fuoroli, "Doris Lessing's 'Game': Referential Language and Fictional Form."

20. Graham Holderness discusses the rediscovered "relevance" of Shakespeare's English history plays, especially *Henry V*, in wartime England. See his "Agincourt 1944: Readings in the Shakespeare Myth."

21. Walker herself prefers the term "womanist" to "feminist," for reasons suggested by her epigraphs to *In Search of Our Mothers' Gardens*.

See also Chikwenye Okonjo Ogunyemi's and Elsa Barkley Brown's arguments in favor of the term "womanist."

22. Other examples of scholarship exphasizing Walker's place in a
tradition of black writers or as a spokesperson for the situation of black
women include: Barbara Christian's *Black Women Novelists* (1980); Faith
Pullin's chapter on contemporary African-American women writers in
A. Robert Lee's *Black Fiction* (1980); Karen Gaston's 1981 essay on "Women
in the Lives of Grange Copeland"; essays in Mari Evans's 1984 anthology, *Black Women Writers (1950–1980)*, by Barbara Christian and Bettye
J. Parker-Smith; Mary Helen Washington's "I Sign My Mother's Name"
in Ruth Perry's and Martine Watson Bradley's 1984 anthology, *Mothering the Mind*; and two 1985 articles in *Signs*—Dianne Sadoff's "Black
Matrilineage: The Case of Alice Walker and Zora Neale Hurston"; and
Chikwenye Okonjo Ogunyemi's "Womanism: The Dynamics of the Contemporary Black Female Novel in English."

23. "Twice, I have heard Alice Walker's novel *The Color Purple*, published in 1982, described as 'a sacred text,'" Stade wrote in the *Partisan
Review*, "once by a true believer, once by a village atheist. Certainly the
extra-textual evidence is with the true believer: the novel has been a
bestseller, first in hardcover and now in paperback; it won the Pulitzer
Prize and the National Book Award; many of the reviews were written
with a hushed and unctuous reverence" (264).

24. At the same time that they absorb black women's writing into
the American canon through their close and attentive reading of a
short story by Alice Walker, the authors also subtly incorporate black
feminist criticism into the "general" or "mainstream" scholarship represented by the *Southern Review*. The impetus for their improvisation
on quilts was the "brilliant essay" on Alice Walker by Barbara Christian
which appeared in an anthology of critical articles on black women
writers (714).

25. Early practioners of women's studies defined their strength in
terms of their marginality. According to the editors of *Female Studies
VI*, it is "because the majority of us have so little stake in existing intellectual institutions and systems [that] we are psychically free to articulate and develop alternatives" (Hoffman, et al. 4).

26. See Gayle Greene and Coppelia Kahn, eds., *Making a Difference:
Feminist Literary Criticism*.

[6] *Playing the Numbers*

1. In 1969, the convention program took up 30 pages in the November issue of *PMLA*; by the mid-1970s the convention program *was* the

November issue of *PMLA*. In 1987 it ran, with advertisements, to more than 300 pages.

2. In chapter seven we discuss two articles that demonstrate these feminist "strategies of rereading," one by Adrienne Munich on Cervantes's *Don Quixote*, the other by Christine Froula on *Paradise Lost*.

3. As in tabulating the figures for table 1, we are relying on papers' titles to indicate the nature of their subjects.

4. The question of "men in feminism" was raised at two sessions at the 1984 MLA and is elaborated in the book that grew out of them, *Men in Feminism*, edited by Alice Jardine and Paul Smith. Elaine Showalter and Jane Marcus also discuss the issue in their contributions to Shari Benstock's collection, *Feminist Issues in Literary Scholarship*. And see the heated response in *Critical Inquiry* by Sandra Gilbert and Susan Gubar to Frank Lentricchia's "Patriarchy Against Itself—The Young Manhood of Wallace Stevens."

5. See Wayne C. Booth, "Freedom of Interpretation: Bakhtin and the Challenge of Feminist Criticism"; Jonathan Culler, *On Deconstruction*; Terry Eagleton, *The Rape of Clarissa*; Lawrence Lipking, "Aristotle's Sister"; and the article by Frank Lentricchia cited in the preceding note.

6. With yet another turn of the theoretical/ideological screw, in 1989 Showalter edited a collection of essays in gender studies. Conceding that "the appearance of this anthology may disturb some readers who worry that 'gender studies' could be a pallid assimilation of feminist criticism into the mainstream (or male stream) of English studies," Showalter nevertheless affirmed her belief "that the fundamental changes have now begun that make the formation of a strong critical community around the issue of gender a genuine and exciting possiblility":

> Like other aspects of literary analysis, talking about gender without a commitment to dismantling sexism, racism, and homophobia, can degenerate into nothing more than a talk show, with men trying to monopolize the [post]feminist conversation. But as the essays in this book demonstrate, the genuine addition of gender as a "central problem in every text" read and taught, "whatever the era and whoever the author," could also move us a step further towards post-patriarchy. That's a step worth trying to take together. ("Introduction" 10–11, brackets in original)

7. And some of that work may not manifest itself directly at the annual convention. Feminist concerns may motivate one's teaching, for example, even if one is doing a different kind of scholarship. Moreover, it is possible to find feminist scholarship valuable, interesting, even exciting, without engaging in it oneself.

8. MLA committees and commissions also arrange meetings, but since the procedures by which they do so are not outlined in "Procedures for Organizing Meetings for the MLA Convention," we have excluded them from our analysis.

9. In 1988, however, the Program Committee recommended changes in the policies and procedures governing allied organizations that, if adopted, would bring them under stricter control by the MLA. It would be more difficult for a learned society or professional association to qualify for allied organization status; once established as such, its status would be reviewed by the Program Committee every seven years; and unless an allied organization had more than 250 MLA members on its rolls, it would be limited to arranging one session per year at the MLA convention, in contrast to the two sessions now permitted all allied organizations ("Meeting of the Council" 340–42). At the 1988 convention, the Delegate Assembly "voted to recommend that this proposal be returned to the Program Committee for further consideration" ("Delegate Assembly" 5).

10. In 1989, when this chapter was revised and updated, 15,057 MLA members were women and 14,455 were men. The gender of 657 could not be determined from their names.

11. We have no way of determining what percentage of articles submitted to *PMLA* are written by women or consider women writers or employ feminist criticism. Thus we are forced to confine our analysis to articles ultimately published in the journal.

12. As Stanton also points out, although author-anonymous reviewing may correct unconscious biases against certain persons or groups of persons, it "cannot remedy bias against certain 'deviant' subjects and methodologies. In most instances," she continues,

> the reader who considers women's studies unscholarly or frivolous, for example, will evaluate a related article negatively. The reader or referee who holds such a priori views and who is usually ignorant of critical contexts and developments in the field should—but rarely does—recommend that an article would be more accurately evaluated by a specialist in Women's Studies. (76 n 17)

Since articles submitted to *PMLA* are sent, for initial review, to one consultant reader and one member of the advisory committee, the increased representation of women on the advisory committee makes it somewhat more likely that feminist scholarship will not be rejected out of hand during the initial screening process. It is not irrelevant to mention that for the last 15 years the managing editor of the journal, who assigns submissions to reviewers, has been a woman.

13. In 1988–89, a subcommittee of the American Association of University Professors' (AAUP's) Committee W on the Status of Women in the Academic Profession wrote the editors of 13 scholarly journals "in the general field of women's studies." They asked, among other questions, what the journal's review process was. All eight of the editors who responded to the subcommittee's request for information reported that their journal had a policy of author-anonymous submission. (The journals were: *Signs, Psychology of Women Quarterly, Hypatia, Sex Roles, Feminist Studies, Journal of Feminist Studies in Religion, Frontiers,* and *Tulsa Studies in Women's Literature.*) One editor wrote that she and her journal's sponsoring organization "have a firm commitment to blind review as a feminist principle" (Sullivan, et al. 39).

14. We did, however, read all the articles in *PMLA* from 1970 through 1987, and the correlation we discovered there between titles and contents of articles suggests that our conclusions about the other journals are firmly grounded.

15. For table 4, we counted only articles. But *Novel* frequently substitutes a review essay for one of its customary 4 to 5 articles per issue. During the 16 years we surveyed, *Novel* published 10 review essays on books of feminist criticism or on books by or about women writers. *Contemporary Literature* regularly publishes interviews and book reviews, in addition to articles. During the 16 years we surveyed, the journal published interviews with the following women writers: Gwendolyn Brooks (1970); Sara Lidman (1971); Marguerite Duras (1972); Nathalie Sarraute, Celia Bertin, Margaret Drabble, and Doris Lessing (1973); Christine Brooke-Rose and Bridgid Brophy (1976); Diane Wakoski and Iris Murdoch (1977); Nadine Gordimer (1981); Joyce Carol Oates (1982); Toni Morrison (1983); and Rosellen Brown (1986).

16. Strictly speaking, as table 4 indicates, there was no article on a woman writer or feminist topic in the 1970 volume of *Contemporary Literature.* But there was an interview with Gwendolyn Brooks, and there were review essays that featured works by Anaïs Nin and Doris Lessing.

17. See the next chapter for our reading of this special issue of *NLH.*

18. *Critical Inquiry's* highest incidence of articles on women writers or feminist topics occurred in 1981, when it published a special issue on *Writing and Sexual Difference.* The second highest incidence occurred in 1985, when a special issue on *Race, Writing, and Difference* featured two articles on women writers and two on feminist topics.

[7]   Who Speaks for the Academy

1. Sidney's characterization of the earth as both mother and nurse is firmly grounded in Renaissance science, as Carolyn Merchant details in *The Death of Nature: Women, Ecology and the Scientific Revolution* (see especially 26–27).

2. Sidney's ambivalence about nature is echoed by Renaissance science which, as Evelyn Fox Keller says, both acknowledged and feared the power of (female) nature: "The alchemists were not feminists. In many ways, they shared in the general contempt for women of their time. But for them, women's procreative powers remained a matter of reverence, awe, and even envy" (*Reflections* 53).

3. Adrienne Rich cites John Crowe Ransom, who calls Emily Dickinson "a little home-keeping person" who, "while she had a proper notion of the final destination of her poems . . . was not one of those poets who had advanced to that later stage of operations where manuscripts are prepared for the printer, and the poet's diction has to make concessions to the publisher's style-book" (*On Lies* 166).

4. In her response to the commentators, Messer-Davidow reveals that Amy Ling

> is one of many women who have been denied tenure. Of the twelve women originally invited to write commentaries on my essay, I know about the personal circumstances of eight. One woman received tenure uneventfully, and one has not come up for a decision. Six were denied tenure: two are appealing their cases, two do not have academic employment, and two gained academic employment and tenure only after difficulty. ("Knowing" 192–93)

5. From writers of fiction like Sara Maitland and Michelene Wandor, who coauthored the novel *Arky Types*, to the women's rock group Tetes Noires, whose members write their songs collectively, to literary and cultural critics like Gilbert and Gubar, the five scholars who wrote *Feminist Scholarship: Kindling in the Groves of Academe* "jointly" (Du-Bois, et al. vii), and the four who "submerg[ed their] individual perspectives for the sake of the collective 'we'" (Belenky, et al. ix) who wrote *Women's Ways of Knowing*, more and more women are discovering the power of collaboration.

6. Note that Goodheart's rational, comprehensible "science" is tacitly being opposed to Messer-Davidow's "magic."

7. And it is contemporary. In Walter Jackson Bate's *Criticism: The Major Texts* (enlarged edition), there is only one woman critic, Virginia Woolf, and she is represented by one of the shortest essays in the book.

Similarly in Hazard Adams's *Critical Theory Since Plato* (1971), only three women are represented, Virginia Woolf once again, Maud Bodkin, and the redoubtable Susan Sontag. None of the women's essays in either of these books is feminist.

8. In "Toward a Woman-Centered University" Adrienne Rich cites Walter Ong to suggest "that the very origins of academic style are peculiarly masculine." Rhetoric, Ong says, is the "rational" equivalent of "the ceremonial combat which is found among males and typically only among males at the physical level throughout the entire animal kingdom." Interestingly, "rhetoric became particularly attached to Learned Latin, which the male psyche appropriated to itself . . . when Latin ceased to be a 'mother' tongue (that is, was no longer spoken in the home by one's mother)" (Ong, quoted in Rich 128).

9. As Jane Marcus points out in "Material Girls," French and French-inspired feminist criticism is engaged primarily "with individual male thinkers, like Freud and Lacan" (289). We would add Derrida and Foucault to her list.

10. Marcus goes on to note, however, that these critics pay insufficient attention to race and sexual orientation.

11. Cf. Belenky, et al.: "In describing connected knowing the women we interviewed used images not of invading another mind but of opening up to receive another's experience into their own minds" (122).

12. In relating this anecdote, we quote from documents lent to us on the condition that the persons involved remain anonymous.

Works Cited

Adams, Hazard. *Critical Theory Since Plato*. New York: Harcourt, 1971.

Adams, Hazard, and Leroy Searle. *Critical Theory Since 1965*. Tallahassee: Florida State UP, 1986.

Aiken, Susan Hardy; Karen Anderson; Myra Dinnerstein; Judy Lensink; and Patricia MacCorquodale. "Trying Transformations: Curriculum Integration and the Problem of Resistance." *Signs* 12 (1987): 255–75.

Allen, Walter. *The Modern Novel in Britain and the United States*. New York: Dutton, 1965.

———. Rev. of *Martha Quest* and *A Proper Marriage*, by Doris Lessing. *New York Times Book Review* 15 Nov. 1964: 5.

Arnold, Matthew. *Complete Prose Works*. Ed. R. H. Super. 22 vols. Ann Arbor: U of Michigan P, 1960–77.

———. From "Sweetness and Light." Bate 466–72.

Atlas, James. "The Battle of the Books." *New York Times Magazine* 5 June 1988. 24+.

Auerbach, Nina. "Engorging the Patriarchy." Benstock 150–60.

Baker, Houston A., Jr., and Charlotte Pierce-Baker. "Patches: Quilts and Community in Alice Walker's 'Everyday Use.'" *Southern Review* 21 (1985): 706–20.

Baldick, Chris. *The Social Mission of English Criticism: 1848–1932*. Oxford: Clarendon, 1983.

Bate, Walter Jackson, ed. *Criticism: The Major Texts*. Enlarged ed. New York: Harcourt, 1970.

Belenky, Mary Field; Blyth McVicker Clinchy; Nancy Rule Goldberger; and Jill Mattuck Tarule. *Women's Ways of Knowing: The Development of Self, Voice and Mind*. New York: Basic, 1986.

Bell, Roseann P., Bettye J. Parker, and Beverly Guy-Sheftall, eds. *Sturdy Black Bridges: Visions of Black Women in Literature*. Garden City, NY: Anchor, 1979.

Benstock, Shari, ed. *Feminist Issues in Literary Scholarship*. Bloomington: Indiana UP, 1987.

Bergonzi, Bernard. Review of *Martha Quest* and *A Proper Marriage*, by Doris Lessing. *New York Review of Books* 11 Feb. 1965: 12.

———. *The Situation of the Novel*. Pittsburgh: U of Pittsburgh P, 1970.

Bloom, Allan. *The Closing of the American Mind: How Higher Education Has Failed Democracy and Impoverished the Souls of Today's Students*. New York: Simon, 1987.

Bloom, Harold. Interview. With Imre Salusinszky. *Criticism in Society*. Ed. Imre Salusinszky. New York: Methuen, 1987. 44–73.

Booth, Wayne C. "Freedom of Interpretation: Bakhtin and the Challenge of Feminist Criticism." *Critical Inquiry* 9 (1982): 45–76.

Boswell, James. *The Life of Samuel Johnson*. Ed. G. B. Hill, rev. L. F. Powell. 2d ed. 6 vols. Oxford: Oxford UP, 1964.

———. *The London Journal, 1762–1763*. Ed. Frederick A. Pottle. New York: McGraw, 1950.

Bowden, Betsy. "The First Professor of English." *PMLA* 104 (1989): 894.

Boxer, Marilyn J. "For and About Women: The Theory and Practice of Women's Studies in the United States." *Signs* 7 (1982): 661–95.

Bradbury, Malcolm. Rev. of *In Search of the English*, by Doris Lessing. *New York Times Book Review* 5 March 1961: 4.

Bronson, Bertrand. "The Double Tradition of Dr. Johnson." *Johnson Agonistes* 156–76.

———. *Johnson Agonistes and Other Essays*. Berkeley: U of California P, 1965.

Brooks, Cleanth, and Robert Penn Warren. *Understanding Poetry*. 1938. New York: Holt, 1976.

Brooks, David. "From Western Lit to Westerns as Lit." *Wall Street Journal* 2 Feb. 1988: 36.

Brown, Elsa Barkley. "Womanist Consciousness: Maggie Lena Walker and the Independent Order of Saint Luke." *Signs* 14 (1989): 610–33.

Bruns, Gerald L. "Canon and Power in the Hebrew Scriptures." Von Hallberg 65–83.

Burney, Fanny (Mme. D'Arblay). *Dr. Johnson and Fanny Burney*. Intro. and notes, Chauncey Brewster Tinker. 1911. Westport, CT: Greenwood, 1970.

———. *The Journals and Letters of Fanny Burney*. Ed. Joyce Hemlow, et al. 10 vols. Oxford: Oxford UP, 1972–82.

Cain, William E. *The Crisis in Criticism: Theory, Literature, and Reform in English Studies*. Baltimore: Johns Hopkins UP, 1984.

Carey, John. "Art and Reality in *The Golden Notebook*." *Contemporary Literature* 14 (1973): 437–56.

———. Letter to the authors. 27 Nov. 1985.

Cheney, Lynne V. *Humanities in America: A Report to the President, the*

Congress, and the American People. Washington, DC: National Endowment for the Humanities, 1988.

Chodorow, Nancy. *The Reproduction of Mothering: Psychoanalysis and the Sociology of Gender.* Berkeley: U of California P, 1978.

Christ, Carol P. *Diving Deep and Surfacing: Women Writers on Spiritual Quest.* Boston: Beacon, 1980.

Christian, Barbara. "Alice Walker: The Black Woman Artist as Wayward." Evans, Mari 457–77.

———. *Black Women Novelists: The Development of a Tradition, 1892–1976.* Westport, CT: Greenwood, 1980.

Cixous, Helene, "Reaching the Point of Wheat, or A Portrait of the Artist as a Maturing Woman." NLH 1–21.

Cohen, Ralph. "Literary Theory in the University: A Survey." *New Literary History* 14 (1983): 409–51.

Contemporary Literature 14.4 (1973). *Special Number on Doris Lessing.*

Cook, Rodney. Review of *Particularly Cats,* by Doris Lessing. *Harper's* July 1967: 95.

Court, Franklin E. "The Social and Historical Significance of the First English Literature Professorship in England." *PMLA* 103 (1988): 796–807.

Cowley, Malcolm. Rev. of *The Memoirs of a Survivor,* by Doris Lessing. *Saturday Review* 28 June 1975: 23.

Culler, Jonathan. "Beyond Interpretation." Adams and Searle 322–29.

———. *On Deconstruction: Theory and Criticism after Structuralism.* Ithaca: Cornell UP, 1982.

Davis, Thadious. "Alice Walker's Celebration of Self in Southern Generations." *Southern Quarterly* 21.4 (1983): 39–53.

"Delegate Assembly." *MLA Newsletter* 21.1 (1989): 5.

De Maria, Robert, Jr. "The Politics of Johnson's *Dictionary.*" *PMLA* 104 (1989): 64–74.

Drabble, Margaret. "Doris Lessing: Cassandra in a World Under Siege." *Ramparts* Feb. 1972: 50–54.

———. "Revelations and Prophecies." Rev. of *Stories,* by Doris Lessing. *Saturday Review* 27 May 1978: 54.

Dryden, John. "An Essay of Dramatic Poesy." Bate 129–60.

DuBois, Ellen Carol; Gail Paradise Kelly; Elizabeth Lapovsky Kennedy; Carolyn W. Korsmeyer; and Lillian S. Robinson. *Feminist Scholarship: Kindling in the Groves of Academe.* Urbana: U of Illinois P, 1985.

Eagleton, Terry. *The Function of Criticism: From the Spectator to Post-Structuralism.* London: Verso, 1984.

———. *Literary Theory: An Introduction.* Minneapolis: U of Minnesota P, 1984.

———. *The Rape of Clarissa*. Minneapolis, U of Minnesota P, 1982.

Edwards, Lee R. *Psyche as Hero: Female Heroism and Fictional Form.* Middletown, CT: Wesleyan UP, 1984.

Eliot, T. S. *On Poetry and Poets.* New York: Farrar, 1957.

———. *Selected Essays.* New York: Harcourt, 1960.

———. "Tradition and the Individual Talent." Bate 525–29.

Elshtain, Jean Bethke. "The Post-*Golden Notebook* Fiction of Doris Lessing." *Salamagundi* 47–48 (1980): 95–114.

Erickson, Peter. "'Cast Out Alone/ To Heal/ And Re-Create/ Ourselves': Family-Based Identity in the Work of Alice Walker." *College Language Association Journal* 23 (1979): 71–94.

Evans, Mari, ed. *Black Women Writers (1950–1980): A Critical Evaluation.* Garden City, NY: Anchor, 1984.

Evans, Sara. *Personal Politics: The Roots of Women's Liberation in the Civil Rights Movement and the New Left.* New York: Vintage, 1980.

Fetterley, Judith. *The Resisting Reader: A Feminist Approach to American Fiction.* Bloomington: Indiana UP, 1978.

Fiedler, Leslie A., and Houston A. Baker, Jr., eds. *English Literature: Opening Up the Canon.* Selected Papers from the English Institute, 1979, n.s. 4. Baltimore: Johns Hopkins UP, 1981.

Fifer, Elizabeth. "Alice Walker: The Dialect and Letters of *The Color Purple.*" *Contemporary American Women Writers: Narrative Strategies.* Catherine Rainwater and William J. Scheick, eds. Lexington: U of Kentucky P, 1985. 155–71.

Fish, Stanley. "No Bias, No Merit: The Case against Blind Submission." *PMLA* 103 (1988): 739–47.

———. "Profession Despise Thyself: Fear and Self-Loathing in Literary Studies." *Critical Inquiry* 10 (1983): 349–64.

Fontenot, Chester J. "Alice Walker: 'The Diary of an African Nun' and Dubois' Double Consciousness." *Journal of Afro-American Issues* 5 (1977): 192–96. Bell, et al. 150–56.

Foster, Ginny. "Women as Liberators." Hoffman, et al. 6–35.

Franklin, H. Bruce. "English as an Institution: The Role of Class." Fiedler and Baker 92–106.

Franks, Joseph. "Spatial Form in Modern Literature." *The Widening Gyre.* New Brunswick, NJ: Rutgers UP, 1963. 3–62.

Freire, Paulo. *Pedagogy of the Oppressed.* Trans. Myra Bergman Ramos. 1968. New York: Continuum, 1983.

"From the Editor." *ADE Bulletin* 88 (Winter 1987): 1–8.

Froula, Christine. "When Eve Reads Milton: Undoing the Canonical Economy." Von Hallberg 149–75.

Frye, Northrop. "The Archetypes of Literature." Bate 601–9.

Fuoroli, Caryn. "Doris Lessing's 'Game': Referential Language and Fictional Form." *Twentieth Century Literature* 27 (1981): 146–65.

Gaston, Karen C. "Women in the Lives of Grange Copeland." *College Language Association Journal* 24 (1981): 276–86.

Gilbert, Sandra M., and Susan Gubar. *The Madwoman in the Attic: The Woman Writer and the Nineteenth-Century Literary Imagination*. New Haven: Yale UP, 1979.

———. "The Man on the Dump versus the United Dames of America; or, What Does Frank Lentricchia Want?" *Critical Inquiry* 14 (1988): 386–406.

———. *The War of the Words*. Vol. 1 of *No Man's Land: The Place of the Woman Writer in the Twentieth Century*. 3 vols. New Haven: Yale UP, 1988.

Gilligan, Carol. *In a Different Voice: Psychological Theory and Women's Development*. Cambridge: Harvard UP, 1982.

Gindin, James. *Postwar British Fiction*. London: Cambridge UP, 1962.

———. Rev. of *A Man and Two Women*, by Doris Lessing. *Saturday Review* 23 Nov. 1963: 42.

Golding, Alan. "A History of American Poetry Anthologies." Von Hallberg 279–307.

Goodheart, Eugene. "Against Coercion." *NLH* 179–85.

Graff, Gerald. *Professing Literature: An Institutional History*. Chicago: U of Chicago P, 1987.

———. "Response to 'The Philosophical Bases of Feminist Literary Criticisms.'" *NLH* 135–38.

Greene, Donald. *The Politics of Samuel Johnson*. New Haven: Yale UP, 1960.

———, ed. *Samuel Johnson*. Oxford Authors Series. Oxford: Oxford UP, 1984.

Greene, Gayle, and Coppelia Kahn, eds. *Making a Difference: Feminist Literary Criticism*. London: Methuen, 1985.

Harris, Trudier. "Folklore in the Fiction of Alice Walker: A Perpetuation of Historical and Literary Traditions." *Black American Literature Forum* 11 (1977): 3–8.

———. "Violence in *The Third Life of Grange Copeland*." *College Language Association Journal* 19 (1975): 238–47.

Hartman, Joan E. "Reflections on 'The Philosophical Bases of Feminist Literary Criticisms.'" *NLH* 105–16.

Hartmann, Geoffrey H. "Literary Commentary as Literature." Adams and Searle 345–58.

Heath, Stephen. "Male Feminism." Jardine and Smith 1–32.

Hemlow, Joyce. *The History of Fanny Burney*. Oxford: Oxford UP, 1958.

Hicks, Granville. "Complexities of a Free Woman." Rev. of The Golden Notebook, by Doris Lessing. Saturday Review 30 June 1962: 16.

Himmelfarb, Gertrude. "Stanford and Duke Undercut Classical Values." New York Times 5 May 1988: A31.

Hirsch, E. D., Jr. Cultural Literacy: What Every American Needs to Know. 1987. New York: Vintage, 1988.

Hodgart, M. J. C. Samuel Johnson and His Times. London: Batsford, 1962.

Hoffman, Nancy, Cynthia Secor, and Adrian Tinsley, eds. Female Studies VI: Closer to the Ground. Women's Classes, Criticism, Programs—1972. 2d ed. Old Westbury, NY: Feminist Press, 1973.

———. "Working Together: The Women's Studies Program at Portland State University." Hoffman, et al. 164–66.

Holderness, Graham. "Agincourt 1944: Readings in the Shakespeare Myth." Popular Fictions: Essays in Literature and History. Ed. Peter Humm, Paul Stigant, and Peter Widdowson. London: Methuen, 1986. 173–95.

Howe, Florence. "Doris Lessing's Free Women." Nation 11 Jan. 1965: 37.

———. "Introduction. Identity and Expression: A Writing Course for Women." Female Studies II. Ed. Florence Howe. Pittsburgh, PA: Know, 1970. 1–4.

———. "A Report from the Commission on the Status of Women in the Profession." PMLA 85 (1970): 644–47.

Howe, Irving. "Neither Compromise nor Happiness." Rev. of The Golden Notebook, by Doris Lessing. New Republic 15 Dec. 1962: 17–20. Sprague and Tiger 177–81.

Hubbard, Ruth. "Constructing Sex Difference." NLH 129–34.

Hynes, Joseph. "The Construction of The Golden Notebook." Iowa Review 4.3 (1973): 100–13.

———. "A Sixties Book for All Seasons." Kaplan and Rose, Approaches 65–71.

Irwin, George. Samuel Johnson: A Personality in Conflict. Aukland: U of Aukland P, 1971.

Jacobus, Mary. "Is There a Woman in This Text?" New Literary History 14 (1982): 117–41.

Jameson, Fredric. The Political Unconscious. Ithaca: Cornell UP, 1981.

Jardine, Alice, and Paul Smith, eds. Men in Feminism. New York: Methuen, 1987.

Jehlen, Myra, and Maureen Quilligan. "Guest Column." PMLA 101 (1986): 771–72.

Johnson, Samuel. Johnson on Shakespeare. Ed. Arthur Sherbo. Intro. Bertrand Bronson. The Yale Edition of the Works of Samuel Johnson. Vol. 7. New Haven: Yale UP, 1968.

———. "Life of Gray." *Rasselas, Poems and Selected Prose.* Ed. Bertrand H. Bronson. 3d ed. San Franciso: Rinehart, 1971.

———. *The Lives of the English Poets.* Ed. G. B. Hill. 3 vols. Oxford: Oxford UP, 1905.

Kampf, Louis, and Paul Lauter. Introduction. *The Politics of Literature: Dissenting Essays on the Teaching of English.* Ed. Louis Kampf and Paul Lauter. New York: Pantheon, 1972. 3–54.

Kaplan, Carey, and Ellen Cronan Rose, eds. *Approaches to Teaching Lessing's The Golden Notebook.* New York: MLA, 1989.

———, eds. *Doris Lessing: The Alchemy of Survival.* Athens: U of Ohio P, 1988.

Kaplan, Sydney Janet. *Feminine Consciousness in the Modern British Novel.* Urbana: U of Illinois P, 1975.

———. "Passionate Portrayal of Things to Come: Doris Lessing's Recent Fiction." *Twentieth Century Women Novelists.* Ed. Thomas F. Staley. Totowa, NJ: Barnes, 1982. 1–15.

Karl, Frederick R. "Doris Lessing in the Sixties: The New Anatomy of Melancholy." *Contemporary Literature* 13 (1972): 15–33.

———. "The Four-Gaited Beast of the Apocalypse: Doris Lessing's *The Four-Gated City.*" *Old Lines, New Forces.* Ed. Robert K. Morris. Rutherford, NJ: Fairleigh Dickinson P, 1976. 181–200.

Keller, Evelyn Fox. *A Feeling for the Organism: The Life and Work of Barbara McClintock.* New York: Freeman, 1983.

———. *Reflections on Gender and Science.* New Haven: Yale UP, 1985.

Kernan, Alvin. *Printing Technology, Letters, and Samuel Johnson.* Princeton: Princeton UP, 1987.

Kolbert, Elizabeth. "Literary Feminism Comes of Age." *New York Times Magazine* 6 Dec. 1987. 110+.

Kolodny, Annette. "Dancing Through the Minefield: Some Observations on the Theory, Practice, and Politics of a Feminist Literary Criticism." *The New Feminist Criticism: Essays on Women, Literature, and Theory.* Ed. Elaine Showalter. New York: Pantheon, 1985. 140–63.

———. "A Map for Rereading: Or, Gender and the Interpretation of Literary Texts." *New Literary History* 11 (1980): 451–67.

———. "Respectability Is Eroding the Revolutionary Potential of Feminist Criticism." *Chronicle of Higher Education* 4 May 1988: A52.

Kostelanetz, Richard, ed. *On Contemporary Literature.* New York: Avon, 1964.

Kronik, John W. "Editor's Note." *PMLA* 103 (1988): 733.

Krupat, Arnold. "Native American Literature and the Canon." Von Hallberg 309–36.

Lauter, Paul. "Race and Gender in the Shaping of the American Literary

Canon: a Case Study from the Twenties." *Feminist Criticism and Social Change: Sex, Class, and Race in Literature and Culture*. Ed. Judith Newton and Deborah Rosenfelt. New York: Methuen, 1985. 19–44.

———, ed. *Reconstructing American Literature: Courses, Syllabi, Issues.* Old Westbury, NY: Feminist Press, 1983.

Leavis, F. R. *Education and the University: A Sketch for an "English School."* 2d ed. 1948. Cambridge: Cambridge UP, 1979.

———. *English Literature in our Time and the University.* 1969. Cambridge: Cambridge UP, 1979.

———. "How to Teach Reading." *Education and the University* 105–40.

———. "Mass Civilization and Minority Culture." *Education and the University* 143–71.

Le Guin, Ursula K. "Bryn Mawr Commencement Address." *Dancing at the Edge of the World: Thoughts on Words, Women, Places*. New York: Grove, 1989. 147–60.

Lentricchia, Frank. "Patriarchy Against Itself—The Young Manhood of Wallace Stevens." *Critical Inquiry* 13 (1987): 742–86.

Lessing, Doris. *The Golden Notebook*. 1962. New York: Bantam, 1973.

———. Interview. With Susan Stamberg. *All Things Considered*. National Public Radio. 25 April 1984. *Doris Lessing Newsletter* 8.2 (1984): 3–4, 15.

Ling, Amy. "I'm Here: An Asian American Woman's Response." *NLH* 151–60.

Lipking, Lawrence. "Aristotle's Sister." *Critical Inquiry* 10 (1983): 61–81.

———. *The Ordering of the Arts in Eighteenth-Century England*. Princeton: Princeton UP, 1970.

Lorde, Audre. "The Master's Tools Will Never Dismantle the Master's House." *Sister Outsider: Essays and Speeches*. Freedom, CA: Crossing, 1984. 110–13.

MacKinnon, Catherine A. "Feminism, Marxism, Method, and the State: An Agenda for Theory." *Signs* 7 (1982): 515–44.

Maddock, Melvin. Rev. of *Briefing for a Descent into Hell*, by Doris Lessing. *Time* 8 March 1971: 80.

Magie, Michael L. "Doris Lessing and Romanticism." *College English* 38 (1977): 531–52.

Maitland, Sara, and Michelene Wandor. *Arky Types*. London: Methuen, 1987.

Marcus, Jane. "Daughters of Anger/Material Girls: Con/Textualizing Feminist Criticism." *Last Laughs: Perspectives on Women and Comedy*. Ed. Regina Barreca. New York: Gordon and Breach, 1988. 281–308.

———. "Still Practice, A/Wrested Alphabet: Toward a Feminist Aesthetic." Benstock 79–97.

McDowell, Deborah E. "The Self in Bloom: Alice Walker's *Meridian*." *College Language Association Journal* 24 (1981): 262–75.

McKay, Nellie. "Response to 'The Philosophical Bases of Feminist Literary Criticisms.'" *NLH* 161–67.

"Meeting of the MLA Executive Council." *PMLA* 103 (1988): 338–46.

Merchant, Carolyn. *The Death of Nature: Women, Ecology, and the Scientific Revolution*. San Francisco: Harper, 1980.

Merod, Jim. *The Political Responsibility of the Critic*. Ithaca: Cornell UP, 1987.

Messer-Davidow, Ellen. "Knowing Ways: A Reply to My Commentators." *NLH* 187–94.

———. "The Philosophical Bases of Feminist Literary Criticisms." *NLH* 63–103.

Moraga, Cherrie, and Gloria Anzaldua, eds. *This Bridge Called My Back: Writings by Radical Women of Color*. Watertown, MA: Persephone, 1981.

Mulhern, Francis. *The Moment of "Scrutiny."* London: NLB, 1979.

Munich, Adrienne. "Notorious Signs, Feminist Criticism and Literary Tradition." Greene and Kahn 238–59.

National Council of Teachers of English. Brochure advertising the 1988 Summer Institute, "Gender Studies and the Canon." Urbana, IL: NCTE, 1988.

National Endowment for the Humanities. *American Memory: A Report on the Humanities in the Nation's Public Schools*. Washington, DC: NEH 1987.

Nelson, Cary. "Against English: Theory and the Limits of the Discipline." *Profession 87.* 46–52.

———. "Feminism, Language and Philosophy." *NLH* 117–28.

New Literary History (NLH) 19.1 (1987). *Feminist Directions.*

Norhnberg, James. "On Literature and the Bible." *Centrum* 2 (1974): 5–43.

Ogunyemi, Chikwenye Okonjo. "Womanism: The Dynamics of the Contemporary Black Female Novel in English." *Signs* 11 (1985): 63–80.

Ohmann, Carol. "Emily Brontë in the Hands of Male Critics." *College English* 32 (1971): 906–13.

Ohmann, Richard. *English in America: A Radical View of the Profession*. New York: Oxford, 1976.

———. *Politics of Letters*. Middletown, CT: Wesleyan UP, 1987.

———. "The Shaping of a Canon: U.S. Fiction, 1960–1975." Von Hallberg 377–401.

Palmer, D. J. *The Rise of English Studies: An Account of the Study of English Language and Literature from its Origins to the Making of the Oxford English School*. London: Oxford UP, 1965.

Parker-Smith, Bettye J. "Alice Walker's Women: In Search of Some Peace of Mind." Evans, Mari 479–93.

Porter, Nancy. "Silenced History—Children of Violence and The Golden Notebook." World Literature Written in English 12 (1973): 161–79.

Poulet, Georges. "Criticism and the Experience of Interiority." Trans. Catherine and Richard Macksey. Reader-Response Criticism: From Formalism to Structuralism. Ed. Jane Tompkins. Baltimore: Johns Hopkins UP, 1980. 41–49.

Prescott, P. S. Rev. of The Color Purple, by Alice Walker. Newsweek 21 June 1982: 67.

"Procedures for Organizing Meetings for the MLA Convention and Policies for MLA Divisions and Discussion Groups." PMLA 102 (1987): 451–61.

Profession 87. New York: Modern Language Association, 1987.

Pullin, Faith. "Landscapes of Reality: The Fiction of Contemporary Afro-American Women." Black Fiction: New Studies in the Afro-American Novel Since 1945. Ed. A. Robert Lee. New York: Barnes, 1980. 173–203.

Radway, Janice A. "The Book-of-the-Month Club and the General Reader: On the Uses of 'Serious' Fiction." Critical Inquiry 14 (1988): 516–38.

———. Reading the Romance: Women, Patriarchy, and Popular Literature. Chapel Hill: U of North Carolina P, 1984.

Raleigh, Walter. Six Essays on Johnson. Oxford: Oxford UP, 1910.

Rich, Adrienne. On Lies, Secrets, and Silences. New York: Norton, 1979.

———. "Taking Women Students Seriously." On Lies 237–45.

———. "Toward a Woman-Centered University." On Lies 125–55.

———. "Vesuvius at Home: The Power of Emily Dickinson." On Lies 157–83.

Rigney, Barbara Hill. Madness and Sexual Politics in the Feminist Novel: Studies in Brontë, Woolf, Lessing, and Atwood. Madison: U of Wisconsin P, 1978.

Robinson, Lillian S. "Feminist Criticism: How Do We Know When We've Won?" Benstock 141–49.

Robinson, Lillian S., and Lise Vogel. "Modernism and History." New Literary History 3 (1971): 177–99.

Rubenstein, Roberta. "The Golden Notebook in an Introductory Women's Studies Course." Kaplan and Rose, Approaches 72–77.

———. Postcard to the authors. 12 May 1987.

Sadoff, Dianne F. "Black Matrilineage: The Case of Alice Walker and Zora Neale Hurston." Signs 11 (1985): 4–26.

Said, Edward W. "Opponents, Audiences, Constituencies, and Community." The Politics of Interpretation. Ed. W. J. T. Mitchell. Chicago: U of Chicago P, 1983. 7–32.

———. *The World, the Text and the Critic.* Cambridge: Harvard UP, 1983.

Sass, Janet. "A Literature Class of Our Own: Women's Studies Without Walls." Hoffman, et al. 79–87.

Schachtel, Ernest. *Metamorphosis.* New York: Basic Books, 1959.

Schaefer, William D. "Anonymous Review: A Report from the Executive Director." *MLA Newsletter* 10.2 (1978): 4–6.

Schlueter, Paul. Letter to the authors. 14 Feb. 1986.

Schmitz, Betty. *Integrating Women's Studies into the Curriculum: A Guide and Bibliography.* Old Westbury, NY: Feminist Press, 1985.

Schweickart, Patrocinio P. "Reading Ourselves: Toward a Feminist Theory of Reading." *Gender and Reading.* Ed. Elizabeth A. Flynn and Patrocinio P. Schweickart. Baltimore: Johns Hopkins UP, 1986. 31–62.

Seligman, Dee. "Help Needed." *Doris Lessing Newsletter* 2.2 (1978): 3.

Shor, Ira. "Anne Sexton's 'For My Lover . . .': Feminism in the Classroom." Hoffman, et al. 57–67.

Showalter, Elaine. "Critical Cross-Dressing: Male Feminists and the Woman of the Year." Jardine and Smith 116–32.

———. "Introduction: The Rise of Gender." *Speaking of Gender.* Ed. Elaine Showalter. New York: Routledge, 1989. 1–13.

———. *A Literature of Their Own: British Women Novelists from Brontë to Lessing.* Princeton, NJ: Princeton UP, 1977.

———. "Women and the Literary Curriculum." *College English* 32 (1971): 855–62.

———. "Women's Time, Women's Space: Writing the History of Feminist Criticism." Benstock 30–44.

Showalter, Elaine, and Carol Ohmann. "Introduction: Teaching About Women, 1971." *Female Studies IV.* Ed. Elaine Showalter and Carol Ohmann. Pittsburgh, PA: Know, 1971. i–xii.

Showalter, English. "Editor's Column." *PMLA* 100 (1985): 139–40.

Sidney, Sir Philip. "An Apology for Poetry." Bate 82–106.

Smith, Barbara Herrnstein. "Contingencies of Value." Von Hallberg 5–39.

———. "President's Column: Curing the Humanities, Correcting the Humanists." *MLA Newsletter* 20.2 (1988): 3–4.

Smith, Patricia Clark. "Concerning Power, Nuclear and Otherwise: A Response to Messer-Davidow." *NLH* 139–50.

Spacks, Patricia Meyer. *The Female Imagination.* New York: Knopf, 1975.

Spilka, Mark. "Lessing and Lawrence: The Battle of the Sexes." *Contemporary Literature* 15 (1975): 218–40.

Sprague, Claire, and Virginia Tiger, eds. *Critical Essays on Doris Lessing.* Boston: G. K. Hall, 1986.

Stade, George. "Womanist Fiction and Male Characters." *Partisan Review* 52 (1985): 264–70.

Stallybrass, Peter, and Allon White. *The Politics and Poetics of Transgression*. Ithaca: Cornell UP, 1986.

Stanton, Domna. "What's in a Name? The Case for Author-Anonymous Reviewing Policies." *Women in Print II*. Ed. Joan E. Hartman and Ellen Messer-Davidow. New York: MLA, 1982. 65–77.

Stein, Sharman. "Writing Coaches Helping to Stamp Out Legalese." *New York Times* 15 Sept. 1989. B7.

Stimpson, Catharine R., with Nina Kressner Cobb. *Women's Studies in the United States*. New York: Ford Foundation, 1986.

Sullivan, Teresa A., Nancy F. Cott, Heidi I. Hartmann, and Lesley Lee Francis. "Valuing and Devaluing Women's Studies." *Academe* July–Aug. 1989: 35–40.

Tate, Claudia. "Alice Walker." *Black Women Writers at Work*. Ed. Claudia Tate. New York: Continuum, 1983. 175–87.

Tillyard, E. M. W. *The Muse Unchained: An Intimate Account of the Revolution in English Studies at Cambridge*. London: Bowes, 1958.

Tompkins, Jane. "Me and My Shadow." *NLH* 169–78.

———. *Sensational Designs: The Cultural Work of American Fiction, 1790–1860*. New York: Oxford UP, 1985.

Tracy, Clarence. "Johnson and the Common Reader." *Dalhousie Review* 57 (1977): 405–23.

Turner, Darwin. "A Spectrum of Blackness." *Parnassus* 4 (1976): 202–18.

Veeser, Cyrus. Letter. *New York Times* 23 June 1988: A22.

Von Hallberg, Robert, ed. *Canons*. Chicago: U of Chicago P, 1984.

Walker, Alice. "The Black Writer and the Southern Experience." *New South*. Fall 1970. Reprinted in *In Search* 15–21.

———. "In Search of Our Mothers' Gardens." *Ms.* May 1974. *In Search* 231–43.

———. *In Search of Our Mothers' Gardens*. New York: Harcourt, 1983.

———. Interview. With John O'Brien. *Interviews with Black Writers*. Ed. John O'Brien. New York: Liveright, 1973. 185–211. Excerpted in *In Search* as "From An Interview" 244–72.

———. "Saving the Life That Is Your Own: The Importance of Models in the Artist's Life." Forum ("Visions of Power in Minority Literature") sponsored by MLA Commission on Minority Groups and the Study of Language and Literature, MLA Convention. San Francisco, 27 Dec. 1975. *In Search* 3–14.

———. "A Talk by Alice Walker '65: Convocation 1972." *Sarah Lawrence Alumni Magazine*. Summer 1972. Reprinted as "A Talk: Convocation 1972" in *In Search* 33–41.

Warner, Michael. "Professionalization and the Rewards of Literature: 1875–1900." *Criticism* 27.1 (1985): 1–28.

Washington, Mary Helen. "An Essay on Alice Walker." Bell, et al. 133–49.

———. "I Sign My Mother's Name: Alice Walker, Dorothy West, Paule Marshall." *Mothering the Mind: Twelve Studies of Writers and Their Silent Partners.* Ed. Ruth Perry and Martine Watson Bradley. New York: Holmes & Meier, 1984. 142–63.

Watkins, Mel. Rev. of *The Color Purple*, by Alice Walker. *New York Times Book Review* 15 July 1982: 7.

Watkins, W. B. C. *Perilous Balance.* Princeton: Princeton UP, 1939.

Wiles, Roy M. *Freshest Advices: Early Provincial Newspapers in England.* Athens: Ohio UP, 1965.

———. *Serial Publication Before 1750.* New York: Cambridge UP, 1957.

Williams, Raymond. *Marxism and Literature.* Oxford: Oxford UP, 1977.

Willis, Susan. "Alice Walker's Women." *New Orleans Review* 12.1 (1985): 33–41.

Winkler, Barbara Scott. "'It Gave Me Courage': What Students Say About Women's Studies." *NWSA Perspectives* 5.4 (1987): 29–32.

Woolf, Virginia. "The Common Reader." *The Common Reader, First Series.* New York: Harcourt, 1925. 1–2.

———. "How Should One Read a Book?" *The Second Common Reader.* New York: Harcourt, 1932. 234–45.

Index

The Canon and the Common Reader was designed
by Dariel Mayer, composed by Lithocraft, Inc.,
and printed and bound by BookCrafters, Inc.
The book is set in Melior and printed on 50-lb
Glatfelter natural.